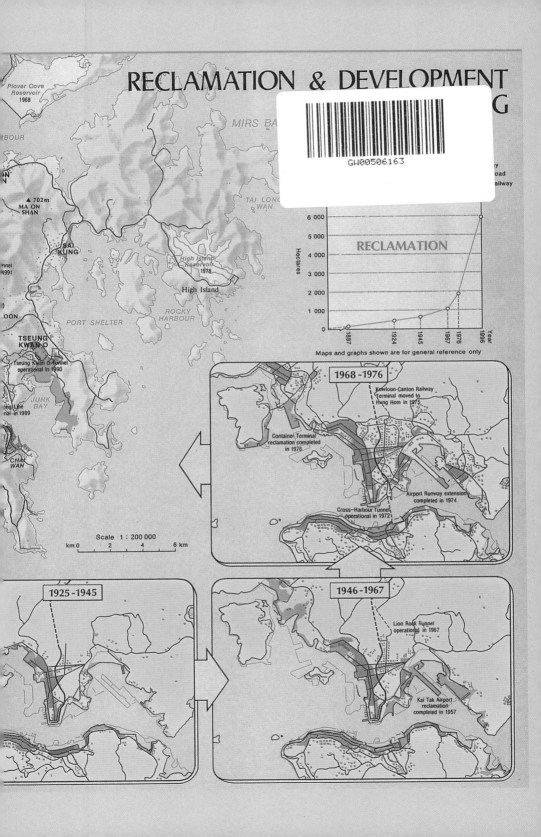

RECLAMATION & DEVELOPMENT

MIRS BAY

Plover Cove
Reservoir
1968

▲ 702m
MA ON
SHAN

SAI
KUNG

TAI LONG
WAN

High Island
Reservoir
1978

High Island

ROCKY
HARBOUR

PORT SHELTER

TSEUNG
KWAN O

Tseung Kwan O Tunnel
operational in 1990

JUNK
BAY

CHAI
WAN

RECLAMATION

Hectares	
6 000	
5 000	
4 000	
3 000	
2 000	
1 000	
0	

1887 1924 1945 1967 1976 1996 Year

Maps and graphs shown are for general reference only

Scale 1 : 200 000
km 0   2   4   6 km

1968 -1976

Kowloon-Canton Railway
Terminal moved to
Hung Hom in 1975

Container Terminal
reclamation completed
in 1976

Airport Runway extension
completed in 1974

Cross-Harbour Tunnel
operational in 1972

1925 -1945

1946 -1967

Lion Rock Tunnel
operational in 1967

Kai Tak Airport
reclamation
completed in 1957

Land Administraton and Practice in Hong Kong

Third Edition

Once again to my wife Priscilla for her continued
and unstinting support

Land Administraton and Practice in Hong Kong

Third Edition

Roger Nissim

香港大學出版社

HONG KONG UNIVERSITY PRESS

Hong Kong University Press
14/F Hing Wai Centre
7 Tin Wan Praya Road
Aberdeen
Hong Kong

© Hong Kong University Press 1998, 2008, 2012
First published 1998
Third edition 2012

ISBN 978-988-8083-80-0

British Library Cataloguing-in-Publication Data
A catalogue record for this book is available from the British Library.

10   9   8   7   6   5   4   3   2   1

Printed and bound by Condor Production Ltd., Hong Kong, China

CONTENTS

PREFACE TO THE SECOND EDITION

I have been both moved and surprised by the overwhelmingly positive response that the first edition of this book has received since it came out in 1998.

A topic such as this one will always be a work in progress because of the continuing stream of new Government Practice Notes and policy reviews, court cases as well as new legislation that all touch on land.

Only Section I of the first edition, which relates to the historical aspects, remains unchanged. There are some substantial and significant changes to the other sections, including a completely new Section IV to describe the very latest development in land administration matters.

I have also taken advantage of the fact that the Hong Kong government is now very much wired to the net and all departments have excellent websites. This has removed the necessity of copying Department Practice Notes as they are easily obtainable on the internet. The following websites are particularly useful:

General Government:	*www.info.gov.hk*
Lands Department:	*www.landsd.gov.hk*
Planning Department:	*www.pland.gov.hk*
Legislation:	*www.justice.gov.hk*

Again my thanks are due to my good friend John Davison for giving me access to his firm's legal library and also for acting as my proof reader to ensure the highest degree of accuracy in my legal interpretations.

Also a big thank you to my secretary Margaret Ho for her unfailing good humour as each chapter was changed, amended and then changed again!

As before if there are any mistakes, they are entirely my responsibility.

December 2007

PREFACE TO THE FIRST EDITION

The motivation to write this book comes from a number of different sources. In the past few years, I have been asked to give lectures to various groups of professionals be they aspiring surveyors, postgraduate architects or practising lawyers on different aspects of land administration in Hong Kong. It was evident by the requests for my lecture notes that there lacked a suitable textbook on this topic to which they could refer. This volume will, hopefully, go some way to rectifying this situation.

Completely separate from this has been my own fascination with Hong Kong's unique position of being internationally acclaimed as one of the best, if not the very best example of a functioning capitalist economy which ironically is founded on what is fundamentally a socialist land tenure system. In Section I of this book, I have tried to unravel how this came to be, who gave the instructions and how they were executed. I hope the readers will find my distillation as interesting as I found the research to be. The principal sources of material for these chapters come from G.B. Endacott's *A history of Hong Kong* (1958) and J.W. Norton Kyshe's twin volumes entitled *The history of the laws and courts of Hong Kong from the earliest period until 1898* (1971).

1997 was of course a momentous year for Hong Kong with the transfer of sovereignty back to China. If you subtract the political arguments that surrounded the handover and the period of transitions the fundamental problem was the expiry of the New Territories leases. Paradoxically, while our leasehold system was the cause of the problem, I believe it was because of our established use of the leasehold system that enabled a practical solution to be found acceptable both to the Chinese and British authorities. Again I explore the background to this, the functioning of the Land Commission and the prospects for the future.

Thanks are in order to my good friend John Davison for giving me access to his firm's legal library which enabled me to obtain the necessary copy of the contemporary legal decisions that are referred to. He was also kind enough to read the final draft to, hopefully, ensure I had not made any egregious errors in my legal interpretations. His thoughtful advice, encouragement and suggestions for improvements to the script have been most welcome.

Thanks are also due to the many of my former government colleagues who willingly answered my questions and requests for information in my attempt to make the text as accurate as possible. If there are any mistakes, they are entirely my responsibility.

I would also like to record my appreciation to both the Main Library of the University of Hong Kong and the Public Records Office for their unfailing help and courtesy in dealing with my many enquiries.

Last and by no means least a special thank-you to my secretary Margaret Ho for typing and retyping the scripts as I constantly redrafted each chapter as more information came to light. She did this all with unfailing good humour for which I am most grateful.

INTRODUCTION

To assist readers the book has been organized in the following way:

Section I
This section contains five chapters which trace the historical development of land administration starting in 1841, through to the present day. This sets the scene to put in context the detail contained in the subsequent sections.

Section II
These chapters deal with the present-day land administration policies with particular reference to the functions of the Lands Department in respect of land disposal, modifications and exchanges with particular emphasis on the control of development through lease conditions. Land management and lease enforcement are also considered.

Section III
In these chapters, some of the more unusual problems associated with land work in the New Territories are investigated.

Sction IV
The second edition of this book contains two new chapters, which reflect the latest development in land administration in Hong Kong.

Appendices
There are some documents which are so lengthy that they would clutter up the main text but nevertheless where a full reference is considered appropriate, the documents will be found in the appendices.

1 | HISTORICAL DEVELOPMENT OF LAND ADMINISTRATION

Section I contains five chapters which trace the historical development of land administration starting in 1841, through to the present day. This sets the scene and puts in context the detail contained in the subsequent sections.

THE FIRST LAND SALES, 1841–1842

It is probable that the first auction of land held on Hong Kong Island on 14 June 1841, was *ultra vires*, not an auspicious start. Why? Although Captain Charles Elliot landed at what is very appropriately named Possession Point on 26 January 1841, under the terms of the Convention of Chuenpi, this was only a preliminary agreement which was never ratified. It was not until the Treaty of Nanking, which was ratified on 26 June 1843, that Hong Kong was formally ceded and the British occupation recognized as being permanent. So for the first two and a half years, the British occupation was temporary and makeshift with no proper authority to deal in land, paragraph 1 on page 13 also refers.

Until the spring of 1842, the British administrative centre for this area had remained in Macao. Elliot was recalled to England in August 1841 and was replaced as Superintendent of Trade by Sir Henry Pottinger who, having been convinced of the need to retain Hong Kong, in March 1842 moved his headquarters to Hong Kong and at the same time declared it a free port. It was about this time that Pottinger received instructions from Lord Aberdeen in England forbidding all further building and grants of land. Elliot, in his enthusiasm to get things started, was considered to have overstepped the limit of his authority.

Maybe Elliot did not have any choice but to take action in order to bring things under control. It appears that speculation in land in Hong Kong started right from the beginning. Immediately following the British possession of Hong Kong in January 1841, sites were occupied and building works started without any form of official approval. Land was sold by Chinese inhabitants without a proper Land Registry for purchasers to check title. The prospect of Hong Kong becoming a permanent British territory encouraged keen competition to get hold of the best sites; in other words, all the necessary ingredients for a speculative market were in place.

Obviously, some immediate action was required by the authorities to ensure a proper and orderly allocation of land for different uses. It was on 1 May 1841 that the principles of land disposal were first announced. Allotments were to be made at public auctions to the highest bidders for the payment of an annual rent, the rent being the subject of the bidding. Elliot safeguarded the rights of the Crown but promised that land holders would be allowed to purchase their allotments in freehold if the home government agreed. Furthermore, the purchasers of town lots could also buy suburban or country lots with choice of site.[1]

The first land sales were announced to take place on 12 June: 'the dimensions of the respective lots will be specified and defined on the spot by the commanding officer of Engineers to whom the parties are referred for further particulars.' Buildings of a certain minimum value fixed at $1000 had to be built on the plots within six months of the date of sale, so it is evident that building covenants have existed from the very first land sales in Hong Kong. The biddings were to be for the annual rate of quit-rent and were to be made in pounds sterling. The upset price was fixed at £10 for each lot and biddings were to advance by 10s. The dollar in all payments was to be computed at the rate of 4s 4d.

The first auction programme was very ambitious as it was intended to offer 100 marine lots facing Queens Road on the seaward side and 100 suburban lots on the opposite side of the road. Not surprisingly, there were difficulties in getting all the plots surveyed in time and although the sale was postponed two days to 14 June,[2] only 35 marine lots were ready for sale, each having 100 feet frontage along Queen's Road and varying in depth to the shore according to the shape of the coastline. It was later discovered that due to the haste with which the sales had been prepared, there were inaccuracies in the survey and the setting out of the lots which, not surprisingly, caused dissension and difficulties later.

Elliot also warned all those who had already begun buildings that all sales of land had to be made through an officer of the government and all native inhabitants claiming land would be required to prove their claims.

In the event, competition for the reduced number of lots was keen and all but one of the lots were sold. Bid rents ranged from £20 to £265 per lot depending on its depth to the sea and location. An article in *The China Mail* reporting retrospectively on this sale gives some insight into the proceedings: 'the first lot sold was numbered 15 in the list, it was knocked down to Mr. Webster at £20 not only without opposition but he was laughed at for giving so much. The next lot No. 14 however fetched £21 ... The sale then proceeded along the Queen's Road at advancing rates which to a certain extent was owing to the less rugged character of the beach and the more central situation.' Lot 1 to 13 were sold for between £38.10s and £80 depending on size and location.

The sale was now moved to the ground that had been cleared by Messrs. Jardine, Matheson & Co., and which was for the most part occupied by their temporary buildings; and it must be noticed, that the proximity of that firm gave an additional value to land in its vicinity. The first lot put up was No. 20, upon which, as already noticed, a house was already in progress. Mr. Matheson begged that this might not impede bidders, and offered at once £150 (the upset price being £10) at which it was knocked down. The two adjoining lots were, after some competition, knocked down to him also at £185 and £230. The remaining ones in that locality were sold at £160, £140, £150, and £111. Prices then began to fall, and the six lots between this spot and what is now called Spring Gardens, ranged from £25 to £67, and all of them except one afterwards lapsed to Government. (*The China Mail*, quoted in Kyshe 1971, p. 267)

The remaining lots were then sold for rents bid between £75 and £265 per lot. The 34 lots realized a total bid rent of £3272.10s, an average of £96.5s per lot.

It was these unexpectedly high figures that three days later prompted Elliot to write to the two principal merchants, Jardine and Dent, saying that he would urge the home government to allow the land to pass to the purchasers outright, that is, freehold, on payment of one- or two-year purchase of the bid ground rent, or else at a nominal quit rent and asked them to circulate this letter to other interested firms. Elliot was obviously keen to establish an impression of permanency as early as possible and also to encourage more new merchants to set up their business in Hong Kong.

When the home government later refused to ratify these terms, it caused further discontent with accusations that Elliot has dishonoured his promises. It is not difficult to see why Elliot had to go and it was even rumoured that the disgruntled merchants had put a price on his head.

In spite of Lord Aberdeen's edict that all land sales were to cease with Pottinger away from Hong Kong, either from a misunderstanding or, more likely because of the intense pressure exerted by the merchant community, the administration announced on 15 October 1841 that 'it is now desirable that persons applying for lots of land for the purpose of building upon, should be at once accommodated upon terms which will be made known to them by application in person to the Land Officer'. The terms referred to were payment of Crown rent at the average rate realized at the first sale on 14 June 1841, and at a rate of £20 per annum per acre for town inland lots and £5 per quarter acre for suburban inland lots. The Land Officer, like the surveyors was a military appointment so as yet there appeared to be no legal input into land sale documents by qualified lawyers! The departure from sales by auction to sales by private treaty probably was to facilitate regularization of existing occupation. This would help avoid the occupier from having to overbid at auction in order to retain his site.

A fairly comprehensive scheme was adopted to classifying sites at appropriate prices into marine and suburban lots. A notification was made in November 1841 that purchasers of lots who failed to abide by the conditions would forfeit their deposits as well as their allotments. Marine lots were defined as those within 200 feet from high water; town lots as certain specified areas in Hong Kong, Wong Nei Chong (Happy Valley), Chek Chu (Stanley) and Chek Py Wan (Aberdeen); suburban lots were all the rest. In addition, some areas were marked out as bazaars to serve the Chinese population.

On his return to Hong Kong in December 1841, Pottinger was naturally displeased to see that his orders had been ignored, but was nevertheless impressed to see the speed of construction and settlement and recognized that in the interests of maintaining 'tranquillity and good government for all persons genuinely residing in the settlement', the administration had probably little or no choice in proceeding as it had done. In any event, he was now persuaded of the need to retain Hong Kong on a permanent basis and soon afterwards removed his headquarters to Hong Kong from Macao. He justified his actions in a letter to Lord Aberdeen saying, 'but I may declare that even that was forced on me by the extraordinary and unparalleled progress which this settlement had made.' He added, 'I had no predilection for raising a colony in Hong Kong or at any other place in China.' Elliot's actions had taken things beyond the point of no return as Pottinger went on to say, 'this Settlement has already advanced too far to admit of its ever being restored to the authority of the Emperor.'

The haste with which the first land sales had been prepared had, as already mentioned, resulted in inaccuracies which needed to be sorted out. On 22 March 1842, Pottinger declared his intention to appoint a committee to investigate any claim that might be pending regarding allotted allocations of ground of whatever description and finally to define and mark off the limits of all locations that had yet been sold or granted upon any other terms. At the same time, it was expressly notified that 'no purchases of ground, by private persons, from natives formerly or then in possession would be recognized or confirmed unless the previous sanction of the constituted authorities should have been obtained, it being the basis of the footing on which the island of Hong Kong had been taken possession of and was to be held pending the Queens Royal and Gracious Commands that the proprietary of the soil was vested in and appertained solely to the Crown.'

Until this time, no lease or other deed of grant of the lots that had been sold had been issued to purchasers. The 'grant' of the lot was simply an entry in a book kept by the Land Officer, showing only the name of the purchaser and the side measurements of the lot purchased. As sales of lots had already begun to take place from one holder to another, difficulties had arisen as to the liabilities of the purchasers to the Crown. As a remedy for these difficulties and to provide for the registration of sales, the following Government Notification signed by the Land Officer was issued on 2 May 1842:

> With a view to the prevention of future misunderstanding and difficulties, His Excellency Sir Henry Pottinger, Bart, is pleased to direct that no sales of land are to be made by the holders of grants to other parties except with the knowledge of the Land Officer, and that any sales that may have been made, or may be made in future, unless registered in the Land Office, shall be held to be invalid. (Quoted in Kyshe 1971, p. 14).

> Purchasers of grants from the individuals before holding them are to understand distinctly that they will be under the same liabilities to Government as the parties from whom they purchase.

Only two weeks after this date, the appointment of Land Officer was temporarily abolished, and further grants of land were prohibited.

On 27 May 1842, a 'Land and Road Inspector' was appointed to do the work of the Land Officer. His instructions with reference to the Crown Lands of the Colony stated that, as the existing prohibition against further grants of land was to continue in full force pending the receipt of commands from Her Majesty's government, it would not even be necessary for him to bring any applications on that subject to the notice of the Deputy Superintendent who would be charged with the Civil Government of the island during the absence of Sir Henry Pottinger. The duties of the new Land and Road Inspector were to prevent encroachments on the unappropriated lands or on the roads, and to register all sales and transfers of land in conformity with the notification issued by the Land Officer on 2 May 1842.

It can be seen that land administration did not get off to a smooth start. The desire to establish a commercial settlement in Hong Kong as quickly as possible was not matched by the establishment of a proper administrative and legal framework to sell and record land titles; problems were thus created from the outset.

Notes

1. The full text of the Public Notice is included in Appendix I.
2. The full text of the Public Notices dated 7 June 1841 and Terms of Sale dated 14 June 1841 are included in Appendix II; both are extracted from the *Report of the Land Commission, 1886–87*.

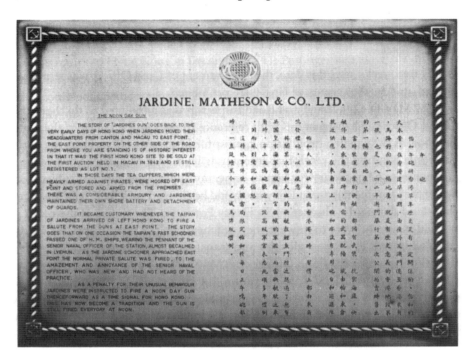

This plaque stands opposite to the World Trade Centre next to the Causeway Bay typhoon anchorage. It is open to the public just after noon each day following the firing of the gun. Note both location and date are wrong!

Plate Courtesy of Alan Macdonald of Architech Audio-Visual Ltd.

2 THE EARLY YEARS, 1843–1898

After the false start of 1841, a proper constitution for the territory was laid down in the so-called Hong Kong Charter on 5 April 1843. This document was also read publicly on 26 June 1843, following the proclamation that the island had become a permanent British territory after the ratification of the Treaty of Nanking. The Governor, assisted and advised by the Executive Council, was among other things empowered to make grants of land.

Instructions and guidelines were received from London on how the Legislative Council was to be constituted and the territory administered. The Legislature was to have the power to pass ordinances covering a wide variety of subjects including land and transfers of land, plus the authority to vote taxes. Importantly, the treatment of property and succession to property were to be in accordance with English law.

It is clear that the Secretary of State for the Colonies in London was firmly in control, issuing instructions, setting out the general principles of administration and calling for information and reports on a regular basis on all issues related to governing the territory.

After the Treaty of Nanking, Pottinger sent home a complete account of the land situation and asked for instructions. In reply, he was told that land must not be granted 'either in perpetuity or for a greater length of time than may be necessary to induce the tenants to erect substantial buildings'. All land must be leased and not sold outright, and the term of the lease was fixed at 75 years, and in the case of land not required for building, for only 21 years; renewals were to be at the discretion of the government. Grants of land were to be made by auction, an allotment being awarded to the person who bid the highest amount as annual payment for the lease. It was also pointed out that no one had any right to grant lands on the island before its cession was recognized by the home government, and no grants made before 26 June 1843, the date the territory was proclaimed, would be recognized as of right and no land rents would be claimed except from that date. It was realized it would be impossible to make a clean start from 26 June 1843 because buildings had been erected on the grants of land that had already been made. In these cases, it was left to Pottinger to decide as a matter of equity what ought to be done. The home government thought the holders should not suffer because of the improvements they had effected, and even went as far as to say that they 'would be disposed to deal more liberally with these people than with others and thus afford them at least such compensation for the disappointment of the expectations which they had been led to entertain'.

The situation was further complicated by the fact that before these instructions arrived, Pottinger had already attempted to deal with some of the abuses himself. A notification of 10 April 1843 called for a full statement and proof of claims to land from each holder, and announced that the Land Officer, who had been again appointed, had been told to prevent the commencement of any further building or the clearance of any site until after final arrangements had been made; all building at whatever stage was to be stopped if proof of ownership of the land was not satisfactory. All encroachments on the future line of roads and streets were to be prevented, and 'all persons were to confine themselves to the exact dimensions of the lots which were originally allotted to them.' In August 1843, Pottinger set up a Land Committee to investigate all claims, fix the rents and arrange for further sale of plots. There was considerable delay in settling the issues, partly due to a dispute between Pottinger and the army over the extent of the military lands, which held up decisions on roads and the amount of land available, and partly due to discussion of the layout of the town.

The Land Committee finally reported in January 1844, and recommended that all marine lot holders should retain their lots on a 75-year lease; it also found that much of the land sold earlier had been at well below its real value and suggested a revaluation, but on this Pottinger delayed taking any positive step. In March 1844, the chief merchants who were holders of most of the original allotments complained strongly against the new conditions and the 75-year leases. Pottinger showed them little sympathy and advised London that 'not one individual in twenty of the purchasers of land at the sales or grants authorised by Captain Elliot or Mr. Johnston had fulfilled the prescribed terms' and that such allotments should have been forfeited and re-auctioned. The merchants continued to protest and later they were to secure substantial concessions, but initially London supported the administration with the following comments which were contained in a dispatch from the Secretary of State for the Colonies, Lord Stanley dated 19 November 1844.

Under these circumstances, after fully reconsidering the matter as brought under my notice in these dispatches, I continue to adhere to the decision expressed in my dispatch of the 3rd January last, that the leases of town and suburban lots for building purposes should not exceed 75 years, subject, of course, to the discretion of the Government to grant renewals from time to time. The reports which I have recently received from you sufficiently show that the terms fixed for the disposal of land in Hong Kong have been no discouragement to building speculations, nor to the purchase of land at high rents. (Quoted in Kyshe 1971, p. 72)

It must be remembered that at this point in time Hong Kong was a burden to the home government who was bearing the total expenses of defence, administration and public works. This position created resentment in the British Parliament and so instructions were issued very early on that Hong Kong was expected to pay its own way as soon as possible. Indeed Pottinger had been informed that he should levy rates on town property for municipal and police purposes, 'confiding to the house-holders the power and the delegation to assess themselves and each other'.

As Hong Kong had been declared a free port, customs duty could not be levied on imported goods. A number of ways to raise revenue were devised including licencing of monopolies for the quarrying of stone and the handling of salt, but the principal source of revenue was to be rent from land.

In order to maximize the revenue from land, roads and streets were built to open up new sites. In an attempt to reduce the effects of speculation by purchasers buying land but not building upon it, government demanded a ten-percent deposit on all sales and arrears of rent if the land was surrendered. For example in 1847, total revenue collected was £31 078, of which £13 996 comprised land rents, representing 45% of the total. However, as expenses that year were £50 959, the deficit had to be made up by a vote from the British Parliament; this situation was to continue for some time which helps explain why London exerted such a strong influence over how affairs were to be run locally.

The 75-year lease term, together with the first rates levy to pay for the police force, was the subject of a complaint letter sent by Hong Kong merchants to London in August 1845. They even claimed it would have been cheaper for them to have stayed in Macao. Gladstone, who had just become Secretary of State for the Colonies, rejected the complaints and supported the governor.

In the meantime, building work was continuing apace. On 28 February 1844, an ordinance was passed for the registration by the Land Officer of all dealings with land and his first report in 1845 gave the number of stone and brick buildings as being 264 European and 436 Chinese.

However, it was not long before Hong Kong experienced its first recession. The local merchants were again moved to write to London in February 1848 on the subject of land, complaining that the rents were too high owing to insufficient land being put up for auction which they claimed had resulted in imbalanced competition that forced up rents. This in effect amounted to the first of what has become a continuing and regular pattern of complaints about the government's 'high land price policy'. They asked for a revision of the leases and a reduction of rent. In support of their case, they quoted from Pottinger's previous dispatch to Lord Stanley dated 4 May 1844, which set out the arguments very clearly:

> Your Lordship will have seen from the copy of the lease, which forms Enclosure No. 11 to my Dispatch, No. 3, of the 23rd January last, that it has been provided for in that document that the buildings shall all become the property of the Crown at the expiration of the 75 years for which the leases are to run; and I am told that this is usually the case in leases of the sort. But there can be no doubt that the strict enforcement of that clause will operate towards deterring people from expending so much money, as they otherwise would do, in improvements, by building quays, docks, etc: and when I look to the high rates of rent at which land of itself has hitherto let in this island, I cannot doubt but a favourable consideration of the prayer contained in the present application would have the most beneficial effect on the future prosperity of the Colony. I should therefore be glad, did it accord with the views of Her Majesty's Government, to see that clause of the lease so modified as to ensure the owners of the different locations, the certainty of retaining possession, subject to such augmented rates of ground rent as the probable increased value of land will then justly authorize. (Quoted in Kyshe 1971, p. 182)

London replied that any reduction in the rents would be unfair to unsuccessful bidders and suggested for consideration an extension of the terms of the leases. In December 1848, after further exchanges of dispatches, London agreed to a very significant concession by allowing the administration to substitute 999 year leases, virtual perpetuity, for those of 75 years. A Gazette Notification dated 3 March 1849 announced the new arrangements: 'it is hereby notified that, under instructions from her Majesty's Principal Secretary of State for the Colonies, all Crown leases heretofore granted for a term of 75 years may be extended for a further term of 924 years. All Tenants of the Crown who may be desirous of availing themselves of the above concession will, on application at the Surveyor General's Office, receive the directions necessary to enable them to obtain a prolongation of their respective leases in conformity with the above instructions.'

Clearly action was necessary because 130 lots had reverted to government, of these 5 were resumed, 49 were purely speculative, and 76 had been held by genuine buyers who gave up their holdings because the territory had not progressed as anticipated. As a result, revenue from land was reduced by twenty percent and a full enquiry was decided upon. A special Land Committee was set up in 1850 and all allotment holders who felt they were paying excessive rents were asked to bring their cases before the committee. In spite of all the fuss and protest of the merchants, only eleven did so, and half the amount of land involved belonged to one notorious speculator, George Duddell. Only five of the applicants had their claims recognized. The outcome was that some relief was given in the rents of seven allotments, and proposals were made for subdividing allotments to facilitate sale.

There was one exception to the decision to only grant land on a leasehold basis and that is the site of St. John's Cathedral in Garden Road. In 1847, the Crown granted a freehold title to the Trustees of the Church of England with the caveat that the estate in fee simple was expressly limited to the land being used for the purposes of a church.[1]

In 1851, London agreed to two important changes in how land was to be dealt with. First, it was agreed that in future biddings for Crown land should not be in the form of advanced rent, but that any such property should be offered for lease at a moderate rent to be determined by the Crown Surveyor, and that the competition should be in the amount to be paid down as a premium for the lease at the rent fixed. However, although this was publicly notified on 25 June 1851 according to the 1886–87 Land Commission Report, this style of sale did not in fact start until 1869.[2] Secondly, it was agreed that lessees could, subject to proper control, be allowed to subdivide their lots and alienate portions of their lands.

All the amendments were reflected in the Crown Leases that were subsequently issued. The following extracts from the lease of Marine Lot No. 1 signed in 1869 are a good example. They contain, *inter alia*, the following:

1. 'AND WHEREAS by certain instructions of Her said Majesty, addressed to the then Governor of Hong Kong, under Her said Majesty's Signet and Sign Manual, and dated Sixth day of April 1843. The said Governor was amongst other things instructed to grant Leases of the land in the said Colony' — this confirms the date when land grants were issued with proper authority, that is, the day following the declaration of the Hong Kong Charter.
2. 'TO HAVE AND TO HOLD the said parcel of ground . . . from the Twenty Sixth day of June AD 1843 for and during and unto the full end and term of nine hundred and ninety nine years . . . ' — interestingly the starting date of the lease and the collection of rent is the same date as the Treaty of Nanking.
3. The yearly rent was fixed at $581.40 and the sum to be spent on construction was set at $5814, that is, ten times the annual rent. The time

period for construction was set at six months which event should occur within the first year of the grant.

4. The buildings to be erected 'shall front and range in an uniform manner with the messuages or tenements in the same Street' — this is the precursor of the design and disposition clause which is discussed later on.[3] The original form of this clause is not considered to be effective on its own in controlling development today on the grounds that its effect has been exhausted in the original buildings on the lot.

5. The offensive trade clause appears in full and again this is discussed later on.[4]

6. The government reserved the right, with three months' notice and on payment of proper compensation, to take back any part of the site 'if required for the improvement of the Colony of Hong Kong or for any other public purpose whatsoever'.

It appears that following the significant changes initiated in 1851, land matters ceased to be a major issue for some time. The cession of the Kowloon peninsula in 1860 did not result in any changes in policy and 999-year leases were granted there in the early years.

Commencing with a dispatch dated 25 April 1863 and concluding with one on 28 November 1864, there was a robust exchange of views between London and Hong Kong on the subject of Hong Kong making a contribution to the upkeep of the garrison stationed here. The main protagonists were the Duke of Newcastle, in his capacity as the Officer Administering the Government of Hong Kong at the Secretary of State for the Colonies, and the Governor, Sir Hercules G.R. Robinson. The gist of the exchange was that in London's view having subsidized Hong Kong for the first fourteen years of its existence as a colony, now that it was at last paying its way, due largely to good land sales revenue, and was even showing surpluses, it was time for Hong Kong to make a contribution towards the costs of defending itself. In the end, London's view, prevailed and it is clear that without good revenue from land sales, this would not have been possible. This is also a major clue as to London's close interest in how land matters were being managed here.[5]

The Commission appointed in 1886 to inquire into and report upon the system of leasing or otherwise disposing of Crown lands and to make recommendations presented its lengthy report to the Legislative Council on 23 September 1887.[6] However, no significant changes were to occur until 1898, which coincided with the leasing of the New Territories, when the following dispatch dated 23 May 1898 was received from the Secretary of State for the Colonies in London, signed by Joseph Chamberlain in his capacity as the Officer Administering the Government of Hong Kong.

Sir,

1. I have the honour to inform you that the policy of giving leases of Crown land in Hong Kong for 999 years, which has prevailed in Victoria for some years, and which the Land Commission of 1886–7 recommended should be extended to Kowloon, is, in my opinion, open to grave objection.
2. Leases for 999 years are practically equivalent to a freehold tenure and the grant of such leases deprives the Government of all control over the land of the Colony, and of all the advantage of any future enhanced value of the land.
3. Subject therefore to any observations in view of special local considerations which you may have to offer, I consider that future leases should be for periods not exceeding seventy-five, or at the outside ninety-nine years, with suitable provisions to meet the objection raised by the Land Commission of 1886–7 viz., that the Crown should not at the expiration of the lease confiscate the whole value of the tenant's improvements.
4. Pending the final settlement of this question, no further leases for 999 years should be granted, at any rate without previous reference to me in each case.

The new instructions from London showed a good appreciation of the benefits of a properly managed leasehold system. They also set the tone for how leaseholds should be treated on expiry of their leases. The author of these instructions could not have possibly conceived of the significance all this would have in the treatment of land under the Sino-British Joint Declaration of 1984, where the precepts of 1898 still hold good.

The reduction of the lease term to 75 years aroused great protest but the only immediate concession that Chamberlain agreed was to make them 75-year leases renewable for one further term. It was the expiry of a large number of these leases in 1973 that led to the Government Leases Ordinance (Cap. 40) which was to introduce the now familiar concept of land leases being renewed, without premium, but with a revised annual rent calculated at 3% of rateable value, all in accordance with the 1898 instructions! Those leaseholders who unfortunately held 75-year or 99-year leases without the right of renewal on expiry were required to pay a full renewal premium based on the current land value. It was not until the coming into force of the Joint Declaration, which is discussed in more detail in Chapter 4 that non-renewable leases were also allowed to be extended, without payment of premium, but with a new annual rent calculated at 3% of rateable value.

Notes

1. Ordinance No. 2 of 1847. See also Ordinance No. 3 of 1850 and the Church of England Trust Ordinance (Cap. 1014) for the present position.
2. Extracts from this report are in Appendix III.
3. See Chapter 9, pp.82, 83.
4. See Chapter 9, pp.83, 84.
5. *British Parliamentary Papers on China*, Vol. 25.
6. Extracts from this report are in Appendix III.

1898 ONWARDS — THE NEW TERRITORIES LEASE

The leasing of the New Territories demanded a completely different approach to land administration than that adopted for Hong Kong Island and Kowloon Peninsula. The principal reason for this, apart from the fact that it was not a permanent cession, was that the earlier cessions were sparsely populated; the estimated population of Hong Kong Island in 1841 being 7450 people including 2000 boat dwellers.[1] By comparison the New Territories had a population of around 100 000 at the turn of the century with some 800 villages.[2] There was no intention to displace so many people; on the contrary, it was decided to make arrangements so that residents could prove ownership and be given title to their land.

The Peking Convention was signed on 9 June 1898, giving Great Britain a 99-year lease of what immediately became known as the New Territories (NT) to begin on 1 July 1898. Physical occupation in fact did not commence until April 1899 and survey work began in November of that year. It was recognized that the most important work to be accomplished after taking over the NT was the allocation and registration of all privately owned land. The survey work was carried out by trained staff lent by the Indian government, which accounts for the place names given to some of the natural features such as the Rivers Indus and Ganges.

The registration of claims was carried out administratively to start with until it was taken over by the Land Courts established under the New Territories (Land Court) Ordinance 1900. It was done hand in hand with the survey work which itself was not completed until June 1903, by which time nearly 41 000 acres of land with about 350 000 separate holdings had been demarcated.[3]

Claimants to lots were at first given a 'chi-tsai' or small slips of paper bearing on their face the lot number and on the back the name of the owner and description of the land in Chinese. After the determination of the claims, these 'chi-tsais' still remained in the owners' hands as the only visible sign of ownership, but they were easily lost and easily transferred. It was therefore decided to issue each landowner a 'Chap-Chiu' or certified extract of his holdings. Chap-Chius were not issued in New Kowloon as owners were expected to register their ownership with the Land Officer in Hong Kong.

Right from the outset, the part of the NT which lies north of Boundary Street and south of the Kowloon Hills became known as New Kowloon. This area was administered from Hong Kong as part of the urban area and enjoyed none of the special privileges and rights to follow Chinese customary law enjoyed by the rural NT to the north. The definition of New Kowloon is to be found in Schedule 5 of the Interpretation and General Clauses Ordinance (Cap. 1) and reads as follows: 'New Kowloon means that portion of the New Territories which is delineated red and shown upon a plan marked "New Kowloon" dated 8th December 1937 signed by the Director of Public Works, countersigned by the Governor and deposited in the Land Registry.' Fortunately, a copy of this plan is on display at the Sales office of the Survey and Mapping Office of the Lands Department if any one wishes to study it.

The NT was divided into 477 Demarcation Districts (DD) for each of which there was a Block Government Lease (formerly called Block Crown Lease) which was executed by the Governor. If a claimant established his title to the satisfaction of the Land Court, his particulars would be entered into the Schedule to the Block Government Lease opposite the Lot Number allocated to his piece of land, together with description of the user of the land at that time, the area of the lot and the amount of Government rent (formerly called Crown rent) payable. These lots are now referred to as Old Schedule lots. The Block Crown Leases were expressed to be 75 years from 1 July 1898 with a right of renewal for a further 24 years less the last three days. These leases and other government leases in the NT containing the same right of renewal were granted extensions for 24 years by the New Territories (Renewable Crown Leases) Ordinance (Cap. 152). It was of course the expiry of all these leases on 27 June 1997 that led to the negotiations which resulted in the Sino-British Joint Declaration of 1984, and the further extension of these leases as agreed in the Joint Declaration was granted by the New Territories Leases (Extension) Ordinance (Cap. 150) enacted in 1988, which extended virtually all these leases until 30 June 2047.

The Block Government Leases are standard and straightforward documents; and their two most important covenants are set out below:

> AND FURTHER that the Lessee or any other person or persons shall not, nor will, during the continuance of this demise, use, exercise or follow, in or upon

the said premises, or any part thereof, any noisy, noisome or offensive trade or business whatever, nor convert any ground hereby expressed to be demised as agricultural or garden ground into use for building purposes other than for the proper occupation of the same ground as agricultural or garden ground without the previous Licence of His said Majesty, His Heirs, Successors or Assigns, signified in writing by the Governor of the said Colony of Hong Kong, or other person duly authorised in that behalf: AND FURTHER that the Lessee or any other person or persons shall not nor will at any time during the said term erect or construct any building or structure of any description on the said demised premises or any part thereof whether demised as agricultural or garden ground or otherwise without first have obtained the approval thereto of the Surveyor to His said Majesty, His Heirs, Successors or Assigns, other person duly authorised by the Governor of the said Colony of Hong Kong, in that behalf . . .

The simplicity of the system would eventually prove to work against the government. The first hint of trouble arose in the case of *Watford Construction Co.* v *Secretary for New Territories* [1978] HKLR 410 where it was held that 'The effect of the covenant was to effect not merely a demise *of* agricultural land but also a demise, pending the lessors permission to build, *as* agricultural land.' The judgement referred to the Schedule to the Block Government Lease which contained in respect of each lease contained in respect of each lot the name of the lessee, the area involved, the term of the Lease and a Description of Lot. Under the heading 'Description of Lot', for the plaintiff's land there appeared the word 'Agricultural'. The plaintiff claimed this was no more than a description of the lot as it existed at the time the Schedule was prepared and did not constitute a restriction of the owner's rights of use. In the later and more famous case *Attorney General* v *Melhado Investment Ltd.* [1983] HKLR 327, this decision was overruled when the Hong Kong Court of Appeal held that 'The use of the land as listed in the schedule to the Crown lease was descriptive only. The purpose of the schedule was to identify the lands to which the lease related. If the schedule had been intended to be other than description it would not have been necessary to include in the body of the lease restrictions on building without a licence. It would be absurd to construe the lease so as to compel a lessee to maintain a lot as a broken latrine for 75 years.' The government had contended that the lot was restricted to agricultural use under the Block Government Lease while the land in question was being used for the storage of steel girders. The effect of the decision was that land described as agricultural under the Block Government Lease was not restricted to that use but could be used for any purpose that did not require a building. This meant that the government could no longer control the use of agricultural land (which made up much of the rural land in the NT) under the Block Government Lease. There was no system of statutory planning for such land at the time. The government did not appeal against the decision, and inexcusably did not plug the loophole with new statutory planning legislation for rural areas in the NT until 1991. This resulted in the proliferation of open storage and other unsightly uses in the flat areas of the NT, particularly in the North West New Territories (NWNT) where large tracts of land are now used for container storage. These unplanned uses have caused much pollution and traffic chaos. Those that existed before 1991 or the date when the first statutory plan for the particular rural area was first published now enjoy established 'existing' use rights. Because of its significance, a full copy of the 'Melhado' appeal judgement is included in Appendix IV.

It has often been asked why the government did not appeal the 'Melhado' decision to the Privy Council. The answer may be found by looking at another related case which was happening at about the same time. Although it was more related to resumption, it nevertheless contained a very significant declaration on the same question. In *Winfat Enterprises (HK) Co. Ltd.* v *Attorney General* [1983] HKLR 211, the High Court considered permitted uses under a similar Block Government Lease. After doing so, Kempster J. made what was in those proceedings the tenth declaration, in the following terms :

> The severed land may be and prior to resumption the resumed land might lawfully have been used for open storage of motor vehicles or any purpose apart from building purposes inconsistent with the proper occupation of the said lands as agricultural or garden land or from any noisy, noisome or offensive trade or business.

The judgement was upheld by the Court of Appeal including the terms of the tenth declaration [1984] HKLR 32 which was later affirmed by the Privy Council [1988] 1 HKLR5.

Of the three decisions related to this case, the one of the Court of Appeal is the most comprehensive as it sets out the full history of the cession of the NT with a chronology of related statutes which provide very useful background information. A full copy of this judgement can be found in Appendix V.

In the light of these decisions, government's only recourse was the planning option, but as already indicated, they were very slow in implementing the necessary legislation.

The Court of Appeal case which considered the points raised in *Winfat Enterprises (HK) Co. Ltd.* v *Attorney General* [1984] HKLR 32 also gave clear guidelines on the status of international treaties, in particular the Peking Convention of 1898, and their relationship with domestic law. Guidelines are also given on the powers of the Governor to administer land in the NT. A brief resume of the case is that although it was in connection with a land resumption in the NT, the plaintiff, hoping to compel the government to pay full market value for the land, commenced an action seeking a series of declarations to the effect that the legislation concerned, namely the Lands Resumption Ordinance (Cap. 124) was *ultra vires*.

The action was dismissed at trial, but on appeal the plaintiff relied on the NT lease treaty of (Peking Convention of 1898) which contains a clause providing that if NT land is required for a public purpose, it should be bought at a fair price (the 'no-expropriation' clause).

The appeal was dismissed for a number of reasons; two of which are particularly important in the context of land administration:

> 'i.   it was not necessary to decide whether the no-expropriation clause had been breached because even if it had, such breach was not capable of redress in the ordinary courts, the right to enforce a treaty remaining with the high contracting parties alone;
>
> ii.   The Governor has authority to deal as he thinks fit with New Territories land, including the power to impose conditions in Crown Leases, because he is the representative in Hong Kong of the Crown, and all land in the New Territories has been vested in the Crown by statute.'

The first reason for dismissal is also of interest as the point crops up again in a subsequent appeal case: *The Home Restaurant Ltd.* v *Attorney General* [1987] HKLR 237 which is discussed in more detail in Chapter 4. The statute referred to in the second reason quoted above is Section 8 of the New Territories Ordinance (Cap. 97).

The other purpose of the Block Government Leases, apart from establishing title, was also to raise revenue by way of Government rent. Agricultural land was classified as 1st, 2nd or 3rd class and rent was assessed at $3, $2 and $1 per acre accordingly, except in New Kowloon where it was $5, $3 and $1.50 respectively. Building land was charged at $50 an acre or 50 cents per annum per house and $100 an acre in the case of more thriving villages. These rates were fixed by a proclamation on 11 July 1906. Initially, there was great resistance to paying these rents, but later it was reported that in 1910, the total rent collected from the NT was $115 448.05.[4]

The Kowloon Walled City

One of the provisions of the Peking Convention permitted the Chinese government to retain control over a small area of land known as Kau Lung Gai — Kowloon City — but subject to the proviso that this should not be inconsistent with the military requirements for the defence of Hong Kong. On 16 May 1899, the British unilaterally invoked the proviso and the Royal Welsh Fusiliers and 100 Hong Kong Volunteers marched into the deserted Walled City, which was by then largely deserted, and hoisted the Union flag. The Walled

City was formally brought under British administration by proclamation on 27 December 1899 and to demonstrate the point, the first New Territories Land Court set up in 1900 was established in the school building within the city. (See Figure 3.1.)

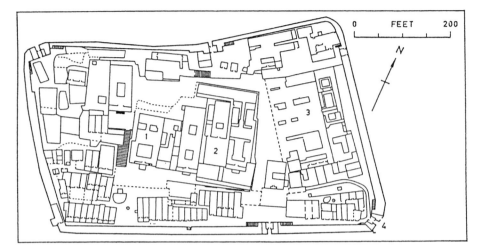

Figure 3.1   The Walled City of Kowloon, 1902

The following can be identified with a fair degree of confidence:
1. Lung Chun Yee Hok, 1847–99; New Territories Land Court, 1900–5
2. Deputy Magistrate's Ya men until 1899; Kwong Yim Home for the Aged, 1902–71; Grace Light School
3. Plague Hospital; Kowloon City Public Dispensary, 1925–33
4. Main gate

The boundaries today are indicated by Tung Tau Tsuen Road to the north and Tung Tsing Road to the east.

Source: 1900–2 Survey, District No. 1, Sheet No. 2; enclosure in Stubbs to Amery, 26 June 1925: CO129/488

However, Kowloon City was to remain an anomaly with the government ambivalent about their authority to administer it like the rest of the territory. Whenever the Hong Kong government attempted to assert its authority, protests were made by the occupants to Beijing, Beijing protested to London and Hong Kong backed off. Thus no rates were ever assessed or levied and municipal services were barely provided. It became a haven for drug addicts and criminals because it was rarely, if ever, policed. The only decisive action government was known to have taken was in 1975 when a building was erected there that infringed the old airport height limits, the Building Authority, without incident, took action to remove the offending storeys. All the buildings apart, from being dangerous and a fire hazard, became appalling slums and an eyesore.

So it came as a great surprise when in 1987 the People's Republic of China (PRC) and Britain announced their agreement that the area should be cleared, the buildings demolished and the land turned into a public park. The government set up a multi-disciplined task force within which the Lands Department ran a specialist team to assess the compensation for the holders of the rather dubious land titles and their tenants (the land was strictly government land and no titles were ever registered). The exercise was successfully completed in 1992 with some 30 000 people compensated and rehoused from the 9000 units that had existed.

All the buildings were demolished in 1993 and an award-winning new park was opened to the public in 1995, thereby closing a curious chapter in Hong Kong's history. A more detailed commentary on this subject can be found in Wesley-Smith (1983) and his article (1973) 3 HKLJ 67.

New Grant Lots

In keeping with the simplified system of land registration devised for existing landowners, an equally simple system of land sales was established. Land was sold by auction with an upset price of one cent per square foot for building land and from 3/4 to 1/4 cent per square foot for agricultural land, plus the Government rent on the scale mentioned above. Lots not exceeding 1000 square feet could be sold by private treaty in districts away from railways or main roads. It was also possible for agricultural land to be let on annual or quinquennial leases with premium.

These sales sites, known as New Grant Lots, were sold subject to standard sets of conditions that were published from time to time in the Government Gazette. Between 1906 and 1946, 14 different Gazette Notifications (GNs) were published. The two that are most frequently referred to are GN 365 of 1906 and GN 364 of 1934. The former provided the first set of very basic standard lease conditions; there were no restrictions on user or site coverage, only a 2-storey height control and a 24-month building covenant period. The latter revoked all earlier GNs and provided slightly more up-to-date conditions. However, there were still no restrictions on user but site coverage was limited to a maximum of 66% of the lot area and the building height was specified at 25 feet with a storey height of not less than 10 feet and a maximum limit of 2 storeys.

Most of the other 12 GNs were to introduce minor amendments to the two principal GNs already referred to. Indeed GN 570 of 1924 revoked GN 365 of 1906 and incorporated all the changes that had been promulgated between times.

GN conditions were widely used in their standard form but were also amended to suit the individual requirements of a particular site. The Government Notification announcing the sale of each lot would specify which of the Special Conditions contained, for example in GN 364, were or were not to apply (see Figure 3.2). Although they are, in theory, standard conditions individual amendments were often made. So care must be taken today when interpreting these types of conditions. It is advisable to go back to the original Government Notification to see exactly what was included or excluded from the sale conditions of each site.

The use of GN conditions was extensive until the Second World War. In the post-war era, they were used less frequently as sites were increasingly tendered or auctioned with their own individual lease conditions. When the Buildings Ordinance (Application to the New Territories) Ordinance (Cap. 322) became effective on 1 January 1961, some conditions of leases that had already been granted subject to GN conditions conflicted with the new law. Those conflicts were dealt with administratively such that the requirement for these owners to submit building plans to the Building Authority was waived. Cap. 322 was repealed and replaced in 1987 by a new Ordinance of the same name and GN lot owners can now make use of these provisions if they so wish.[5]

These gradual changes reflected the changing character of the NT and how the government administered land. Until as recently as 31 March 1982, the District Officers had remained the land authority. It was not until 11 May 1985 under GN 1409 that the use of GN conditions was formally revoked for all future sales. Qualified surveyors were seconded from the former Crown Lands and Survey Office in increasing numbers during the 1960s and 1970s to assist the District Officers particularly, as the New Town development programmes gradually built up momentum and the need for more professionalism became apparent. The first major changes in the NT were the construction of the big reservoirs that resulted in many villages being removed and agricultural land losing its natural water supply if they fell in the water catchment area, and the construction of the first of the new towns in Tsuen Wan from 1960 onwards. An expanded new towns programme which started in the early 1970s resulted in massive land resumptions and disrupted traditional rural life. With improved access and increases in population, the character of the NT inevitably changed. District Land Officers who are all qualified surveyors took over the day-to-day management of the NT from 1 April 1982, so it can be seen that professional land management in the NT is a relatively new phenomenon.

One interesting development in land policy that has arisen in recent years is in regard to columbaria and whether the standard NT leases or GN conditions, which prohibit the storage of 'human remains' on the lot, are breached by columbarium use when the legislation governing crematoria and columbaria does not treat human ash as 'human remains'.

Currently Lands Department takes the view, based on their own internal legal advice, that human ash equates to human remains and therefore would charge a premium for any columbarium use. This approach could stymie the Governments stated desire to increase the number of private columbaria throughout the Territory in order to meet the overall public demand.[6] Some new thinking will be required to overcome this obstacle, perhaps by charging a concessionary land premium in order to encourage such developments.

The contrast with Hong Kong Island and Kowloon Peninsula could not be greater. In these two areas, there was no recognition of Chinese customary law with regard to land ownership, transfer of land or succession; indeed it was explicit in the instructions from London that British law should apply. In comparison with the one used on Hong Kong Island and in Kowloon Peninsula, the system devised for the NT was the simplest one available. It was also closest to the system which the local inhabitants were used to. The District Officers, who in NT land matters acted as the Land Officer for their district, were given, and exercised, very wide powers in the appointment of trustees and in the settlement of land disputes to the extent that lawyers were not allowed to appear in land cases without their express permission. Even if disputes needed to go to court, Section 13 of the New Territories Ordinance (Cap. 97) expressly stated that 'the courts shall have power to recognize and enforce any Chinese custom or customary right affecting such land'.

It is evident that in terms of land administration, there has long been in existence a version of 'one country — two systems' ever since the NT was taken over. This observation will be reinforced when this chapter is read together with the chapters in Section III.

Notes

1. See G.R. Sayer 1937 (Reprint 1980), p. 203.
2. Report on the New Territories 1899–1912 laid before the Legislative Council, 22 August 1912.
3. Extracts from 'Notes for Use in the District Land Offices New Territories', 1908.
4. Report on the New Territories 1899–1912 laid before the Legislative Council, 22 August 1912.
5. Refer to Chapter 14 (p. 118) for details.
6. Review of Columbarium Policy Public Consultation Document, 6/7/2010, at Food & Health Bureau website www.fhb.gov.hk.

No. S. 51. — It is hereby notified that the following Sale of Crown Land by Public Auction will be held at the District Office, South, Queen's Building, 2nd floor, Hong Kong, at 11 a.m., on Friday, the 16th day of February, 1940.

The Lots are sold for the term of seventy-five years from the 1st day of July, 1898, with the right of renewal for a further term of 24 years less the last 3 days at a re-assessed Crown Rent Serial Nos. 1 to 3 as Building Lots, and Serial Nos. 4 to 12 as Agricultural Lots, subject to the General Conditions of Sale published in Government Notification No. 364 of 1934, Serial Nos. 1 to 3 are further subject to Special Conditions Nos. 2 (a) and (b), and Serial Nos. 4 to 12 are further subject to Special Conditions Nos. 1 (a) and (b), in the above Government Notification.

The amounts to be spent on the building lots in Serial Nos. 1 to 3 in rateable improvements under the General Condition No. 5 are $1,500, $250 and $1,750 respectively.

Full Particulars and Conditions may be obtained at this Office.

PARTICULARS OF THE LOTS.

Registry No.				Boundary Measurements						
No.	D.D.	Lot.	Locality	N.	S.	E.	W.	Contents in Acres or Square feet	Upset price	Annual Crown Rent
									$	$. ct.
1	441	106	Tsing I.	As per plan deposited in the District office, South.				2,500 S.F.	50	6.00
2	2	577	Mui Wo.	,,				435 ,,	9	.50
3	4	605	,,	,,				2750 ,,	55	3.50
4	,,	606	,,	,,				.08 acre.	8	.10
5	2	578	,,	,,				.06 ,,	7	.10
6	445	409	Ha Kwai Chung.	,,				.13 ,,	29	.20
7	,,	668	,,	,,				.12 ,,	25	.20
8	,,	670	,,	,,				.58 ,,	126	.60
9	451	129	Lo Wai.	,,				.18 ,,	39	.20
10	453	915	I Pe Chun.	,,				.28 ,,	61	.30
11	453	892	,,	,,				.44 ,,	96	.50
12	,,	893	,,	,,				.06 ,,	13	.10

H. J. Cruttwell,
District Officer, Southern District

2nd February, 1940.

Figure 3.2 Typical Government Notification (GN) for Sale of Land

4

THE SINO-BRITISH JOINT DECLARATION 1984 AND BASIC LAW 1990

The Joint Declaration

The principal reason behind the negotiations that resulted in the signing of this document on 19 December 1984 was the fact that the NT, which comprises 92% of the total land area of the territory, was held on a fixed lease that was to expire on 30 June 1997. Paragraph five of the Introduction to the *White Paper* published by the British government on 26 September 1984 (which coincided with the initialling of the Draft Agreement) inviting public comments on the agreement spells out the background position very clearly:

> In the later 1970s, as the period before the termination of the New Territories lease continued to shorten, concern about the future of Hong Kong began to be expressed both in the territory itself and among foreign investors. In particular there was increasing realization of the problem posed by individual land leases granted in the New Territories, all of which are set to expire three days before the expiry of the New Territories lease in 1997. It was clear that the steadily shortening span of these leases and the inability of the Hong Kong Government to grant new ones extending beyond 1997 would be likely to deter investment and damage confidence.

In other words, because of the fundamental basis of the leasehold land system, Britain had no option but to formally ask the PRC that the question of the expiring NT lease be resolved. Keeping Hong Kong Island and Kowloon Peninsula on their own was completely untenable and therefore the issue had to be addressed so that there would be a legal basis for continuing to grant extended land leases.

The Joint Declaration states that the rights concerning the ownership of property, including those relating to acquisition, use, disposal, inheritance and compensation for lawful deprivation (corresponding to the real value of the property concerned, freely convertible and paid without undue delay) shall continue to be protected by law.

The significance of land in the overall negotiations is reinforced by the fact that an entire annex was required to set out in detail how land leases were to be dealt with and to state the new policies that were to apply to the treatment of land leases which were due to expire on or before 30 June 1997. Due to its importance, Annex III is reproduced in full below:

Land leases

The Government of the United Kingdom and the Government of the People's Republic of China have agreed that, with effect from the entry into force of the Joint Declaration, (27th May 1985) land leases in Hong Kong other related matters shall be dealt with in accordance with the following provisions :

1. All leases of land granted or decided upon before the entry into force of the Joint Declaration and those granted thereafter in accordance with paragraph 2 or 3 of this Annex, and which extend beyond 30 June 1997, and all rights in relation to such leases shall continue to be recognized and protected under the law of the Hong Kong Special Administrative Region.

2. All leases of land granted by the British Hong Kong Government not containing a right of renewal that expire before 30 June 1997, except short term tenancies and leases for special purposes, may be extended if the lessee so wishes for a period expiring not later than 30 June 2047 without payment of an additional premium. An annual rent shall be charged from the date, adjusted in step with any changes in the ratable value thereafter. In the case of old schedule lots, village lots, small houses and similar rural holdings, where the property was on 30 June 1984 held by, or, in the case of small houses granted after that date, the property is granted to, a person descended through the male line from a person who was in 1898 a resident of an established village in Hong Kong, the rent shall remain unchanged so long as the property is held by that person or by one of his lawful successors in the male line. Where leases of land not having a right of renewal expire after 30 June 1997, they shall be dealt with in accordance with the relevant land laws and policies of the Hong Kong Special Administrative Region.

3. From the entry into force of the Joint Declaration until 30 June 1997, new leases of land may be granted by the British Hong Kong Government for terms expiring not later than 30 June 2047. Such leases shall be granted at a premium and nominal rental until 30 June 1997, after which date they shall not require payment of an additional premium but an annual rent equivalent to 3 per cent of the ratable value of the property at that date, adjusted in step with changes in the ratable value thereafter, shall be charged.

4. The total amount of new land to be granted under paragraph 3 of this Annex shall be limited to 50 hectares a year (excluding land to be granted to the Hong Kong Housing Authority for public rental housing) from the entry into force of the Joint Declaration until 30 June 1997.

5. Modifications of the conditions specified in leases granted by the British Hong Kong Government may continue to be granted before 1 July 1997 at a premium equivalent to the difference between the value of the land under the previous conditions and its value under the modified conditions.

6. From the entry into force of the Joint Declaration until 30 June 1997, premium income obtained by the British Hong Kong Government from land transactions shall, after deduction of the average cost of land production, be shared equally between the British Hong Kong Government and the future Hong Kong Special Administrative Region Government. All the income obtained by the British Hong Kong Government, including the amount of the above mentioned deduction, shall be put into the Capital Works Reserve Fund for the financing of land development and public works in Hong Kong. The Hong Kong Special Administrative Region Government's share of the premium income shall be deposited in banks incorporated in Hong Kong and shall not be drawn on except for the financing of land development and public works in Hong Kong in accordance with the provision of paragraph 7(d) of this Annex.

7. A Land Commission shall be established in Hong Kong immediately upon the entry into force of the Joint Declaration. The Land Commission shall be composed of an equal number of officials designated respectively by the Government of the United Kingdom and the Government of the People's Republic of China together with necessary supporting staff. The officials of the two sides shall be responsible to their respective governments. The Land Commission shall be dissolved on 30 June 1997. The terms of reference of the Land Commission shall be:

   a) to conduct consultations on the implementation of this Annex;
   b) to monitor observance of the limit specified in paragraph 4 of this Annex, the amount of land granted to the Hong Kong Housing Authority for public rental housing, and the division and use of premium income referred to in paragraph 6 of this Annex;
   c) to consider and decide on proposals from the British Hong Kong Government for increasing the limit referred to in paragraph 4 of this Annex;
   d) to examine proposals for drawing on the Hong Kong Special Administrative Region Government's share of premium income referred to in paragraph 6 of this Annex and to make recommendations to the Chinese side for decision.

   Matters on which there is disagreement in the Land Commission shall be referred to the Government of the United Kingdom and the Government of the People's Republic of China for decision.

8. Special details regarding the establishment of the Land Commission shall be finalized separately by the two sides through consultations.

The establishment of the Land Commission in 1985 gave the PRC a good and lengthy insight into how land was administered in Hong Kong. Arguably it was the organization that operated the most efficiently during the transition period during which time they probably came to understand why Britain had no choice but to formally approach them on the question of the expiring NT lease. It had plenty of work to accomplish starting with the vetting of the legislative changes that were required to implement the policies that had been agreed.

Lease Extensions

The only practical way of extending all the leases in the NT was by legislation. On 21 January 1988, the New Territories Leases (Extension) Ordinance (Cap. 150) was enacted which automatically extended all leases in the NT, with the exception of short-term tenancies and leases for special purposes, from their existing expiry dates until 30 June 2047 without requiring payment of a premium, but with an annual rent to be charged as described in paragraph 2 of Annex III.

On 1 February 1990, the Lands Administration Office issued Practice Note 1/1990 to Authorized Persons, Solicitors and Chartered Surveyors reminding them of the general policy that was to be applied to *the extension of leases not containing a right of renewal in the urban areas*, it reads as follows:

> The purpose of this Practice Note is to remove any doubt relating to the general policy on the treatment of Government leases not containing a right of renewal that expire before 30 June 1997 in the urban area and which are not 'short term tenancies' or 'lease for special purposes'. This policy is that such leases will normally be extended beyond their expiry date unless the site is required for a foreseen Government use or other public purpose. There has been no change in this policy since the entry into force of the Sino-British Joint Declaration.

> Annex III of the Joint Declaration provides that the term of such leases may be extended, if the lessee so wishes, for a period expiring not later than 30 June 2047 without payment of an additional premium but subject to an annual rent from the date of extension equivalent to 3% of the rateable value of the property at that date, adjusted in step with any changes in the rateable value thereafter. (Prior to the Joint Declaration, if leases not containing a right of renewal were regranted, this was done on payment of a full market value land premium.) The Joint Declaration enables the Government to extend such leases in the way described above but does not oblige it to do so.

For the purposes short term tenancies are defined as leases which were originally granted for a term of not more than seven years, and special purpose leases are defined as those which contain a permanent prohibition against assignment.[1] There were 842 special purpose leases, granted by private treaty for specific purposes such as public utilities, special industries, schools, welfare facilities, recreational clubs, churches and so on. Each of these leases was examined individually, and virtually all of them were extended, without premium, but on payment of the new annual rent. The very few that were not extended had either ceased to be using the land for the original purpose it was granted, or the land was needed for some known public purpose.

The enactment of this legislation was a significant step in implementing one of the major principles laid down in the Joint Declaration.

The Hong Kong Special Administrative Region Government (HKSARG) currently collects over $5 billion annually as a result of these revised rents. It is not an insignificant sum that will go some way to compensate for the fact that Britain occupied the NT for 99 years rent free!

The 50-Hectare Quota

Pargraph 4 of Annex III limited the amount of new land that could be granted in any one year to 50 hectares. However, paragraph 7 b) and 7 c) of the same Annex set out the terms of reference for the Land Commission; they clearly indicated that with proper consultation additional areas beyond the stated limit could be approved. The British had asked for a higher figure when negotiating the agreement, but it is understood the PRC was insistent on the 50-hectare limit. They knew that, by insisting on this limit, there would, every year, be requests for extra quota. By requiring that all additional quota had to be justified to the Land Commission, they could exercise a major influence on how and when land was granted. In the event, as Figure 4.1 indicates, the 50-hectare quota was exceeded in every year of the transition; this shows that a prudent and practical approach was adopted.

There were comments expressed from time to time that the 50-hectare quota was an artificial constraint on land supply. Apart from the land for luxury housing, the facts do not bear this out because during the 12 years of transition, the property market was, by and large, growing steadily with none of the dramatic fluctuations that were experienced in 1973–4 and 1981–2. There were some relatively minor setbacks to the market in 1989–91 and also 1993–4, which were reflected in the lower take-up rate of land. But more importantly, when the property market started to experience much stronger growth in the last two years of the transition, the Land Commission responded by agreeing to a significantly higher quota for sale, particularly in the residential sector.

However, there was one weakness in the system as the land quota was given in terms of land area rather than permitted gross floor area. As a consequence, the Lands Department were naturally reluctant to sell sites with a low density of development as they would consume comparatively more of the quota. This fact probably contributed to the shortage of supply at the luxury end of the market experienced in 1996 and 1997.

The financial implications were not lost sight of either. At the time the Joint Declaration was signed, it was estimated that the Land Fund established under paragraph 6 of Annex III would, with interest accrued, probably reach $25 billion at prices then prevailing. By the time the Land Commission ceased to

Land Disposal Programme (hectares)
(including supplementary figures if applicable)

User category	85/86	86/87	87/88	88/89	89/90	90/91	91/92	92/93	93/94	94/95	95/96	96/97
Private commercial[1]	16.39	18.53	27.54	24.16	22.07	20.31	26.67	25.22	21.67	32.20	44.45	50.20
Assisted housing[2]	2.76	19.64	18.87	19.81	18.44	19.68	15.52	16.87	24.65	35.81	37.04	42.64
Infrastructure[3]	6.87	13.99	12.23	12.44	10.64	8.91	9.87	14.65	5.85	5.21	9.39	16.31
Special requirement[4]	28.72	6.39	11.51	91.50	8.92	71.85	5.63	33.72	55.95	1305.98	85.19	201.02
Total	54.74	58.55	70.15	147.91	60.07	120.75	57.69	90.46	108.12	1379.2	176.07	310.17

1 including residential and industrial development.
2 e.g. Home Ownership Scheme, Sandwich Class Housing Scheme, Private Sector Participation Scheme, etc. (excluding any land for public rental housing)
3 including public utilities, education, welfare, religious and recreational uses.
4 e.g. Chek Lap Kok new airport (1248 hectares) in 94/95.

Figure 4.1 Land Disposal Programme, 1985/86–96/97

operate, the actual figure was a remarkable $197 billion which would all help in giving the new HKSARG an excellent financial foundation. This sum, together with all subsequent premium income from land transactions, is credited to the Capital Works Reserve Fund under the Public Finance Ordinance (Cap. 2)

Annex III of the Joint Declaration was referred to by one lessee in a Court of Appeal case *The Home Restaurant Ltd.* v *Attorney General* [1987] HKLR 237. The case raised two interesting issues; the first was related to the status of international agreements in domestic law while the second was related to the principle of legitimate expectation. The following extracts summarize the points raised and the decision given:

> This was a dispute over the terms on which a Crown lease, which had expired in 1978, would be renewed. The Crown had offered, in 1986, to renew the lease until the year 2047 on terms which would require payment of a substantial premium as well as annual rent. The lessee contended that it was entitled, under the Sino-British Joint Declaration on the question of Hong Kong, to a renewal without payment of premium. Paragraph 2 of Annex III of the joint declaration provides that leases expiring prior to the reversion of Hong Kong to Chinese rule in 1997 may be renewed on terms requiring payment of an annual rent equivalent to three per cent of the rateable value of the land, 'without payment of an additional premium'.

> Held, allowing the Attorney General's application for an order that the lessee's proceedings be set aside, (1) the Joint Declaration, its annexes and accompanying government announcements are within the realm of treaties, and as such are not justiciable in the courts of Hong Kong; (2) government announcements to the effect that it intended to implement the joint declaration did not give rise to a justiciable legitimate expectation (*Attorney General v Ng Yuen-shui* [1983] 2 AC 629 distinguished).

> #### The Status of international agreements in domestic law

> The common law has long held that international agreements, being the fruit of the Crown's exercise of its prerogative in respect of foreign affairs, are not justiciable in the ordinary courts of the land unless and until they have been given the force of law in implementing legislation (*Attorney General of Canada v Attorney General of Ontario* [1937] AC 326). There is no doubt that rule is in force in Hong Kong (*Winfat Enterprises (HK) Co. Ltd v Attorney General* [1985] AC 733) and the lessee in this case cannot seriously have hoped that the court would find in its favour on this point. Although it is true that in *Council of Civil Service Unions v Minister for the Civil Service* [1985] AC 374 the House of Lords opened the door to judicial review of the manner of exercise of prerogative powers, giving the force of domestic law to unimplemented treaties would be quite another thing.

Legitimate expectation

The lessee's related argument, that the Joint Declaration gave rise to a justiciable legitimate expectation did not, however, have the weight of authority bearing against it. The lessee relied on *Attorney General v Ng Yuen-shiu* [1983] 2 AC 629 in which the Privy Council held that the Hong Kong Government was bound to act in accordance with its public pronouncements in connection with the treatment of illegal immigrants on termination of the 'reach base' policy in 1980. Here, however, the court held that it would be impossible to find a justiciable legitimate expectation without a detailed examination of the Joint Declaration, the very thing it cannot do.

In any event, given that the Crown lease in this case expired six years before the signing of the Joint Declaration, it is difficult to see how, on the facts, the lessee could assert a legitimate expectation arising from the Joint Declaration.

It is not surprising that the lessee wanted to argue the point because the financial implications were enormous. The premium required for the lease renewal was quoted at about \$8.5 million. However, 3% of rateable value would have given a new annual rent of only \$21 600. Adopting an investment rate of 5%, this would give 20 years purchase resulting in an equivalent premium of a mere \$432 000!

This one case alone gives a very clear indication of the significant concession that lessees of both renewable and non-renewable lease received as a result of the Joint Declaration.

It was evident that the signing of the Joint Declaration had an immediate beneficial impact as the local property market had experienced a severe slump starting in 1981–82 which lasted through until this time. There was the collapse of the Carrian Group, the closure of a number of banks, interest rates were close to 20% and if one added to this the political uncertainties about Hong Kong's future, it is not surprising that the property market was dead. In this environment, it was pointless for land to be put up for auction because there were simply no bidders. Instead, the Lands Department had a policy whereby sites that were ready for sale were published on what was called a 'reserve list'. If any developer was interested in a particular site, they could contact the department. Provided that they paid an agreed deposit in advance to guarantee they would make the opening bid, the auction conditions would be prepared and a sale date fixed. It seems that over the Christmas holidays of 1984, the development industry read and digested the Joint Declaration, and liked what they saw. Immediately after the resumption of business in the new year of 1985, numerous enquiries were received for sites on the reserve list to be put up for sale, the most prominent ones being those that now comprise the development at Pacific Place. Perhaps the economic cycle had completed its circuit but there can be no doubt that the Joint Declaration and Annex III in particular had a very positive effect on the property industry and the property market.

The Basic Law

The Basic Law was adopted by the National People Congress of the PRC on 4 April 1990 and spells out, in effect, the new constitutional arrangements for the HKSAR which came into effect on 1 July 1997. The six articles set out below are the ones relevant to property ownership and land:

Article 6   The Hong Kong Special Administrative Region shall protect the right of private ownership of property in accordance with law.

Article 7   The land and natural resources within the Hong Kong Special Administrative Region shall be State property. The Government of the Hong Kong Special Administrative Region shall be responsible for their management, use and development and for their lease or grant to individuals, legal persons or organizations for use or development. The revenues derived therefrom shall be exclusively at the disposal of the Government of the Region.

Article 120 All leases of land granted, decided upon or renewed before the establishment of the Hong Kong Kong Special Administrative Region which extend beyond 30 June 1997, and all rights in relation to such leases, shall continue to be recognized and protected under the law of the Region.

Article 121 As regards all leases of land granted or renewed where the original leases contain no right of renewal, during the period from 27 May 1985 to 30 June 1997, which extend beyond 30 June 1997 and expire not later than 30 June 2047, the lessee is not required to pay an additional premium as from 1 July 1997, but an annual rent equivalent to 3% of the rateable value of the property at that date, adjusted in step with any changes in the rateable value thereafter, shall be charged.

Article 122 In the case of old schedule lots, village lots, small houses and similar rural holdings, where the property was on 30 June 1984 held by, or, in the case of small houses granted after that date, where the property is granted to, a lessee descended through the male line from a person who was in 1898 a resident of an established village in Hong Kong, the previous rent shall remain unchanged so long as the property is held by that lessee or by one of his lawful successors in the male line.

Article 123 Where leases of land without a right of renewal expire after the establishment of the Hong Kong Special Administrative Region, they shall be dealt with in accordance with laws and policies formulated by the Region on its own.

Article 6 protects all existing landowners subject to current legislation which may in future be amended or changed. Article 7 converts all the former Crown or government land into state owned property and gives the HKSARG the authority to grant new leases and manage such land. Articles 120, 121, 122 and 123 are a reaffirmation of the essential paragraphs contained in Annex III of the Joint Declaration. Article 120 reaffirms paragraph 1 and Articles 121, 122 and 123 reaffirm paragraphs 2 and 3.

Following the rulings handed down in *Winfat Enterprises (HK) Ltd.* v *Attorney General* [1985] AC 733 and *The Home Restaurant Ltd* v *Attorney General* [1987] HKLR 237, it is clear that the provisions of the Basic Law do not confer on the owner of a Government lease the automatic right to a renewal of that lease; this would apply in particular to Article 123.

Paragraph 2 of Annex III to the Joint Declaration now embodied as Article 121 of the Basic Law represented a very significant concession to the holders of non-renewable leases, particularly to leaseholders in the urban area. As discussed in the decision of the case *The Home Restaurant Ltd.* v *Attorney General* above, where the lease had expired in 1978, a substantial premium had been charged for the right to renewal. Looking at Article 123 of the Basic Law, those leaseholders who have non-renewable lease which expire after 1 July 1997 will be very happy that as early as 15 July 1997, the new Executive Council of the HKSARG agreed that the same concession will be applied to them so that these leaseholders now know where they stand.

Note

1.   See New Territories Leases (Extension) Ordinance (Cap. 150).

HONG KONG SPECIAL ADMINISTRATIVE REGION GOVERNMENT

Up until 30 June 1997 under Article XIII of the Hong Kong Letters Patent, the Governor had the power to make and execute grants and disposition of land in the territory. This power was, in turn, delegated down to the Director of Lands and his senior staff. During the very first hours of 1 July 1997, the Hong Kong Reunification Ordinance was enacted to ensure a seamless legal and administrative transfer from the old to the new administration. As regards land administration, Sections 27 and 32 of this ordinance are particularly relevant and are quoted below in full:

Delegations relating to land

All delegations to public officer of the power of the Governor to grant or dispose of land which were in force immediately before 1st July 1997 shall on and after that date continue in force and be deemed to be delegations to the corresponding public officer in the HKSAR of the power of the Chief Executive to lease or grant State land.

Lease or grant of land and natural resources

The Chief Executive may on behalf of the Government of the HKSAR lease or grant land and natural resources within the HKSAR which are State property.

There was welcome news for the property industry when just 15 days after the transfer to sovereignty, the Executive Council of the HKSARG approved the new policies that were to apply to the granting, modifying, renewing and extending of land leases. In essence, the policies that were applicable in the twelve and a half year transition period leading up to the transfer of sovereignty were very quickly reaffirmed which not only resulted in consistency but perhaps more important certainty for everyone involved in the development field. The basic principles that are applied by the Lands Department are as follows:

1. **New leases**

    These are granted, except for new special purpose leases for recreational purposes, petrol filling stations, public utility companies or franchises and short- term tenancies, for a period of 50 years *from the date of grant*, at a premium and subject to payment from the date of the land grant of an annual rent equivalent to 3% of rateable value of the property at that dated, adjusted in step with any changes in the rateable value. The exemptions from the liability to pay such rent in respect of certain rural holdings as permitted in accordance with Annex III of the Joint Declaration will continue.

    New recreational leases and petrol filling stations are granted on 21-year leases. Public utility companies or other companies with a franchise or operating licence will normally receive a grant for the same length of time as their franchise or licence.

2. **Modifications of lease conditions**

    Again there were no significant changes in policy. Modification cases which do not involve any realignment of the boundaries of the lot(s) in question are executed by modification letters with all the conditions previously applicable to the lease, including the lease term and rent remaining unchanged, with the exception of the conditions being modified. In all other modification cases executed by surrender and regrant, that is, land exchanges the new term is for 50 years *from the date of the Conditions of Exchange are executed* subject to an annual rent equivalent to 3% of the rateable value of the property, adjusted in step with changes in the rateable value thereafter, and payable from the date of regrant.

    As before the premium to be charged for modifications and land exchanges will be equivalent to the difference between the value of the land under the previous conditions and its value under the modified conditions.

3. **Non-renewable leases**

    Leases not containing a right of renewal , upon expiry, should, at the sole discretion of the HKSARG, be extended for a term of 50 years, without payment of an additional premium but an annual rent is charged from the date of extension equivalent to 3% of the rateable value of the property adjusted in step with any change in the rateable value thereafter.

    The phrasing of this statement makes it clear that lessees do not have an automatic right of renewal and, as previously, if for example the lessee has ceased using the land for the original purpose it was granted, or was not making the most efficient use of the land in question by serious under-utilization, or if the land was required for a planned public purpose, then it may be reasonable to expect that the HKSARG would not renew such leases.

There is one case in this category which is a cause for concern because the government has, without giving reasons, decided not to renew the lease of Kowloon Permenant Pier No. 83, otherwise known as Ocean Terminal. Furthermore, the government has stated that on expiry of the lease, it will in due course dispose of the development by open competition. The current lease term is for 21 years from 17 June 1966 renewable, at a premium, for a further term of 25 years; it will therefore expire on 16 June 2012. Under the terms of the lease, the lot is to be used as a commercial ocean terminal with such other associated facilities as the lessee shall think fit. Not surprisingly, in view of the massive financial implications running into billions of dollars, the current leaseholder made an application for Judicial Review (HCAL 14/2005) which was granted on 3 February 2005.

The gist of the leaseholder's case is as follows:

The Secretary for Planning, Environment and Lands, in a press release (which had been approved by the Executive Council) on 15 July 1997, made the following statements (**'1997 Policy Statement'**) about the manner in which the government shall deal with land leases and related matters in exercise of its authority under Articles 7 and 123 of the Basic Law:

> Non-renewable leases will, upon expiry and at the Government's sole discretion, be extended for a term of 50 years without payment of an additional premium. However, an annual Government rent of three per cent of the rateable value will be charged from the date of extension to be adjusted in step with changes in the rateable value.

> It is also important to emphasize that the lessees do not have an automatic right of renewal of their non-renewable leases. Such extension of non-renewable leases will be at the Government's sole discretion, i.e. the Government may, if circumstances require in the public interest, decide not to extend certain leases.

> We expect however that most of the non-renewable leases will be renewed.

The Applicant argued that the 1997 Policy Statement applies to the Lease and asked for:

(a) an Order directing the Director of Lands to give reasons for the Decisions;

(b) a declaration that the 1997 Policy Statement applies to the renewal of the Lease and/or the proposed surrender and re-grant;

(c) a declaration that the Applicant has a legitimate expectation that once the District Lands Conference has approved in principle the application for the proposed surrender and re-grant, it will not thereafter be rejected by the Lands Department or any other governmental body without submission to the Chief Executive in Council;

(d) a declaration that the Director of Lands' decision that 'the development will be disposed of by open competition in due course' is contrary to the 1997 Policy Statement; and

(e) a declaration that the disposal of land by open competition is not a relevant 'public interest' as stated in the 1997 Policy Statement that 'the Government may, if circumstances require in the public interest, decide not to extend certain leases'.

It is worth noting the non-standard nature of both the lease term and the user which may have encouraged the Lands Department to act as it has done. On the other hand, the leaseholder will point to the fact that there have been no substantive breaches of the existing lease and that the lot is being used in conformity with the current statutory land use zoning plan.

There was a curious but inconclusive end to this affair when the lessees withdrew their application for Judicial Review in July 2007 because the government's counsel advised the judge that the administration had merely decided not to allow an early surrender of the lease in exchange for a new 21-year, implying that it had not completely ruled out the possibility of granting an extension closer to the date of expiry of the current lease in 2012. Unfortunately this still leaves a high degree of uncertainty in a matter that demands clarity and consistency for all future lease renewals.

Separately, the Hong Kong Institute of Certified Public Accountants have for the purposes of amortization (depreciation) promulgated their own determination on the same issue. With effect from 24 May 2005, they advise that 'lessees shall not assume that the lease term of a Hong Kong land lease will be extended for a further 50 years, or any other period, while the HKSAR Government retains the sole discretion as whether to renew'.

4. Extension of special purpose leases

The same principles set out in paragraph 3 above are to be applied to this category of leases where, again following the previous policy, it is now agreed that special purposes leases other than those specified below may, on expiry and at the HKSARG's sole discretion, be extended for a term of 50 years without payment of a premium, but an annual rent shall be charged from the date of extension equivalent to 3% of the rateable value of the property at that date adjusted in step with any changes in the rateable value thereafter. The exceptions to the arrangements, which again are unchanged from before, are as follows:

(a) leases for recreational purposes may not be extended for a term exceeding 15 years;

(b) leases covered by franchises or operating licences should normally be extended for a term to be the same as that of the franchise or licence;

(c) leases for petrol filling stations may not be extended; new leases for a term of not more than 21 years may, however, be granted to the existing owner on payment of a premium; and

(d) leases for kerosene stores may not be extended; however, short-term tenancies at full market rental may be offered to the existing owner for an initial term of three years.

5. Short-term tenancies

As previously these are to be considered separately from leases and are normally granted for periods of not more than seven years. This is, of course, consistent with the definition of short term tenancy which is contained in the New Territories Leases (Extension) Ordinance 1988 (Cap. 150), for the purpose of that Ordinance.

A couple of interesting and significant points arise as a result of the promulgation of these new policies. First, new leases and renewed leases are now for a period of 50 years from the date of grant or renewal. Prior to 1 July 1997, all new leases and renewals could only be up until 30 June 2047, but with this new announcement it means that the new and extended leases and presumably the HKSARG itself are going to go on beyond that date? Again, this is very encouraging news for anyone who is involved, or who wishes to get involved not only in the local property industry but in Hong Kong as a whole. The second point relates to statements with regard to modification and land exchanges. Again it is the application of these new policies in the NT that may start to throw up anomalies. All the NT leases were extended until 30 June 2047. So if only a modification is now required, there will be no extension of the lease term. However, if a modification is to be carried out by land exchange, a fresh term of 50 years will be given from the date the Conditions of Exchange are executed. Initially this will not pose too many problems, but in another 10 or 15 years' time, it will be more attractive to go for a land exchange rather than a modification because of the longer tenure available.

Now that the land policies have been set down by the new administration and are operating, one final point emerges. Back in 1973, the previous administration first had to struggle with, and find a solution to, the problem of how to treat non-renewable leases that were due to expire but the sites of which had been developed and sold into multiple undivided shares representing individual ownership of flats. The relatively simple formula of charging 3% of rateable value was devised and enacted. This enabled those individual owners to remain without paying a single huge premium, but instead an enhanced annual rental to the landlord, that is, the government, in recognition of their leases being extended. The same formula was again applied by statute to the NT leases that were all going to expire on 27 June 1997. The formula has been working well so far. Non-renewable leases are now generally renewed or extended for 50 years without payment of premium but on payment of an increased annual rent, presumably in lieu of premium, to reflect the benefit conveyed to the lessee by the lessor, that is, the government. Is it right then that the government should also charge this 3% of rateable value in respect of those leases where a full market premium has been realized either at auction or tender, or by assessment as a result of a modification or land exchange? In practice, this 3% of rateable value will usually be borne by the new owners of the undivided shares of finished flats once they have been sold. In effect, they are being required to pay the equivalent of their renewal rent in advance of the expiry of their particular lease. Perhaps this means that what has now been established in Hong Kong is a land tenure system which is, in effect, a perpetual leasehold.

On 17 April 1998, the government gazetted the Adaptation of Laws (Crown Land) Ordinance No. 29 of 1998 to make amendments to the laws of Hong Kong, in connection with references in those laws to the Crown in relation to land, to make them conform with the Basic Law. As the title implies, all existing ordinances have now been amended to delete all references to the word 'Crown', usually by substituting it with the word 'Government'. The following ordinances have had their short title amended as indicated:

- Land (Miscellaneous Provisions) Ordinance —
  formerly Crown Land Ordinance (Cap. 28)
- Lands Resumption Ordinance —
  formerly Crown Lands Resumption Ordinance (Cap. 124)
- Government Leases Ordinance —
  formerly Crown Land Leases (Cap. 40)
- Government Rights (Re-entry and Vesting Remedies) Ordinance —
  formerly Crown Rights (Re-entry and Vesting Remedies) Ordinance (Cap. 126)

- New Territories (Renewable Government Leases) Ordinance —
  formerly New Territories (Renewable Crown Leases) Ordinance (Cap. 152)

A noticeable feature of the new HKSARG is the increasing intrusion of politics into every strata of the government. There is now a tendency for every decision to be challenged by local politicians, civic groups, or the Director of Audit, and complaints are frequently made to the Commission of Administrative Complaints and/or the media. These intrusions have resulted in a noticeable drop in efficiency of the whole administration as civil servants become ultra cautious about making mistakes or being accused of collusion or inadvertently conferring benefits without proper charge. All these result in a slowing down of the service they provide.

The dictionary definition of collusion is 'fraudulent secret understanding'; so if it does exist, and can be proved, this would be a serious criminal matter for the Independent Commission Against Corruption to investigate. Thus such accusations should not be made lightly.

The Lands Department has not been immune to the change, as evidenced by the Director of Audit's criticism in Chapter 6 of Report No. 43, October 2004 concerning the development of Discovery Bay. In the 1970s and 1980s the administration had approved major changes to the Master Layout Plan (MLP) which resulted in a change of use and development intensity without having charged a premium. This case is an historical anomaly in that the original grant was made some 30 years ago and, to the writer's knowledge, is the only time a lease was issued containing no restrictions as to permitted gross floor area, with development density controlled through the approved MLP. Such arrangement no longer occurs because contemporary leases contain clear statements as to user, permitted gross floor area (gfa), and a whole host of other development parameters.

From 1994 onwards changes to the MLP were permitted subject to the payment of premium, implying perhaps that the earlier changes did not warrant charging. However, the Director of Audit recommended in his report that the Director of Lands when drawing up lease conditions should explicitly state that premium will be charged on making changes to an approved MLP. The Director of Lands' position is that whether a consent fee will be charged will depend on whether there is any enhancement in value. On the basis of established case law (*Hang Wah Chong Investments Co. Ltd.* v *Attorney General* [1981] HKLR 336, [1981] WLR 1141) he is already entitled to charge a premium for consenting to alterations to MLPs and stating as such in MLP clauses serves no purpose other than to explicitly remind the owner of the position. The Director of Lands has also reassured the property industry that this change is not intended to indicate any change in policy on the exercising of that right.

We will have to wait and see but inevitably there will be delays in future amendment submissions as Lands Department staff pore over the plans looking for anything resembling a chargeable enhancement.

It is also apparent that since the Director of Audit's report, the Lands Department has started to state in public that it perceives its role as a protector of the public purse and that it will pursue premium collection wherever possible as an important source of public revenue. This is also evident in the department's attitude to charging premium for what are called 'incentives' to encourage the design and construction of buildings that will improve and protect the built and natural environment. How can it be called an incentive if it has to be paid for? If the administration as a whole is sincere in its desire to promote the principle of sustainable development, then these 'incentives' should be precisely that and not charged for! This change in attitude is disturbing because the role of the Lands Department has always been twofold — ensuring good development control first, and revenue collection second. It would be a great shame if the department abdicates the first and simply focuses on the second.

Another concern is the administration's lack of belief and trust in the operation of an open market for the sale of government land. Since 2004, despite the market's overall recovery, the administration abandoned the regular land auction programme, whereby two or three parcels of land were offered for sale every two to three months. Instead there is a procedure for land sale under an application system, spelt out in Lands Department Practice Note No. 1/2007, whereby developers can select sites from the Application List and offer a guaranteed minimum price; provided this price is 80% or more of the department's own assessment of Open Market Value this will be accepted as a trigger to initiate an auction or tender. During the financial year 2004/05, six sites were triggered for sale in four separate auctions. In 2005/06, three sites were triggered and sold in a single auction.

In 2006/07 a further nine sites were triggered for sale in six separate auctions. The 18 sites over the three years sold, on average, at over 85% of the trigger price; the lowest number of bids was 24 and the highest number 221! This all indicates significant pent-up demand and a healthy market response. Up until the end of 2010 only 41 sites with a total site area of 43.54 hectares were sold under the application system. This miserly release of land, averaging 6.2 hectares per annum over seven years, should be compared with the more generous and healthier land disposal programme from 1985 until 1997 set out in Figure 4.1 on page 32.

The shortage of land supply has resulted in a significant drop in the number of newly completed flats for sale with only 8000 and 8200 new units started in 2008 and 2009 respectively. Flat sale prices now have risen to close, or even beyond, their 1997 peak exacerbated by the shortage in land supply.

The 2011-12 land sale programme has 64 sites available, 52 of which are for residential use. Initially only four of these sites were to offered at Government initiated auction and four were to be tendered. However in a welcome change of heart, in part stimulated by private developer interest, the Government in the April to June quarter ended up auctioning or tendering nine sites and for the July to September quarter has taken a further six sites off the application list to be auctioned without the need to be triggered. However in light of the most recent international financial crisis in the autumn of 2011 their third quarter land sales will all be by way of tender.

The relationship between land supply and flat production has been clearly demonstrated in the previous paragraphs and the Chief Executive in his 2011–12 Policy Address has finally admitted there has, in recent years, been an inadequante supply of land that Government needs to remedy in order to ensure a healthy and stable development of the property market. A number of initatives have been suggested but these will inevitably take time to make on impact.

Land Revenue Reform?

One of the problems that has occurred over time is the significant change in the balance between land premium and ground rents. In broad terms on lots that were sold before the Second World War the capitalized fixed ground rent for a 75-year lease equated to the same as the bid premium, ie a 50–50 split. Compared with today where a 50-year lease is required to pay 3% of adjustable rateable value in ground rent so in effect 97% of the land value is in the up-front premium and 3% is collected over the life of the lease.

This high-premium-low-rent structure has some of the following consequences:
1. Only a handful of large developers have big enough balance sheets to afford large-scale projects on their own, reducing competition;
2. The Government receives lump-sum revenue in return for future land use, rather than recurrent ground rents that would smooth out revenues and allow it to better match future expenditure with income;
3. The Government earmarks land premiums in a separate account called the 'Capital Works Reserve Fund' (CWRF) and feels obliged to spend it on one off, sometimes of dubious economic value, infrastructure projects; and
4. The high land costs are naturally reflected in the sale price of newly built buildings of all use categories.

It would therefore be prudent for the Government to seriously consider shifting the balance back towards ground rents that could have the following benefits:

1. The up-front premiums to develop are reduced lowering the barriers to entry thereby increasing competition;
2. The Government would receive smaller premiums but would build up stronger and reliable annual recurrent revenues that could be directed, for example, towards education, welfare, health care and nature conservation;
3. Higher ground rents would go the General Reserve not the CWRF, hopefully, reducing wasteful infrastructure projects; and
4. The lower land premiums should be reflected in lower sale prices enhancing affordability across the board.

Implementing such radical changes will not be easy, for example at what level should the new ground rents be set: 5%, 10%, 15% or even 30% of rateable value? However unless such possibilities are explored the current 'high land price policy' will prevail.

II | PRESENT-DAY LAND ADMINISTRATION

These chapters deal with the present-day land administration policies with special reference to the functions of the Lands Department in respect of land disposal, modifications and exchanges. Particular emphasis is placed on the control of development through lease conditions. Land management and lease enforcement are also considered.

As land is a scarce commodity, it is essential to have an effective and professional land administration system in order to keep pace with the fast rate of growth.

Under Article 7 of The Basic Law, the Hong Kong Special Administrative Region Government is responsible for the management, use and development of land and for granting leases to individuals, legal persons or organizations for the use or development of land. In practice, this power is delegated from the Chief Executive to the Secretary for Development, who provides the key policy guidelines, and then down to the officers of the Lands Department which is the government's executive arm for land disposal, land acquisition and land management.

The Lands Department, which is headed by the Director of Lands, is responsible for all aspects of land administration. The department plays a major role in the entire property development cycle: granting leases, arranging public auctions, tenders and private treaty grants of government land. It is also involved in the approval of building plans and monitoring development performance.

There are specialist sections that deal with the acquisition of private land for public projects including urban renewal and environmental improvement schemes, lease extensions, regrants and renewals of private leases. Among its other responsibilities are valuations for government land transactions and projects involving a change in land use.

For land administration purpose, the HKSAR is at present divided into 12 districts, 4 in the urban area and 8 in the NT. Each district is looked after by a District Lands Officer (DLO), who provides a wide range of professional services related to land matters in the district. Large one-off public work projects, such as the construction of the new airport off Lantau, require specialist land teams to be formed and dedicated to supporting and implementing the project. A similar team was also formed for the Mass Transit Railway Corporation's (MTRC) West Rail project.

Legal advice on land transactions and conveyancing services for disposal and acquisition of land are provided by the department's own in-house solicitors, who are members of the Legal Advisory and Conveyancing Office (LACO). LACO provides legal support and services to the Director and other senior members of the department. It also maintains sub-offices in the territory to provide legal support to each of the District Lands Officers.

The chapters of this section cover an outline of the history and background information regarding land reclamations. There are also discussions on how the Lands Department functions under administrative law, and its policies on land disposal, land exchange and modification methods. There is also a review of how development is controlled under new and old lease conditions and their interrelationship with planning and building legislation.

ECONOMIC BACKGROUND, LAND NEEDS AND RECLAMATIONS

Economic Background

Prior to the beginning of the Second World War, Hong Kong was a thriving port — the main deep sea port of Southern China with a population of 1.6 million. By the end of the war in 1945, the population had fallen to 500,000. However, people began to return after the war at a rate of almost 100 000 a month, and by the end of 1947, the population stood at 1.8 million. By 1950, it had increased to two million.

In the 1950s, Hong Kong began to develop as a manufacturing centre, at first on the basis of cotton textiles, then adding woollen and man-made fibres and made-up garments as the major part of our domestic exports. Subsequently electrical and electronic products, watches and clocks, toys, plastics and other light industries became major contributors.

There were further surges of population; many people had come from the PRC in the 1950s, the mid-60s and late 70s when the population grew at about one million each decade.

China's open-door policy, introduced in the late 1970s, has had a profound effect on the economy of Hong Kong. Significant expansion of the manufacturing base has occurred in the Pearl River Delta (PRD) and there is now more emphasis on Hong Kong's role as an entrepot, a centre for finance and other business-related services. Tourism has now become a significant industry, particularly with the opening of Hong Kong Disneyland in September 2005. Figures and estimates vary, but between 10 and 12 million people now work in Hong Kong-owned factories in the PRD; this clearly indicates the shift of manufacturing into the PRC.

Land Needs

As the population and industrial activity increased, so did the demand for land for both housing and industry. Initially, factories were developed in the old warehouse areas around the harbour. In the 1960s, new industrial areas were established in Tsuen Wan and Kwun Tong, both on the outskirts of old Kowloon. Supporting housing development, both private and public, also took place in these areas, with Tsuen Wan being regarded as the first new town.

A stock-taking exercise in the early 1970s showed that 1.8 million people needed better housing and that the supply of industrial land was falling far short of demand. As land in the traditional urban areas of Hong Kong and Kowloon was scarce, it was decided to develop three more new towns in the NT, namely, Shatin, Tai Po and Tuen Mun. These towns were planned to be balanced developments which provide accommodation, jobs and a full range of community facilities including schools and hospitals. This programme has since been expanded with a total of eight new towns which now provide housing for about three million people.

The new town development programme met most of the land needs in the 1970s and 1980s, but shortfalls in land supply have become apparent in the 1990s. Territorial Development Strategy (TDS) studies began to identify additional sites around the wider harbour area to allow development to continue into the next century. Detailed planning of these areas had to be abandoned due to the Protection of the Harbour Ordinance (Cap. 531) (PHO) discussed in the next section. Alternative sources of land supply will now need to be found including resumption and land use conversion of agricultural land in the New Territories, particularly in the north-west.

Currently the Planning Department is conducting a wide ranging consultation exercise entitled 'Hong Kong 2030, Planning Vision and Strategy'. The report on the third round published in December 2004 can be viewed at their website www.info.gov.hk/hk2030. A number of significant issues have emerged that potentially could have a major impact on future land needs. The first relates to the population assumptions. Currently our population is about 7 million. The Census and Statistics Department predicts a population of 8.7 million by 2030, whereas the planners have chosen to use a higher number of 9.2 million. During the course of the third round of consultation, both these figures were criticized as being unrealistically high, given the low fertility rate and the rapidly ageing population (the percentage of population over 60 years old is predicted to increase from 15% to 28% over the next 15 years). During one of the consultation focus meetings, respected academics from the University of Hong Kong demonstrated that our population may have already peaked and suggested we could even experience a drop in population similar to cities like London and New York. This view is supported by the announced results of the 2006 by-census, which gives us a total population of 6.9 million; more importantly the figures indicate that the growth rate has slowed to 0.4% over the past five years, compared to 0.9% over the years 1996–2001 when the last full census was taken. Clearly this is an important issue that needs a clearer resolution because of the implication on future land use needs for housing, education, health care and related issues which are all highly dependent on accurate population predictions.

Another issue is the need to improve the quality of the urban living environment in the metro area. This can be achieved by implementing lower density of development and by directing future development areas to the NT. In the latter case, higher density of development can be allowed along the rail networks already in place. (The MTRC's West Rail is rather under-utilized in this respect.) A similar view emerged during the Council for Sustainable Development's Engagement Process on the topic of Urban Living Space under ULS Principle 2 reported in February 2005 at www.susdev.org.hk/en/Report/Report_ch3.htm/

Reflecting the decline of the older industrial areas, the Planning Department has completed a major rezoning exercise over the whole of Hong Kong by introducing a new 'Other Uses (Business)' — OU(B) — category to over 100 hectares of redundant industrial land in the Urban area and to over 150 hectares in the NT. This new zoning will, subject to suitable lease modification arrangements, permit any use other than residential, that is, offices, retail or hotel use. This huge reservoir of brownfield development land should provide a more than adequate supply for these three uses for the foreseeable future — assuming a plot ratio of 10, this has potential, over time, to generate some 25 million square metres of new commercial floor space. Given the acute shortage of land for housing, serious thought should be given to rezoning some of these sites in order to permit residential use.

The next major infrastructure project that is going to have a significant impact on future land needs is the bridge link across from Lantau to Zhuhai and Macau. This project is now at an advanced state of planning and approval to start tendering for the building of this bridge is expected soon. As with the opening up and the easing of travel restrictions to the eastern side of the PRD, the completion of this bridge is expected to have a similar impact as access to the western side of the PRD will become much easier.

Reclamations

The lack of natural flat land has plagued Hong Kong from the beginning and supports Lord Palmerston's famous description of Hong Kong as 'a barren island with hardly a house on it' when it was first ceded.

Consequently, land reclamations have been a feature of Hong Kong's development right from the outset. The very first lots sold along Queen's Road Central were at the seashore and resulted in some reclamation, albeit illegal. The sketch plan in Figure 6.1 is taken from Cameron (1979). It demonstrates how the boundaries along the north shore of Hong Kong Island have evolved. This can be further illustrated by the observation that when built in the early 1900s, the trams on Hong Kong Island ran along the waterfront, some parts of which had been reclaimed earlier.

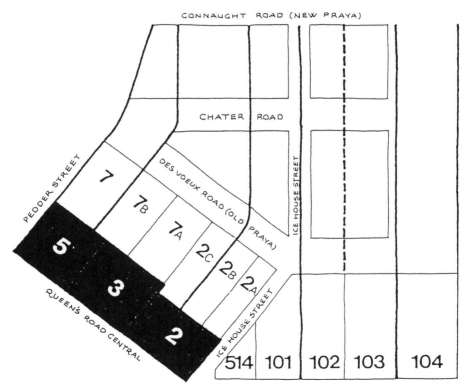

Figure 6.1   A sketch plan showing how the original Marine Lots 2, 3, and 5 accumulated reclaimed land, first to the Old Praya at Des Voeux Road, and then to Connuaght Road with the Central Reclamation.

In total, approximately 6000 hectares of land has been added to the original land areas of Hong Kong, Kowloon and the New territories (see map on inside front cover). By 1967 the figure was around 1000 hectares; it had risen to nearly 2000 hectares by 1976, with a massive 4000 hectares added in the last twenty years. Most of the new towns relied on large areas of reclamation to provide flat development land. The development began initially in Tsuen Wan and Kwai Chung, then in Sha Tin, Tai Po and Tuen Mun, and more recently in Ma On Shan, Tung Chung and Tseung Kwan O.

The site of Hong Kong International Airport at Chek Lap Kok, probably the largest single land grant at 1248 hectares, was 75% reclaimed.

Reclamations at present are governed by the Foreshore and Seabed (Reclamations) Ordinance (Cap. 127) but this is essentially an ordinance to protect people or landowners who may be adversely affected by a proposed reclamation and to enable them to claim compensation. There are requirements for proposed reclamations to be gazetted, for objections to be made and considered.

The current planning system is weak in this area because at present there is no proper statutory procedure whereby the proposed land uses that are planned for the new reclamation are required to be considered and approved by the Town Planning Board (TPB) with full and proper consultation *before* the reclamation is gazetted. This is fundamentally wrong because it is putting the cart before the horse for a reclamation to be gazetted before the planned land uses have been properly considered and agreed. This flaw in the current planning system needs to be properly addressed and correct procedures should be enacted in any future amendments to planning legislation.

The weakness in the present planning system coupled with increasing public objection against further reclamations resulted in a private member's bill which sought to prevent further reclamations, specifically in Victoria Harbour, without the prior approval of the Legislative Council, being enacted as the PHO. This piece of legislation now provides for protection of the harbour and also served as a useful lesson to the government on the strength of public opinion on this subject.

In its final form, the Ordinance provides that 'the central harbour is to be protected and preserved as a special public asset and natural heritage of Hong Kong people and for that purpose there shall be a presumption against reclamation of the central harbour'.

Enacted in 1997, this Ordinance quickly became the centre of a fierce debate between the government and civic society led by the Society for the Protection of the Harbour Ltd. (SPH) which culminated in a referral to the Court of Final Appeal in the case of *Town Planning Board* v *SPH* [2004] 1 HKLRD 396. In view of the significance of this case, the following extracts are included to assist readers' understanding:

The TPB decided to submit a plan (the Plan) which proposed reclaiming 26 hectares from Victoria Harbour (the harbour) to the Chief Executive in Council for approval. The respondent brought successful judicial review proceedings on the basis that in making, *inter alia,* that decision the Board has misinterpreted the PHO (Cap. 531), in particular s.3. Section 3(1) provided that '(1) The harbour is to be protected and preserved as a special public asset and a natural heritage of Hong Kong People, and for that purpose there shall be a presumption against reclamation in the harbour. (2) All public officers and public bodies shall have regard to the principle stated in sub-s. (1) for guidance in the exercise of any powers vested in them.' The TPB appealed to the Court of Final Appeal. It argued it had applied the correct construction of s.3, namely, that the decision-marker must consider the presumption against reclamation (the presumption) as a compulsory material consideration and must undertake a weighing exercise to decide whether the public benefits of the proposed reclamation outweighed the need to preserve the harbour.

Held, dismissing the appeal and remitting the matter to the TPB, that:

(1) Section 3(1) established a statutory principle recognizing the harbour as a special public asset and a natural heritage of the Hong Kong people and prescribing that it was to be protected and preserved as such an asset and such a heritage. It was recognized as something extraordinary. By representing the harbour in such special terms, the Legislature was giving legal recognition to its unique character and the great public need to protect and preserve in having regard to such character. The legislative intent so expressed was to establish the principle of protection and preservation as strong and vigorous one.

(2) Section 3 (2) was in mandatory terms and imposed on public officers and public bodies the statutory duty, not only to have regard to the principle, but also to have regard to the presumption in exercising their powers.

(3) The Board's construction relegated the presumption to no more than a planning consideration required by statute to be taken into account and must be rejected.

(4) On a true construction, the presumption could only be rebutted by establishing an overriding public need for reclamation. This included economic, environmental and social needs of the community. A need was only overriding if it was a compelling and present need: compelling so that it has the requisite force to prevail over the strong public need for protection and preservation; and present in that it would arise within a definite and reasonable time frame. Such need went far beyond something which was

desirable, preferable or beneficial, but it would be going much too far to describe it as a last resort or something which the public could not do without.

(5) Where there was a reasonable alternative, an overriding need for reclamation would not be made out. In considering what was a reasonable alternative, all the circumstances should be considered including the economic, environmental and social implications.

(6) The overriding public need test was a demanding one and there must be cogent and convincing materials before the decision-maker to satisfy him that it was met. Thus, the burden on those seeking to rebut the presumption was a heavy one.

Why had the SPH taken the government to court in the first place? The answer is that in spite of the PHO, the government assumed it could continue its reclamation programme unabated with proposals for 190 hectares at Green Island, linking it to the western tip of Hong Kong Island, 30 hectares filling in Tsuen Wan Bay and originally same 300 hectares in Kowloon Bay in and around the old Kai Tak Airport. These three projects, which have now had to be abandoned in the light of the above decision, were in addition to the one in Central on which the legal challenge was based.

This decision has now had the effect of defining in a permanent way the boundaries of Victoria Harbour, enabling the water's edge to be properly planned and completed.

It also brings to an end the government's cheap source of land supply and will require a more thoughtful use of redundant industrial land and all other 'brownfield' sites whether they be privately or publicly owned.

7 LANDS DEPARTMENT FUNCTIONS UNDER ADMINISTRATIVE LAW

Administrative Law

Arising from a lease modification case came a very significant decision from the Privy Council in respect of *Hang Wah Chong Investment Co. Ltd.* v *Attorney General* [1981] HKLR 336, [1981] WLR 1141, that provides the foundation of how the government, that is, the Lands Department, administers land. What the decision essentially states is that each lease executed is a private transaction with appropriate contractual rights and that such transactions cannot be considered as performing an executive function and therefore are not susceptible to judicial review.

In other words they are, for the most part, dealt with in the framework of private law, not public law. There are, however, exceptions to this as in the case of *The Hong Kong and China Gas Co. Ltd.* v *Director of Lands* [1997] HKLRD 1291. When the Director of Lands declined to renew a special purpose lease held by the applicant under the New Territories Leases (Extension) Ordinance (Cap. 150), Mr Justice Keith in the Court of First Instance held that 'in view of the competing interests which the Director of Lands had to balance in the context of the application of an important policy statement relating to the extension of large numbers of Crown leases in the New Territories I have concluded that his decision whether or not to extend the Company's lease was made by him in the exercise of his public function and is therefore amendable to judicial review'.

Furthermore, *Hang Wah Chong* established the broad principle that where a tenant seeks a concession from his landlord in relation to the development of land leased, the landlord is entitled to make the granting of that concession conditional upon the payment of a premium. Perhaps most significant is that there is no requirement for the government to establish reasonableness in the exercise of its discretion as landlord, whether or not to grant the modification and what level of premium it may wish to charge. In fact the latter point was addressed in the much earlier case of *Crozet v Attorney General* (unreported MP No. 409/1973) when the court posed itself the question "Is there to be implied into the special condition in the lease a further provision that special approval will not be unreasonably withheld?" The answer to this question is "No.". All this puts the Lands Department in an extremely strong negotiating position in every land transaction. Because of the significance of the Hang Wah Chong case, the full text of the decision is included in Appendix VI.

All the main principles established in *Hang Wah Chong* have recently been re-affirmed in the Court of Appeal decision in *Anderson Asphalt Ltd and Secretary for Justice* [2010] 5 HKLRD 490. Those principles can now be taken as settled law.

Notwithstanding the Lands Department's seemingly invincible position, they do recognize the need to provide a service to the public, and this is spelt out in their vision and mission statements:

Vision

We strive to achieve excellence in land administration in Hong Kong for the greater benefit of the community.

Missions

- To keep pace with economic and market trends in a local and regional context.
- To continuously review policies and employ best practices to meet the changing needs of the community.
- To develop and sustain a culture of transparency and professionalism.
- To use up-to-date technology and optimize human resources to enhance productivity and efficiency.

These statements are reinforced by a number of performance pledges that have been given by the Lands Department in which they commit to perform certain specified tasks within a target time frame and these are referred to, as appropriate.

Land Disposal

The disposal of land has always been one of the Lands Department's principal functions and is currently achieved through its annual Land Sale Programme under which they publish a list of sites available for sale upon application known as the Application List. The list contains information on lot number, location, use, site area and estimated earliest available date for each of the sites; Practice Note 5/2005 refers.

Land leases stipulate the obligations and duties of the owner, and the planning engineering and development requirements that need to be met. The following conditions are usually included:

- Lease term — normally 50 years from the date of grant, with an annual rent assessed at 3% of rateable value.
- Permitted uses — these generally correspond to the land use zoning for the lots as shown on the relevant outline zoning plan. In residential zones usually only private residential use will be permitted. If the site is zoned for commercial/residential (C/R), then mixed uses are permitted and the user clause is usually written allowing non-industrial uses, with certain exceptions such as petrol filling stations.
- Maximum building heights.
- Minimum and maximum gross floor area (gfa).
- Maximum permitted site coverage (SC).
- The period required for construction, known as the building covenant (BC) — for most sites, 48 or 60 months is specified although longer periods may be granted if appropriate;
- Master layout plan (MLP) requirements (for large schemes).
- Design, disposition and height control (DDH).
- Car parking, loading and unloading requirements.
- Restrictions on vehicular ingress and egress.
- Landscaping, tree felling and environmental requirements — the importance now attached to the proper compliance with landscape clauses is spelt out in the Lands Department Practice Note No. 6/2003 and Joint Practice Note No. 3.
- Much more attention is now given to the question of tree felling as set out in Practice Note No. 7/2007. This Practice Note sets out a much more stringent set of rules and guidelines regarding the processing of tree felling applications. In addition penalties and fines are now being levied for any breach of tree felling clauses in leases, again indicating the seriousness of the government's intentions in this matter.
- Recreational facilities — in residential sites recreational facilities are permitted and indeed are encouraged by virtue of the fact that the gfa and site coverage of the buildings that house these facilities are permitted in addition to the gfa and coverage allowed for the residential development itself. The floor area for these facilities is not usually specified but as a

guideline should not exceed 5% of the residential gfa with each case being considered on its merits.Lands Department Practice Note 4/2000 entitled 'Recreational Facilities in Domestic Development' sets out the criteria.

In *Secan Ltd.* v *Attorney General* [1995] 2 HKLR 523, the applicant challenged one of the special conditions included in a land grant. The Court of Appeal applied the principles established in *Hang Wah Chong Investment Co. Ltd.* v *Attorney General* [1981] HKLR 336 that it was not legitimate to apply a requirement of reasonableness into the decision-making process. However, if a statutory official was named as an authority to give an approval under a lease, he could not act capriciously. Unfortunately the Director of Lands is not a statutory official. A summary of the case is in Appendix VIII.

Land is now sold by either auction or public tenders. Tender are always used in cases of very specialized uses such as petrol filing stations or where the development conditions are so complex, usually as a result of the government requiring certain public facilities to be incorporated into the scheme, that in fairness to the developers they are given time to design a scheme and then make a bid through the tender process.

Private Treaty Grants (PTGs) are reserved principally for public utility companies and non-profit-making organizations. As public utility companies are run on commercial principles, they are required to pay a premium normally assessed by assuming an equivalent industrial land value for the location, and applying it to the actual gfa of the building to be erected. Non-profit-making organizations such as schools, welfare facilities and hospitals usually qualify for a nil or heavily subsidized premium to reflect their status. These grants will typically include special conditions that restrict the use of the land to the purposes of the grantee's operation only and will also prohibit any alienation or sale. Policy issues arise when such older lots become redundant or the grantee wishes to redevelop but has no cash. Because of the highly restricted nature of these leases, any modification will usually require the approval of the Chief Executive in Council (ExCo) and the payment of a full land premium.

There are some exceptional circumstances when a PTG is made to commercial profit-making users such as for Hong Kong Disneyland or the grant of the air space development rights above the Mass Transit Railway stations. These cases usually need the approval of ExCo; sometimes it is necessary to go back to ExCo if approval is needed for any subsequent modification or alienation of the lot in question.

Lease Conditions

Government leases come in many different forms, be they Conditions of Sale, Conditions of Exchange, Conditions of Grant, Conditions of Tender, Conditions of Regrant or a full Crown or Government lease. For ease of reference, the term 'lease conditions' is used throughout whatever the nature of the document is. It is important to understand the reasoning behind the imposition of some of the more significant lease conditions which are now considered below.

Building Covenant (BC)

A full review of the government's policy on building covenants can be found in the High Court judgment in the case of *Shun Shing Hing Investment Co. Ltd.* v *Attorney General* [1983] HKLR 432 where it was noted that 'building covenants have been a central feature of life in Hong Kong since the present administration started'. It also mentions that a BC was included in Marine Lot No. 1, see pp. 13–14 and Appendix II.

The main purpose of the BC is to ensure that the site in question is developed with an acceptable amount of floor space within a reasonable period of time. Generally the volume of floor space required to be completed in order to fulfil this condition is 60% of the maximum floor space permitted to be built within the time frame stated, usually 48 or 60 months. BCs previously contained a monetary value to be spent on construction but this is no longer included.

If at the end of the BC period there has been no progress on site with no building plans approved, the government is likely to exercise its rights to re-enter the site and take it back without any payment of compensation.[1] It should be noted that the grantee would also be in breach of the standard maintenance covenant in the lease conditions that would give a right of re-entry. If building plans have been approved and works are in progress at the time the BC is due to expire, then it is possible to obtain an extension to the BC period on payment of a premium, by applying to the local DLO. These premiums are calculated on a fixed formula, with progressively higher penalties being charged on longer periods of extension. For instance, 2% of the assessed land value will be charged for the first year (or part thereof); 4% for the second year; 8% for the third year and so on.[2]

Whilst 48 months is the standard BC period, longer or shorter periods may be imposed depending on the nature and scale of development. For example, if the gfa is less than 10 000m^2, a 36-month BC may be imposed. For large projects covered by a Master Layout Plan, a longer BC period, which may be phased to reflect a specific development programme, may be given.

At the expiry of a BC period where development is well advanced, yet incomplete, an extension at premium is normally offered. However, in the event that at the expiry of the BC period, the Authorized Person (AP)[3] is able to certify that there is a reasonable expectation of an Occupation Permit (OP) being issued within three months, the grantee may apply for a three-month extension with payment of a premium in the form of a deposit. Such deposit will be refunded, without interest, only if the OP actually issued within the said additional three month period.

At the time of the economic downturn in 1982–83, the government, in recognition of the problems being faced by developers, introduced administratively a number of measures to assist owners of property under development.[4] One of these measures was to permit the first-year extension of the BC to be at nil premium, thus giving developers more flexibility in programming both the construction and selling of their flats. Again in 2003 similar concessions were offered to developers for a one year period to reflect the difficult economic climate at that time.[5]

For special purpose leases such as grants for schools, churches, public utility companies and recreational clubs the standard BC clause will not be used. It will be replaced with a clause requiring the grantee to 'bring into operation' the proposed facility within a specified time frame, which is usually calculated in the same way as a BC period. Again compliance is achieved by the issuance of the OP from the Building Authority. Another important activity related to compliance with the BC is the issuing of the Certificate of Compliance (CC). Without the CC, developers cannot complete the sale of their new units. Thus, there is a lot of pressure on the AP to ensure it is issued on time.

Deeds of Mutual Covenant (DMC)

The vast majority of developments in Hong Kong comprise high-rise buildings, be they residential, offices or factories. There are also mixed user developments with commercial uses in the podium and residential or offices above. The individual units are usually disposed of as undivided shares in the lot but in mixed user developments, it is not uncommon for the developer to retain the ownership of the podium whilst disposing of the units above. The purpose of the DMC is ensure that a fair balance is struck between the interests of all parties, including future purchasers with regard to responsibilities and costs for the long-term management and unkeep of the building. All DMCs have to be submitted to and approved by the Legal Advisory and Conveyancing Office (LACO) and this process forms an integral part of LACO's Consent Scheme for the sale of uncompleted developments. Provisions regarding DMCs are also found in the Building Management Ordinance (Cap. 344).

Some private development sites have lease conditions that require the developer to provide certain government, institutional or community (GIC) facilities. Experience has shown that in these types of case there can be considerable delays in getting the DMC approved. The government has now recognized the problem and new procedures are to be put in place to try and overcome them.

Certificate of Compliance (CC)

When a lot is disposed of with a building covenant, a restriction on alienation prior to compliance with all the positive lease conditions will also be imposed. Assignment prior to such compliance is only permitted in closely defined circumstances under the 'Land Officer's Consent Scheme'. The CC is an administrative measure whereby the Lands Department confirms to the registered owners and LACO that all the positive obligations imposed by the General and Special Conditions (including the BC) have been complied with to the satisfaction of the Director of Lands. Responsibility for verifying such compliance rests with the District Lands Office concerned. All applications and correspondence concerning the issue of a Certificate of Compliance should be addressed direct to the District Lands Officer concerned.

The CC can be issued when:
1. all *positive* obligations have been complied with, to the satisfaction of the DLO and/or other departments concerned;
2. a temporary or final OP has been issued;
3. all sums payable under the conditions have been demanded and paid, except:
   (a) any sums due in respect of excess or deficiency in area (if applicable)and
   (b) if the premium is payable by instalments, any instalments of premium not due as at this date.
4. if the conditions make provision for the Director of Highways to confirm his acceptance of any area as a public road, when the Director of Highways has so accepted the area.

It is understood that the government is considering whether or not negative covenants also need to have been complied with before issuing the CC. This idea is causing concern within the development industry because of all the uncertainties this will generate.

The issuance of the Certificate of Compliance is also significant in terms of the legal title of the lot on which the building stands. Until the early 1970s, it was the practice of the government to issue a Crown Lease (now Government Lease) when the CC under the lease conditions had been issued. Thus the sequence was clear: lease conditions, development of the lot, followed by a Crown Lease replacing the lease conditions. This is no longer the case and land continues to be held under lease conditions after the time when a Government Lease should properly have been issued, that is, after the receipt of the Certificate of Compliance. In practice, owners of land held under lease conditions are treated on an equal footing with those holding land under a Government Lease. However, strictly speaking at law, only the Government Lease gives a legal estate whereas lease conditions confer only an equitable interest which is deemed to be equivalent to the legal estate on the issue of the Certificate of Compliance. Legally, the lease conditions are a contract by the government to grant the owner a Government Lease when the conditions for the grant have been performed. Section 14 of The Conveyancing and Property Ordinance 1984 (Cap. 219) clarified this process of converting the equitable interest of those landowners with lease conditions into a legal estate, by defining that a Certificate of Compliance would be evidence of the conversion and the date of conversion, and deeming a Government Lease to have been issued on receipt of a Certificate of Compliance. As at 1 November 1984, Government Leases for all land held under lease conditions issued before 1 January 1970 were deemed to be issued and the owners became holders of a legal estate. For lease conditions issued after 1 January 1970, the performance of the conditions precedent to the entitlement to the Government Lease, as evidenced by the issue and registration of the Certificate of Compliance, will trigger the deemed issue of the Government Lease and the conversion of the owner's equitable interest into a legal estate.[6]

The timely issuing of CCs is one of the Lands Department's performance pledges which is spelt out as follow:

> On receipt of applications for Certificates of Compliance, the appropriate District Lands Office will, within 3 months, either issue the Certificate, or indicate by letter, non-compliance setting out the reasons why the Certificate cannot be issued.

Guidance on how to apply for a CC is contained in Lands Department Practice Note No. 1/1987 to architects, surveyors and engineers with Practice Note No 8/2000 giving a useful checklist to help streamline and simplify the process.

Master Layout Plan (MLP)

Conditions of Sale for large-scale developments usually contain a requirement for the submission and approval by DLO of Master Layout/Concept Plans. However, it is now policy, in order to avoid duplicated effort and to reduce the time of approvals, that new leases will not require this submission where the MLP has already been submitted for approval under the Town Planning Ordinance (Cap. 131) (TPO).

The purposes and objectives of a Master Layout /Concept Plan are:

1. to ensure that the nature and layout of a particular large scale development are acceptable to the government;
2. to ensure that the whole site is developed in an orderly and composite manner;
3. to enable the developer to submit his proposals and receive an early indication that the general nature of the development and the proposed layout thereof are acceptable.

Master Layout/Concept Plans are called a variety of names, for example, Master Plan, Layout Plan, Preliminary Concept Plan, Layout and Master Plan, General Layout Plan, but the objectives are the same.

To achieve the objectives of a Master Layout Plan, sufficient information has to be provided either in the form of plan, sketches or written statements. Information to be included in a Master Layout Plan will be specified in the Conditions of Sale and will usually include the following:

1. the formation levels of the site and the position, widths and levels of any proposed roads, emergency accesses, footbridges and pedestrian ways;
2. the nature, height and gfa of the buildings proposed, including their disposition location and distribution;
3. the vehicular ingress and egress arrangements;
4. an indication of the locations for the parking of vehicles;
5. any communal open space and an indication of landscaping and recreational facilities proposed; and
6. the stages or phases of the development.

When approving MLPs, the DLO will usually advise that the approval of the MLP only indicates that the general design concept is acceptable; it should not be construed that every detail shown thereon is in all respects in compliance with the lease conditions.

It was held in the case of *Canadian Overseas Development Co. Ltd.* v *Attorney General* [1991] 1 HKC 288 that following the principle laid down in *Hang Wah Chong Investment Co. Ltd.* v *Attorney General* [1981] HKLR 366, the government in deciding whether or not to approve on MLP was exercising a contractual right rather than performing an executive function governed by public law, the decision was therefore not susceptible to judicial review.

However, the approval of development plans under lease condition is now included as one of the Lands Department's performance pledges, as follows:

On receipt of development plans for approval under lease conditions, the appropriate District Lands Office will, provided the application complies with the relevant Department Practice Notes, give a substantive reply within the following periods:

Master Layout Plans — 10 weeks
General Building Plans — 10 weeks
Landscape Plans — 8 weeks
Lands Department Practice No. 5/2002 also refers.

Gross Floor Area (gfa) and site coverage (SC)

One problem that occurs for developers and their consultants is that the definition of gfa and SC that is given in lease conditions can differ as compared with the definitions under the Buildings Ordinance (Cap. 123) or the TPO. Ideally the government should adopt a common definition throughout in order to minimize the problems that do arise. Lands Department have issued a Practice Note for architects, surveyors and engineers APSRSE No. 1/98 entitled 'Accountable and Non-Accountable Gross Floor Area under Lease', and with regard to site coverage, Practice Note 1/2004 advises on how to proceed if the Building Authority gives concessions which then result in the site coverage permitted under lease being exceeded. This topic is also covered in a later section of this chapter under the heading of Joint Practice Notes.

Height Limits

There are three basic forms of height control that occur in lease conditions and guidelines on their interpretation are set out below:

1. **Airport Height Limit**
   These are absolute height limits which are imposed without any concession being granted. Where such limits are imposed, no plans may be approved if there is any breach, however minor that breach may be. The original standard clause provides that 'no part of any structure to be erected on the lot shall exceed a height of . . . metres above Hong Kong Principal Datum' More recent conditions refer to height controls specified in orders that are made under the Hong Kong Airport (Control of Obstructions) Ordinance (Cap. 301).

   With the closure of Kai Tak Airport following the opening of Hong Kong International Airport in July 1998, most of these controls in the Urban area became redundant and can now be modified subject to payment of a premium. Lands Departments Practice Note No APSRSE 1/96 refers.

2. **Special Height Limit**

   (a) The height of a building should be measured from the formation level upon which the building stands to the roof slab level, with the formation level being taken as the lowest formation level on which any part of the building stands. The roof level is normally taken as the top of the highest roof slab within the proposed building. While this is the general rule, some tolerance is allowed where there are minor projections above or below the specific height limits which result from architectural features. This means that where, for architectural reasons, only the height limits are exceeded in a very minor way, approval can be given provided that the building itself, without the architectural feature, could be built within the specified height limits. In such cases, DLO staff have to seek approval from their internal Building Conference.

   (b) It is an established practice to allow vertical projections above these specific height limits for stairhoods, water tanks and parapet walls. In most circumstances, no approval will be given to such structures where they exceed a height of 3 m above the main roof level. Where the structures do not exceed 3 m and are of reasonable size, they may be recommended for approval. Careful attention will be taken in considering roof top projections to ensure that they cannot be easily illegally converted. Lift motor rooms are not encouraged at roof level and wherever possible, the architects will be advised to locate them at the bottom of the lift shaft. Drying shelters at roof level are usually included in height calculations.

   (c) Where a specific building height is imposed under the lease conditions for a sloping site, there could be situations where a single building height measurement can cause problems. The general rule is that the formation level in respect of a sloping site is taken as the mean level of the site for a single building. In the case of buildings to be erected on platforms at various levels, the building height should be measured, in respect of each building from the platform level upon which each building will stand.

3. **Design Disposition and Height Clause (DDH)**

   This clause exists in various forms with the present wording as follows:

   > The design disposition and height of any building or buildings erected on the lot shall be subject to the special approval of the Director.

   The clause can be used to govern site coverage, height and therefore plot ratio.

   It is current Lands Department's policy that this clause should not be used to achieve payment of a premium but only to control development in order to conform with town planning requirements. The Director of Lands has an absolute discretion under this clause and the Director's decision cannot be challenged in the Courts; see *Crozet Ltd v Attorney General* (unreported M.P. No. 409/1973). This point was restated in *Polorace Investments Ltd v Director of Land* [1997] 1 HKC 373, which also serves as a reminder that the Director acts as the government's agent in its capacity as landlord; so the matter of charging a premium under covenants in the lease was clearly governed by private and not public law and was not susceptible to judicial review. The conclusion is that there could be a change of policy in future with the administration deciding to charge for such approvals.

To assist architects, surveyors and engineers in preparing building plan submissions where the lease contains a DDH clause, the Lands Department issued Practice Note No. APSRSE 1/99 which identifies the aspects that would generally be considered in the exercise of their discretion under this clause.

The extent of the contractual discretion conferred on the Director of Lands by the DDH clause was further considered in the case *Ying Ho Co. Ltd. and others v Secretary for Justice* [2005] 1 HKLRD 135, sometimes referred to as the 'Nina Towers' case. The Court of Final Appeal's decision has some helpful comments on the treatment of both DDH and MLP clauses:

(1) Where a condition of grant of land was concerned, principles such as those identified in the English case *Equitable Life Assurance Society v Hyman* [2002] 1 AC 408 could and should be given effect by preventing, or awarding a remedy for, any derogation from grant. Here, the project for which the appellant eventually obtained approval would utilize the full plot ratio and gross floor area available under the grant, and would be no less valuable than what they had planned as the tallest building in the world. In the present circumstances, there was no derogation from grant.

(2) Upon a true construction of the Conditions, both SC (5) and the DDH clause were intended to expressly reserve to the Director a power to control the height of the buildings. The existence or absence of statutory height restrictions were relevant considerations in the exercise of that discretion. Therefore, the DDH clause was not purely procedural. When the Director (for public interest reasons including aviation safety) specified the height limit, he was not depriving the appellant of any right under the Conditions. There was simply no right to build to whatever height they wanted and in the circumstances of this case, no legitimate expectation that no height restrictions would be imposed (*Hang Wah Chong Investment Co. Ltd. v A-G of Hong Kong* [1981] HKLR 336 considered).

(3) Performance of the obligations imposed on the parties under the Conditions required each to cooperate in good faith with the other. To give the

Conditions business efficacy the Government had: (a) to deal with the MLP and to give or refuse approval with reasonable dispatch; (b) if rejecting an MLP, to inform the appellant (applicant) of the respects in which it is deficient.

Height controls are specified in the notes to many Outline Zoning Plans. Even in cases of minor relaxation of building height, it may be necessary to submit a S.16 Application seeking Town Planning Board's approval irrespective of whether it may be permitted under the lease.

Hong Kong Principal Datum (HKPD)

Airport height limits and other development control height limits are invariably expressed as being so many metres above HKPD (some older leases refer to 'Colony Principal Datum' or 'CPD') which has its definition hidden away in Schedule 1 of the Interpretations and General Clauses Ordinance (Cap. 1) as part of the description of the Boundaries of the City of Victoria! It reads as follows:

> . . . a level 17.833 feet below the benchmark known as 'Riflemans' 'Bolt' the highest point of a copper bolt set horizontally in the east wall of the Royal Navy Office and Mess Block Naval Dockyard. . .

The name comes from the Her Majesty's Surveying Vessel *Rifleman* which came to Hong Kong in 1866 to assist in the mapping of the territory. The original 'Bolt' was removed from the Dockyard in 1959 and relocated to Tamar Basin, but when that in turn was reclaimed it was removed altogether thus requiring a redefinition of HKPD.

In 1995 the Land Boundary Survey Committee of the Survey and Mapping Office agreed to a new definition in order to bring Hong Kong into line with worldwide practice; it reads as follows:

> The Hong Kong Principal Datum (HKPD) is the vertical or height datum used for land surveying in Hong Kong. It is based on the Mean Sea Level (MSL) derived from 19 years (1965–1983) of tidal observations taken at the automatic tide gauge at North Point and is 1.23 metre below MSL.

The consequential amendment to Cap. 1 will no doubt occur in due course.

In order to assist land surveyors in this matter there are currently some 1500 Bench Marks scattered around Hong Kong.

Photographs of the Rifleman's Bolt (Copper Plaque, Stone Plaque and Copper Bolt), courtesy of the Survey and Mapping Office of the Lands Department. Both these items are now kept in the Survey and Mapping Office Training School.

Joint Practice Notes (JPNs)

Recognizing the need for the three principal departments involved with development control — Planning Department, Buildings Department and Lands Department — to unify their approach as far as possible, there has been a new trend of issuing Joint Practice Notes (JPNs) which are signed off by all three departments.

The first of these JPNs was issued in February 2001 and covers the topic of 'Green and Innovative Buildings' in order to introduce incentives to encourage the design and construction of buildings that will improve and protect the built and natural environment. In February 2002 the second JPN was issued introducing the second package of such incentives.

Although these two JPNs were announced as providing incentives to encourage better design and construction, they have to some extent been negated by the Lands Department's insistence that where appropriate they should charge a premium for such exemptions if they result in the granting of additional gfa. Their Practice Note No. 6/2001 relates to JPN No. 1 and No. 3/2003 refer to JPN No. 2. The standard rates adopted are reviewed from time to time with the latest figures announced in Practice Note No. 2/2005. If these premiums are too great they could well be a disincentive to go along with the new ideas which would totally counterproductive! Clearly an overall policy directive is needed to deal with this contradiction.

The third JPN is entitled 'Re-engineering of Approval Process for Land & Building Developments' and was issued in August 2003 and relates very much to the processing of landscape plans and landscape master plans.

JPN No.4, entitled Development Control Parameters, was first issued in November 2008 and revised in January 2011 and promulgates the practices adopted by the Buildings Department (BD), Lands Department (Lands D) and Planning Department (Plan D) in respect of some development control parameters that are commonly encountered in the development process.

In general in processing building plan submissions Plan D would follow BD's practice in GFA calculation and granting GFA concessions, subject to specific provisions in relevant statutory plans. However owing to the variance of development parameters between individual leases and properties, each case will be considered on its own merits by Lands D. In paragraph 9 of this JPN the Director of Lands emphasizes their right, acting in the capacity of lessor/landlord, not to be bound by the wording of this JPN. This caveat puts into doubt the underlying purpose and effect of this JPN?'

Notes

1. Also refer to Chapter 12, pp. 99–101.
2. Lands Department Information Note No. 1/1985.
3. Authorized Person (AP) as defined in the Building Ordinance (Cap. 123).
4. Lands Departments Information Note Issue No. 1/1983.
5. Lands Department Practice Note No. 5/2003.
6. See also (1985) 15 HKLJ 48 and generally Sarah Nield 1997.

LAND EXCHANGE AND LEASE MODIFICATIONS

Lease Modifications

In Annex III of the Joint Declaration, there was a distinction made between new land and existing land. Lease modifications applied to existing land but importantly, the land areas involved did not form part of the 50-hectare quota although the premium received by the government had to be shared in the same way that revenue from land auctions and grants of new land had to be shared.

It is the government's policy in certain areas to modify old lease conditions which severely restrict the development permitted on a lot, so that redevelopment that complies with current town planning requirements can take place. A premium equivalent to the difference in land value between the development permitted under the existing lease and that permissible under the new lease is charged for any modification granted. A good example of this would be where an existing lease has the old 35-foot height restriction, but the current Outline Zoning Plan permits a plot ratio of 5 with medium/high rise residential development. An application from, or on behalf of, the registered owners to the local District Lands Officer would be circulated through the government and basic terms and conditions, including premium would be offered. These terms and conditions which can be negotiated on before they are finally accepted, will look very similar to be conditions outlined on pp. 59–60 for new auction sites. In other words, the government takes the opportunity to rewrite the development control sections of the old lease.[1]

When applying for a lease modification or land exchange, it is important to remember that the government will only accept such applications from the registered owners of the land, or their formally appointed agents who have written instructions to act on their behalf. In order to assist in speeding up the time taken to process land transaction, architects, surveyors and solicitors were in 1991 advised to include in their applications a copy of the up-to-date lease conditions together with a location plan to the scale of 1:1000.[2] In addition, applicants are now requested to accompany their applications with two sets of the following documents:

1. a computer printout containing the historical and current ownership particulars of the subject property; **and**
2. a complete copy of the Government Land Grant (including all modifications and attachments thereto) affecting the subject property.

One set of these documents needs to be certified by either the Land Registry or by the solicitor acting for the applicant. The other set can be a photocopy of the certified documents.[3]

Lease Modification Documentation

Modification Letter/Deed of Variation

Modifications affecting Conditions in respect of lots held in single ownership and where there are no changes proposed to the lot boundaries are effected by a Modification Letter, and where a government lease has been issued, a Deed of Variation will be used. The treatment of lease modifications is covered by a Lands Department's performance pledge, which reads as follows:

1. A reply to an application for lease modification, advising the applicant whether the case can be entertained or not and identifying the case officer, will be given within 3 weeks from receipt of the application.
2. In straightforward cases, a letter offering the basic terms including the premium payable, or a letter rejecting the application, will be issued within 26 weeks from receipt of the application. More time is usually required for non-straightforward and complicated cases.
3. Once the offer has been accepted, the legal document in respect of straightforward cases will be issued for execution within 13 weeks from receipt of the acceptance.

'No Objection' Letter

This is used where a lot has been subdivided into undivided shares with exclusive rights to the use and occupation of various units in the building thereon, and a modification in respect of one unit or part of the building only is to be effected. In such cases, it is not practical to modify the conditions by the usual Modification Letter, which requires to be executed by all the co-owners, and thus a 'no objection' letter requiring only the acceptance of the unit owners concerned is issued. Frequently the no objection letter will state that it only applies for the lifetime of the building currently standing on the lot.

Extension Letter/Conditions of Extension

There are occasions when an existing or parent lot is allowed to be expanded by adding additional adjoining government land. If the lot is subject to conditions, an Extension Letter will be used but if it is subject to a lease, then Conditions of Extension may be used. A full premium will be assessed to reflect the enhancement in value to the parent lot. Today the most frequent application of this method is to allow lot owners to extend their boundaries for the purpose of slope stabilization works, thereby ensuring that the right party not only carries out the necessary works but, as important, is responsible for the future maintenance of these slopes. It is often very difficult to assess a premium in such cases unless a significant saving in cost can be identified as a result of the granting of the extension area.

Prior to 1985, parcels of land suitable for use as garden were granted by way of extension, but they became a casualty of the 50-hectare land disposal quota previously discussed in Chapter 4. Consequently the policy was changed and garden land is now dealt with by direct grant of tenancies. As the 50-hectare quota is no longer an issue, the Lands Department could, on application, consider reverting to the old policy of granting permanent extensions where appropriate. By their Practice Note No 7/2002 the Lands Department advised that swimming pools could now be built on Garden lots without the need for a modification.

Contemporaneous Exchange

Cases in the following categories are dealt with by way of a contemporaneous exchange:
1. case involving a major readjustment of lot boundaries;
2. cases involving the amalgamation of lots;
3. cases involving major amendments to the existing lease including up-dating of the conditions.

In the past, land exchange ratios for the NT had generally been at the ratio of 5:2 for agricultural to building land. More recently however, in the light of circumstances prevailing in individual cases, lesser ratios have sometimes been permitted; in low density development areas, a 1:1 ratio has been adopted.

It has now been decided that a ratio of 1:1 is appropriate in all cases and will be adopted with immediate effect. For the purposes of land development zoned for comprehensive redevelopment on the relevant outline zoning plan, the government may be prepared to consider a lesser ratio.[4]

The following criteria, which apply equally to both extensions and exchanges, have to be met before the Lands Department will be prepared to consider the granting of additional government land; these criteria require that the government land applied for must:

(a) be incapable of reasonable separate alienation or development;

(b) have no foreseeable public use; and

(c) attract a premium, to be assessed at full market value, which should be no less than if the land was theoretically sold separately.

There are two categories of land exchange: *in-situ* or non-*in-situ*. For *in-situ* exchanges a portion of the land to be surrendered in the 'before' situation must physically overlap the land that will form part of the new lot in the 'after' situation. For non-*in-situ* exchanges the land to be granted will be physically separate from the land to be surrendered. In the cases of non-*in-situ* exchange it follows that it will be extremely difficult to satisfy the first of the three criteria given above. In practice therefore it is extremely rare for a non-*in-situ* exchange to be granted to a commercial profit-making organization, although they are now being considered, in exceptional cases for conservation sites as discussed in Chapter 20. However, it may be given to non-profit-making organizations which are forced to be relocated in order to implement a public project.

Until 1990 there was an administrative rule governing the amount of additional government land that could be added to an existing lot; it was limited to 25% of the lot area being enlarged. Today there is no such restriction provided that the three criteria mentioned above are met. In theory this should give the Lands Department considerably more flexibility when considering applications. However, in the current climate of not wishing to be seen as giving developers anything that could be perceived as an unwarranted benefit, there is a tendency now for the Lands Department to revert to a strict one-for-one exchange ratio. This way the department will avoid criticism but may frustrate some good projects.

The procedures for considering a modification by way of exchange are considerably more lengthy than any of the other methods above and so should only be used where they are completely appropriate and essential. In addition, for those cases involving the amalgamation of lots in different ownership, unity of title is a prerequisite before the DLO will entertain an application for a land exchange.

Land exchanges are implemented by Conditions of Exchange which involves the surrender of the applications' 'old' lots and the contemporaneous grant of a 'new' lot. For this reason, such an exchange is sometimes referred to as a 'surrender and regrant'. These should be distinguished from Conditions of Regrant which were used to extend non-renewable leases.

Lands Department makes frequent use of Practice Notes to advise practitioners of charges in its policy. Examples can be found with No. APSS 2/94 which advised on the criteria for imposing building covenants in lease modification/exchange cases for residential development and Practice Note No.5/2008 which further advises the criteria for imposing building covenants in such cases involving non-residential development.

There is one very important 'administrative' rule within the Lands Department to the effect that no significant modification will be entertained within the first five years of any new lease; these include change of user, increase in plot ratio, and so on. Only minor technical modifications or extensions to the building covenant period will be considered.

The rationale behind the five-year rule is that it would be unfair to the other bidders or tenderers for a particular site if the winner were granted a significant modification even when that modification attracted a full premium. The unsuccessful applicants could rightly claim that if they had known a subsequent modification was going to be allowed, they might well have bid a higher figure; thus the five-year rule ensures a level playing-field for all developers to compete for land and therefore must be retained.

Roads: It is most important that the implications of the Roads (Works, Use and Compensation) Ordinance (Cap. 370) are fully understood in the context of land administration.

There are occasions, particularly when dealing with a big land exchange, when requirements to improve existing roads or even the construction of completely new roads arise as one of the conditions. In some cases, this will require the full gazetting procedure under this ordinance which can be a very time-consuming exercise requiring preparation and submission of engineering plans, consultation with the local District Council and the Rural Committee in the NT, together with the handling of objections. Normally the DLO will not complete the valuation and make the full offer of terms until all these issues have been resolved. In some cases, the procedures can delay a project by over a year. Therefore, if one can avoid gazetting, one should follow that route.

Premium Assessments for Modification/Land Exchanges: The long established practice adopted in the assessment of premia for these types of transaction has been to assess the value of the site only in both the 'before' situation, that is, in accordance with the original lease conditions, controls and restrictions, and the 'after' situation which would be in accordance with the new lease conditions. The premium is taken as being the difference between the 'after' and the 'before' values. In addition to the premium, a modest administrative fee is also charged.

As observed by the Court of Final Appeal in *Director of Lands* v *Yin Shuen Enterprises Limited and Nam Chun Investment Company Limited* [2003] 2 HKLRD 399, 'The Government's right to charge the full value of the modification has not been and could not be challenged. Its policy is informed by the philosophy, which formerly underlay the ownership of land in Hong Kong while it remained a Crown Colony. Land in Hong Kong was regarded as belonging to the Crown, which parted with its ownership only for the duration of the lease and for the user specified in the lease. Subject thereto, it remained the undisposed property of the Crown. In granting a modification of the user covenants in the lease, therefore, the Crown in effect made a further disposal of the land for which it was entitled to charge full value.'

Assessing the 'after' value on a cleared site basis, that is assuming the site has been cleared of all buildings and people is obviously correct, but is such an approach appropriate in the 'before' situation? In circumstances where there is an existing building on the site which has some economic value, several points arise. To begin with, if the building has some intrinsic value, and in particular, if the site has recently been acquired by a developer, that value, together with a degree of hope value for the enhanced development potential, will have been reflected in the purchase price. Secondly, if the existing building is occupied, there will also be the question of payments for tenants compensation and other costs, including demolition costs, which will be incurred to get to a cleared site situation. Under the present policy, none of these costs are allowed for in the premium calculation which appears to be patently inequitable.

In the urban area, the assembly of sites occupied by older buildings is complex and difficult, and many of them are subjected to protected tenancies. If there is no proper credit given in the premium assessment for legitimate costs entailed in obtaining vacant possession in order to get to a cleared site situation, it will merely be a further disincentive for developers to attempt this type of redevelopment. It should not be seen as a concession but as a proper and equitable approach to this type of valuation. If the government wishes to give concessions, it could consider reverting to the policy that existed prior to 1 July 1973 when full modification premia were assessed but only charged at 50%! Perhaps this type of incentive would encourage more developers to attempt the more difficult urban renewal type projects?

Now that many existing industrial areas have been rezoned for OU (B) development, the same questions will arise if these industrial lots, many of which have existing buildings, are to be modified. A fair and equitable approach to the assessment of the modification premium will not only encourage developers to participate, but should also help speed up the process. Furthermore, there is the societal benefit of urban renewal as each old industrial building will be replaced by a modern office cum commercial building. There are occasions when the standard before and after valuation techniques cannot produce a positive premium, but it is acknowledged that the modification or exchange does have benefit to the owner. In these cases, the Lands Department will charge an empirical premium which is reviewed annually. Currently, the base figure is around $70,000, with discretion to charge a higher figure if warranted.

In those cases where the modification is purely technical in nature and there is no discernible enhancement in value, only a modest administrative fee will be charged for the transaction.

Lands Departments Practice Note 1/2006 sets out in some detail their new procedure for premium assessment relating to lease modifications and land exchanges. In the initial assessment stage, no direct negotiation will be permitted although applicants and agents are allowed to submit information and clarifications considered relevant to the assessment. If subsequently a premium offer is not accepted and an appeal is made, the applicant (or the applicant's agent) will be invited to attend the meeting of the Valuation Conference to present the applicant's case, Practice Note 4/2009 also refers. Nevertheless, the final decision on premium still rests with Lands Department. Practice Notes 5/2006, 5/2007 and 3/2008 outline a Fast Track Procedure for Processing Second Appeals and Practice Note 3/2009 extended this to third appeals!

Easements

Easements, being permanent in nature, are usually granted by way of a Deed of Easement. A full market value premium reflecting the enhancement in value to the benefiting lot(s) will be assessed and charged. Sometimes an easement clause will exist or be included in a modification or exchange, often for the purposes of giving a right of way to the lot in question. Usually, the owner of the lot that has the benefit of the easement will be given a non-exclusive right of access and will be solely responsible for the maintenance even though others may be permitted to use it. This topic is also considered in Chapter 10.

Another example of their application is to cover the provision of a permanent footbridge over government land that often links two private lots in the same ownership. It, for any reason, a permanent easement cannot be granted, a licence will be issued instead.

The Procedures

Once an application for a land exchange or lease modification has been received and accepted, the DLO will act as a clearing house for all other interested government departments to comment on. Typically, an application will be circulated by the DLO to the following departments: Buildings, Civil Engineering, Drainage Services, Environmental Protection, Highways, Town Planning, Territories Development, Transport and Waterworks. Once their comments have been received, the DLO will prepare a submission for the District Land Conference (DLC) where the terms and conditions will be hammered out and agreed. With so many departments to consult, there is plenty of scope for disagreement which can cause delay.

Following the promulgation of Practice Note No. 4/2001, it has been the practice for the applicant (and/or the applicant's authorized representative) to be invited to attend the DLC that considers the applicant's case. This gives an excellent opportunity to explain the background and answer any questions that may arise.

Following the DLC's approval, the applicant will receive a letter from the DLO setting out what are called 'basic terms'; these terms will reflect all the technical and planning issues raised, discussed and agreed at the DLC as well as those that the government wishes to impose as conditions for the land exchange/modification. These conditions can be negotiated, but this can cause delay because any resultant changes may need to be referred back to the DLC for ratification before the case can proceed to the next important step — the premium assessment. For those cases that have associated road works imposed as one of the conditions by the DLC and need to be gazetted under the Roads Ordinance, these procedures will take place after the DLC and before any premium assessment is made in order that all the financial implications of the project are clearly understood.

When the premium has been assessed and agreed by the Lands Department's valuers, the DLO will then be in a position to offer the full terms and conditions including a comprehensive draft set of the proposed new lease conditions. These terms have to be accepted, usually within four weeks of the date of the offer letter and such acceptance has to be accompanied by a receipted demand note for 10% of the agreed premium and acceptance will be regarded as having entered into a binding contract that has to be completed within three months.[5]

The 10% deposit will be forfeited in the event the applicant fails to complete the transaction. If applicants do not find the premium acceptable they may, as discussed earlier, appeal but they are reminded that the re-assessment will be at values prevailing as at the date the appeal is considered, so in a rising market there is a risk the premium could, in fact, increase!

These relatively new arrangements for offer and acceptance of terms for lease modifications and land exchanges are to better protect the government's position, after the government lost its appeal in the case of *Humphreys Estate (Queens Gardens) Ltd. v Attorney General and Another* [1986] HKLR 669. [The text of the Court of Appeal decision can be found in Appendix VIII.] In essence, what happened was that in spite of a considerable measure of performance by both parties, including occupation and payment of premium by the applicant, the wording of the offer letters were 'subject to contract' and the licence to occupy the site was specifically worded so that it did not commit the government to the permanent grant. Both the High Court and Court of Appeal held that the applicant could withdraw from the agreement and was entitled to a refund of the premium.

Notes

1. Refer to *Hang Wah Chong Investment Co. Ltd. v Attorney General* [1981] HKLR 336, Appendix VI.
2. Lands Department Practice Note 2/1991.
3. Lands Department Practice Note APSS 2/98.
4. Lands Department Practice Note APSS 1/94.
5. Lands Department Practice Notes APSS 2/99 & No. 9/2000.

9 DEVELOPMENT CONTROL IN OLDER LEASE CONDITIONS

It is important to remember that in the early years of development in Hong Kong there was little or no statutory planning and therefore the most effective method of control that the government could exercise was through the lease conditions.

As discussed in Chapter 11, Town Planning is now fully operative throughout the territory and together with certain sections of the Buildings Ordinance (Cap. 123) can, because of their statutory authority, be used to override the development rights conferred in the private contract that may exist between the government as landlord and the land owner as lessee.

Nevertheless, it is essential to understand the basics of lease interpretation in order to correctly assess the before value in the premium assessment, particularly in the case of older leases where a modification may be granted. As this is a legal matter, any cases of uncertainty or dispute should be referred to solicitors for advice and guidance. It is important that lease conditions are read as a whole, including both the General Conditions and the Special Conditions, because they sometimes contain implied covenants in favour of the government, individual clauses should not be read in part or in isolation from the main body of the text. It should also be remembered that in spite of the government's best efforts to standardize as much as possible, each set of lease conditions will be unique and therefore each case has to be treated on its individual merits.

It is also important to bear in mind a fundamental principle of lease interpretation — that the meaning of a word, phrase or clause in a lease should be determined on the basis of what the word, phrase or clause meant at the date the lease was granted, *Gold Shine Investments Ltd. v. Secretary for Justice* [2010] 1 HKC 212, 83.

The following clauses appear in older lease conditions and their current broad definitions are outlined in some cases assisted by a judicial ruling, but in any event these definitions are strictly for guidance purposes only. Lands Department Practice Note 3/2000 also refers.

1. **House(s)**

This word is normally given a very wide interpretation and can mean a multi-storey development for non-industrial use. However, when used in the singular, the building must have only one main entrance; a secondary entrance is sometimes permissible if it is not intended to provide normal access. Thus, a residential development with one main entrance to the lift lobby and a back entrance for tradesmen or for fire-escape purposes would conform with the definition of the term 'house'. A multi-storey residential/commercial development with shops on the ground floor would not normally comply with the definition of one house if each shop has its own separate entrance to the road. Neither would a terrace of town houses when each has its own separate access. Often the expression 'shall not erect other than one house' is found; in these circumstances this means exactly what it says. A joint development, having the characteristics of one house constructed over two lots, each containing a clause stating that the owner 'shall not erect other than one house', will not be permitted. Conversely, where a lease stipulates that no building other than two houses of a European type should be built a single multi-storey building would be considered as being in breach as decided in *Jasmine Enterprises Ltd.* v *Chan Yuk Hon* [1998] 2 HKLRD 131.

In the case of *Wah Yick Enterprise Co. Ltd.* v *Building Authority* [1997] HKLRD 1177, the judgement, which is essentially planning argument as to the definition of the word 'house' within an area zoned Village on an OZP, included the following comments: 'The word "house" had a distinct fluidity of meaning and it was best construed in relation to the context in which it was found, and in relation to the objects and purposes of the Ordinance or of the section of the Ordinance in which it was used. Whether a particular building did or did not fall under the word "houses" was a mixed question of law and fact; insofar as it was necessary to ascertain all the relevant facts relating to the building, and law insofar as the application of the word "houses" to those facts involved the construction of the Ordinance.' The judgement went on to say that 'It was not necessary to formulate a definitive definition of "house" in this case. It sufficed in the context in which it appeared, the use "house", properly construed, did not include the 33 storey block of flats P (the plaintiff) proposed to build . . . '.

Both the above cases were referred to in a more recent decision in the case of *Fully Profit (Asia) Ltd.* v *Secretary for Justice for and on behalf of the Director of Lands,* HCMP 82/2010. In this case the Plaintiff owned 5 adjoining lots, each with a separate lease granted in 1965, that contained a restriction not to erect or allow to be erected more than one house on each lot. The redevelopment plans showed that the existing 5 houses were to be replaced by one composite multi-storey building with some 26 storeys that would straddle all 5 lots in question. The District Lands Officer/Kowloon East contended that this form of development would be in contravention of the each of the Government leases and would therefore require lease modifications (land exchange?) in order to proceed. The Plaintiff challenged this decision but the court found in favour of the Government and dismissed their Originating Summons.

2. **Dwelling House**
The word 'dwelling' does qualify the word 'house' to a considerable degree as the house(s) may only be used for residential purposes, with flatted development permitted.

3. **Private Dwelling House**
In the singular, this would only permit a single private house and precludes flatted development. Reference is drawn from *Wong Bei-Nei* v *Attorney-General* [1973] HKLR 582, summarized as follows:

> In 1931 a lot was sold by the government at public auction subject to General and Special Conditions of Sale. Special Condition 6 provided that 'the purchaser shall not erect any buildings other than detached or semi-detached residential premises of European type . . . no building erected on the Lot shall be used otherwise than as a private dwelling house'. The purchaser wished to erect a block of flats on the lot.
>
> The court held that a building containing a number of flats would be in breach of the condition that no building erected on the lot should be used otherwise than as a private dwelling house, since it was intended by that condition that a house when built was to be maintained private to the purchaser. To allow the house to be used by several persons in separate tenements would put an end to that privacy.

4. **Messuage(s) and Tenements**
This term has been interpreted as having no building or user restriction.

5. **Villa(s)**
Proper legal advice should be sought on the meaning and effectiveness of any clause containing the above term. Sometimes the wording in the lease is villa residence(s), which would probably bring it into the next category. It usually precludes multi-storey buildings provided that the condition is still enforceable, see p. 78. Reference is drawn from *T.S. Cheng & Sons Ltd.* v *Attorney-General* [1986] HKC 607, summarized as follows:

Land in Old Peak Road was leased by the government in 1860 for 999 years to the predecessor in title to the plaintiff. The government lease contained a clause which provided that the lessee would expend at least $416 in the erection of 'one or more villa residences' on the site. The present owner wished to construct a block of flats and maintained, *inter alia,* three arguments: first, that the building covenant was spent, since a villa had already been erected on the site; secondly, since there was a rate and range provision in the government lease and blocks of flats had been constructed close by, the lessee was prohibited from erecting a villa on the site and the covenant must be disregarded; finally, that a block of flats could still be classified as a villa.

The court rejected all three contentions.

6. **Residence(s)**

This term, when used in the plural, would normally permit development similar to that allowed under the 'house' definition. However, the user will be restricted to residential purposes only. When used in the singular, it would only permit the building to be used for the occupation of one family. Reference is drawn from *Loi Po Investment Co. Ltd.* v *Real Reach Co. Ltd.* [1986] HKLR 643, summarized as follows:

Three government leases each contained a covenant not to erect on the land more than one residence and the defendants as owners of the leases joined together to sell their land to the plaintiff, a development company, in order to construct a block of flats on the combined lots. By an originating summons the parties sought to determine whether, on the construction of the government leases, a block of flats could be constructed on the land.

The court held that the word 'residence' should be given its ordinary meaning and a block of flats clearly involved the construction of more than one residence. The proposed development was, therefore, contrary to the terms of the government leases.

7. **European**

Often the term will be used in conjunction with the term 'house' or 'residence', however it does not normally alter the interpretation in any way. It was intended originally to distinguish houses in European style from those in traditional Chinese style; this distinction is no longer of importance.

8. **Rate and Range Clause**

This clause is only found in old government leases. It required the buildings to be built on the lot to 'rate and range' (or sometimes 'front and range') in a uniform manner with buildings immediately adjacent or in the same street.

It was an early form of town planning that led to rows of houses of similar height and of uniform character.

It is always followed in the government lease by a repairing covenant and a covenant requiring the lot and the building on it to be surrendered and yielded up to the government on expiry of the lease term. When reference is made to a Rate and Range clause, it actually refers to the three clauses read together and all three clauses must be taken into account.

The first clause, the one that actually uses the phrase 'rate and range', was exhausted by the fulfilment of the original building covenant (which usually precedes the three clauses in the government lease) and is no longer effective. However, certain forms of the repairing and surrender covenants (the form may vary from lease to lease and needs to be checked carefully) can in certain circumstances be used by the government to control redevelopment of the lot.

Usually, the government does not use an effective Rate and Range clause to charge premium, but merely prevent a development it does not approve of (for example, on traffic grounds) where there are no other legal means available to the government to do so.

If in doubt, legal advice should be obtained.

9. **Height Limits**

Buildings not to exceed 35 feet in height is a common restriction in older leases. If a higher building is now permitted, a lease modification will be necessary for which a full premium will be charged to reflect the enhancement in land value.

10. **Design Disposition and Height Clause**

There are two forms of the clause, one contained in older leases and the new form presently in use. The obvious difference between the two is that in the older version, 'design' relates not to the buildings as such but merely to the 'exterior elevations' of the building whereas in the 'newer' version, the word 'design' relates specifically to the building or buildings.

(a) The older form of the clause without the word 'height' reads: 'And will not erect on the said piece or parcel of ground any buildings other than houses of European type the design of the exterior elevations and the disposition thereof to be subject to the special approval of the said Director'. This clause may be said to give some control over site coverage but could not be used to control plot ratio or height. Each case would, however, need to be looked at on its individual merits.

(b) The older form of the clause with the word 'height' included could certainly be used to control height and may possibly be used to govern site coverage, so in effect plot ratio could also be controlled. Again, each case would need to be looked at on its own merits.

Again these clauses should not be used by the government to achieve payment of a premium but only to control development in accordance with current planning requirements.

11. The Offensive Trade Clause

There is no better explanation of this clause than that provided by Roberts (1975) as follows:

> This is a beautiful example of archaic terminology finding its way into modern legal documents. It was probably taken in its entirety from an eighteenth-century book of conveyancing precedents, and is worth reproducing in full, it reads :
> The lessee his Executors, Administrators, or Assignees, or any other person or persons, shall not nor will, during the continuance of this demise, use, exercise or follow, in or upon the said premises or any part thereof, the trade or business of a Brazier, Slaughterman, Soap-maker, Sugar-baker, Fellmonger, Melter of tallow, Oilman, Butcher, Distiller, Victualler, or Tavern-keeper, Blacksmith, Nightman, Scavenger, or any other noisy, noisome or offensive trade or business whatever . . .
> Many of these trades or businesses are no longer offensive or noisy, for example, a fellmonger (originally a seller of animal skins, especially sheepskin — the modern equivalent is a furrier, one of the most luxurious and non-offensive of all traders); an oilman (originally a maker or seller of oil from animal fat or vegetable matter; now, for example, a proprietor of a petrol filling station); and a victualler (a seller of food).
> Sugar-baker is an obsolete term, whose last known use according to the Oxford English Dictionary was in 1688. Clearly the compilers of the dictionary could not predict its use in leases issued in Hong Kong today.
> Other trades have virtually disappeared from the general urban scene, but in the seventeenth century must have been socially offensive — brazier, a worker in brass; slaughterman, whose functions are almost completely taken over by modern abattoirs; soap-maker, whose product is always manufactured nowadays in factories; melter of tallow (who used hard animals fat for making candles). Government sanitary services have long ago supplanted the need for a nightman to empty cess-pools by night. (pp. 16–17)

It is found in the standard form in government leases and is implied into all Conditions and recently there has been some discussion as to the effectiveness and enforceability of this clause.

The leading modern English case with a very similar clause is *Mount Cook Land Ltd.* v *Joint London Holdings Ltd. and Market Place Investments Ltd.* [2006] IP. & C.R. DG 14 (CA) ('the Mount Cook case'). In that case two experts gave evidence that from the 1790s onwards there was a progressive build-up of restrictions contained in the standard form of leases used on the great London estates. The form of lease used in the Estate that was the subject of the

Mount Cook case had included a restriction against use as a 'victualler, vintner, tavern-keeper' from the 1790s, a prohibition against acting as a vendor of malt liquors from the second half of the nineteenth century and a prohibition against restaurant use shortly after the First World War.

The particular offensive trade clause in the subject case was used in a 1950 lease and, except that there was a longer list of prohibited trades, the clause was pretty well identical with the Hong Kong version. Note the very important point that despite the old-fashioned language and references to what appeared to be obsolete trades, the clause has to be interpreted in accordance with 1950 conditions and the words given the meaning they would have borne in 1950 — not in 2005 when the case was heard.

There was extensive discussion of the meaning of 'victualler' and 'licensed victualler'. The judges held that the 1950s meaning of 'victualler' was a person who supplied food and drink and that 'licensed victualler' was a different expression meaning a person who ran a public house. The word 'victualler' could not be limited to a 'licensed victualler'. I see no difference between the meaning of these words now, in the twenty-first century, from the meaning these judges gave them for the 1950s.

In the light of this very recent decision, there is every reason to believe that the prohibition in the Hong Kong leases, in particular 'oilman', 'victualler' and 'tavern -keeper', are effective and the words would be given meanings consonant with current usage and that those meanings would apply for most of the dates for which interpretation has to take place.

Previously land owners could apply for a modification or no objection letter to delete the following categories of offensive trades from leases on payment of a technical modification fee: oilman, tavern-keeper, victualler, butcher and sugar baker. For example some of the hotels on Hong Kong Island are built on lots with leases containing this clause; it was necessary to remove the tavern-keeper and victualler uses before the hotels could operate. Now by virtue of Lands Department Practice Note No 6/2007 such applications will be dealt with by the granting of a licence. For hotel developments the lot can only be alienated as a whole and the letting of individual rooms is restricted to a maximum period of 12 months with no right of renewal.

ACCESS ARRANGEMENTS AND RIGHTS OF WAY

Access Arrangements

When considering older leases, it is most important to check the access arrangements. Sometimes these are indicated on the old grant plans as rights of way, with or without dimensions, and they may also be referred to in the text of the lease conditions. The width of such rights of way can have a significant impact on the density of development that may be permitted and in this connection a proper understanding of Building (Planning) Regulation 19 is essential. The following principles are relevant:

1. Building (Planning) Regulation 19(2) states: 'Where a site abuts on a street less than 4.5 m wide or does not abut on a street, the height of any building or buildings to be erected thereon and the maximum site coverage and plot ratio to be permitted in respect of such building or buildings shall be determined by the Building Authority.' Where the Building Authority has to rule on such cases, it is normal for them to restrict redevelopment to 'existing bulk'. It is, therefore, very important to know when Building (Planning) Regulation 19(2) applies and in each case where it would appear to apply, it will be necessary to apply to the Building Authority for ruling on the volume of the existing bulk or such other redevelopment that they may permit.

2. Notwithstanding whether Building (Planning) Regulation 19(2) could be applied, it has been ruled that where a lot is separated by a strip of government land running the length of the lot's frontage which is reserved for future road widening, such widening would mean that the lot will abut the future road. Thus, Building (Planning) Regulation 19(2) may be used to restrict redevelopment to existing bulk provided that no modification of lease conditions is otherwise required or, if necessary, the Lands Department has agreed to permit a modification. Again it would be prudent to apply

to the Building Authority for a ruling in such cases in order that the true position is known.

Improvements of Rights-of-Way on Government Land to Private Lots

1. Cases arise where greater development of a lot than otherwise permissible under the Lease/Conditions of Grant, can only be undertaken after the approach road (over a right of way on government land) is brought up to the standards laid down under the Building (Private Streets and Access Roads) Regulations (Cap. 123). Normally where there is inadequate access, the Building Authority will limit redevelopment to the 'existing bulk' of development. To permit greater development often necessitates changing the alignment of the existing right of way, or granting an extended right of way over government land. The question of whether it is appropriate to charge a premium for the provision of a right of way which will enable an owner to develop a lot to the maximum within the limits imposed by the lease and the Building Ordinance and Regulations, depends on whether:
    (a) the lot is held under conditions wherein an imprecise phrase such as 'on a line to be approved' was used when referring to the original right of way grant. In such cases, it will be difficult for the government to state categorically that additional land is required and so normally no premium is required; and
    (b) the lot is held under Conditions or Lease where a specific right of way is shown on the plan.

2. In the first type of case, it could be that no premium will be charged. In the second type, the owner is only entitled to the defined right of way and will have to pay for any 'extra'. Such premium will reflect the difference between the before and after land value.
    Each case must be dealt with on its individual merits and legal advice should be sought if there is any doubt.

3. In modification cases, the 'no greater bulk' ruling would affect the assessment of the 'before' value. However, in the 'after' value, it is likely that the assessment of maximum development would automatically include the benefit of any revised right of way required, and therefore, any benefit derived from this improved right of way would already be included in the modification premium.

The requirement of the government to honour any rights of way granted under lease was upheld in the Court of Appeal in the case of *Wisename Ltd. v The Secretary for Justice* [1998] 1 HKLRD 71. In this case, the plaintiff was in 1957 given a right of way to his lot of sufficient width for vehicles to use. In spite of the fact that the loss of vehicular access occurred over 12 years earlier, it was held that the Limitations Ordinance (Cap. 347) could not be invoked and that the government had by its actions derogated from its grant.

TOWN PLANNING CONTROLS AND DEVELOPMENT RESTRICTIONS IN LEASE CONDITIONS

The first TPO was not enacted until 1939, but because of the Second World War, it was not brought into effect until 1947. The Ordinance applied to the urban areas of Hong Kong Island and Kowloon as the NT was still essentially rural and undeveloped.

Until 1973 the planning restrictions that did exist were confined to controlling the use that land could be put to with no attempt to control the density or volume of development. The density of development was controlled either by the lease conditions or, in the case of unrestricted leases, by the First Schedule to the Building (Planning) Regulations Cap. 123.

Where lease conditions could be used to regulate and control the density of development, broad Density Control Areas were designated together with some specific Areas of Special Control whereby the predecessor to the Lands Department, the former Crown Lands and Survey Office, could administratively control the density and volume of development that was permitted. For example in some areas such as the Mid-Levels, no modifications were permitted that would result in more intensive development.

The obvious weakness in this system of administrative control arose in those older urban areas where the lease conditions were unrestricted. On 13 April 1973, the Draft Peak Area Outline Zoning Plan was exhibited and became the first area where the government introduced statutory density control specifying a maximum plot ratio of 0.5, or if the bulk of the existing buildings was higher than 0.5 pr, then the redevelopment would be allowed to equal the existing plot ratio. Coincidentally, during 1973 outline zoning plans for three new towns in the NT were also exhibited thus introducing statutory planning control there for the first time.

The power of the government to impose statutory plot ratio controls under the TPO was immediately challenged and in the case of *Crozet Ltd.* v *Attorney*

General (unreported MP No. 409/1973); the Courts upheld the government's position. The same question arose in the Court of Appeal decision in the case of *Attorney General* v *CC Tse (Estate) Ltd.* [1982] HKLR 7 (CA) when again the government's position was upheld.

With the backing of these two decisions, it became the government's policy for all the old Density Control Areas and Areas of Special Control to be incorporated into their respective Outline Zoning Plans (OZP) and this has been achieved progressively. The current practice is to specify the maximum permissible plot ratio, site coverage, building height or any combination of them in the 'Remarks' column of the Notes to each statutory plan. In this way, even if the lease is unrestricted, any building proposals which contravene the stated development restrictions will be rejected by the Building Authority under the provisions of Section 16 (1) (d) of Cap. 123.

As the authority of the Planning Department has increased, the authority of the Lands Department has been reduced as gradually the full effect of statutory planning control took over from the previous arrangements for administrative control. However, where a proposed development is permitted under the draft or approved plan but would contravene a covenant in the lease, the developer must still apply for a variation of the lease and may have to pay a premium for such variation. In the words of Deputy Judge Cruden in *Mexx Consolidated (Far East) Ltd* v *The Attorney General* [1987] HKLR 1210:

> No matter what approval the Town Planning Board may have given under its statutory powers, that would not have affected or reduced the Crown's contractual powers under the Crown lease. They are two quite distinct concepts . . . if the Town Planning Board — which is a wholly Government administrative body and not a judicial or quasi-judicial tribunal — approved of the changed use, the Crown might then, in its contractual capacity, more favourably deal with an application by the lessee for the waiver or modification of the user covenant.

Similarly, even if consent to build is given under the Buildings Ordinance (Cap. 123), such consent will not serve as a waiver of any restrictive term in the government lease or conditions.

Section 14(2) of the Buildings Ordinance says:

> Subject to section 28B(4), neither the approval of any plans nor the consent to the commencement of any building works or street works shall be deemed . . .
>
> (b) to act as a waiver of any term in any lease or licence.

The wording of Deputy Judge Cruden's decision is worth close examination. The critical section is '. . . the Crown *might* then, in its contractual capacity, more favourably deal with an application by the lessee for the waiver or modification of the user covenant'. However, in view of the much quoted decision in *Hang Wah Chong Investment Co. Ltd.* v *Attorney General* [1981] HKLR 336, the government as the land authority equally *might not* favourably consider such an application and, not having the need to act reasonably, could frustrate a scheme which had received planning approval.

Conversely there could be situations when, for example, as a result of a rezoning exercise or amendments are made to an OZP, the TPB's decision could result in a landowner's development rights as stated in the lease being diminished. At the moment, there are no statutory provisions for compensation in the event of an adverse or down-zoning situation unless the new zoning is for a public purpose in which case the government can usually be persuaded to resume. The question of compensation for partial loss of development rights was one of the topics considered by the Special Committee on Compensation and Betterment, chaired by Mr John Todd, a former senior Hong Kong Government Officer, whose report, published in March 1992, concluded that the status quo should remain and that in general there should be no compensation paid in such circumstances. It seems to be inequitable that on the one hand when there is a change in a statutory plan that results in an increase in development potential, the government is only too happy to permit that to happen and collect a land premium for any lease modification that may be required. However, when the reverse occurs, they refuse to pay any compensation, relying on the decision in the case of *Lam Kwok Leung* v *Attorney General* [1979] HKLR 145, when it was held that planning or other statutory powers adversely affecting a lessees' rights do not amount to any derogation of grant.

The other way of tackling this problem is to challenge the validity of the change in land use zoning in the first place, where it would bring the owner into a conflict with the user as permitted under the lease. In the case of *Fine Tower Association Ltd.* v *Town Planning Board* [2006] 2 HKC 507, the applicant sought a Judicial Review of the TPB rejection of their objection to the planning limitations proposed to be imposed on their land. The following extracts from the case report are considered to be relevant:

> 1. The applicant's two pieces of land, which are adjacent to each other, are leasehold properties. They are subject to restrictive covenants which include the following:
>
> (i) the land may only be used for industrial and/or godown purposes, this to include the bulk storage and distribution of petroleum products;
> (ii) one of the pieces of land may only initially be developed as an oil depot, and
> (iii) any structures built on the land may not exceed a maximum height of 85.19mPD.

2. The restrictive covenants state that any failure to abide by these (and other) restrictions will entitle the Government, as landlord, to enter upon and take back the land without obligation to pay compensation. The Government, as landlord, constrained by private not public law, may of course agree to a variation of the special conditions but it is not obliged to do so. Any variation must be the result of commercial negotiations. If such negotiations are successful – and that must always be uncertain — I understand that they will invariably involve the payment by the applicant of premium.

3. When the applicant acquired the two pieces of land they were zoned for 'industrial' and government, institution or community' use on the Draft Quarry Bay Outline Zoning Plan No. S/H21/6.

4. In April 2003, the Draft OZP was exhibited for public inspection under s.5 of the Town Planning Ordinance.

5. In terms of the Draft OZP, the zoning of the applicant's two pieces of land was changed so that 44% of their total area was to be designated as 'open space' while the balance of 56% was to be designated as 'other unspecified use', more specifically, as the explanatory statement to the Draft OZP explained, for the purposes of 'cultural and/or commercial, leisure and tourism related uses.'

So one of the applicant's principal objections was that the limitations imposed by the Draft OZP in respect of the permitted uses of the two pieces of land were directly at odds with the uses permitted by the covenants (i.e. the special conditions of exchange) governing the applicant's ownership of the land. The conditions of the Draft OZP, if approved, would prohibit the applicant from using its two pieces of land in accordance with the covenants while the conditions of the land grants prohibited it from using the land in accordance with the Draft OZP. Accordingly, so it was argued, the limitations as to use imposed by the Draft OZP, allied with other limitations (such as the more rigorous height limitation), prevented the applicant from developing its two pieces of land and amounted to a *de facto* deprivation of the applicant's rights in that land.

On the question of deprivation of property, paragraph 51 of the decision includes a very useful reference to the principle involved:

> As a statement of relevant principle, I do not believe it is possible to improve on the words of Lord Hoffmann in the Privy Council judgement of *Grape Bay Limited* v *Attorney General of Bermuda* [2000] 1 WLR 574, at 583:
>
> > 'it is well settled that restrictions on the use of property imposed in the public interest by general regulatory laws do not constitute a deprivation of that property for which compensation should be paid. The best example is planning control *(Westminster Bank Ltd.* v *Beverley Borough Council*

[1971] A.C 508) or, in American terminology, zoning laws (*Village of Euclid v Ambler Realty Co.* (1926) 272 U.S. 365). The give and take of civil society frequently requires that the exercise of private rights should be restricted in the general public interest. The principles which underlie the right of the individual not to be deprived of his property without compensation are, first, that some public interest is necessary to justify the taking of private property for the benefit of the state and, secondly, that when the public interest does so require, the loss should not fall upon the individual whose property has been taken but should be borne by the public as a whole. But these principles do not require the payment of compensation to anyone whose private rights are restricted by legislation of general application which is enacted for the public benefit. This is so even if, as will inevitably be the case, the legislation in general terms affects some people more than others. For example, rent control legislation restricts only the rights of those who happen to be landlords but nevertheless falls within the general principle that compensation will be payable. Likewise in *Penn Central Transportation Co.* v *New York City* (1978) 438 U.S. 104, the New York City's Landmarks Preservation Law restricted only the rights of those people whose buildings happened to have been designated historic landmarks. Nevertheless the Supreme Court of the United States held that it was a general law passed in the public interest which did not violate the Fifth Amendment prohibition on taking private property without compensation.

Whether a law or exercise of an administrative power does amount to a deprivation of property depends of course on the substance of the matter rather than upon the form in which the law is drafted.

So whether there has been a deprivation of property is, therefore, to use the words of *Lord Hoffmann*, a matter to substance not a matter of formality. The following points are also made in paragraphs 59 and 60:

But indeed what must be remembered is that the applicant has no right in law to demand a change in the restrictive covenants nor has the Government any obligation to act reasonably in considering any request for change. In this regard, the definitive statement as to the position has been given by *Lord Millett NPJ* in *Director of Lands* v *Yin Shuen Enterprises Ltd. and Another* [2003] 2 HKC 490, at 500:

'Two further considerations are relevant at this point. First, the user covenants in the Crown leases are absolute. They are not qualified by any requirement that the Crown's consent is not to be unreasonably withheld; and the statute law of Hong Kong does not subject user covenants in leases to any such requirement. Secondly, in deciding whether to grant or withhold its consent to a modification of the terms of a lease, the Government does not exercise a public law function but acts in its private capacity as landlord: see *Hang Wah Chong Investment Co. Ltd.* v *A-G* [1981] HKLR 336 (PC). It thus has an absolute right if it chooses to demand a premium, however large, for granting a modification of the terms of the lease, or to withhold its consent altogether, however unreasonably: see *Tredegar (Viscount)* v *Harwood* [1929] AC 72.'

Government is not therefore obliged to act reasonably in respect of an application for modification of the user covenants which presently apply to the applicant's land.

A reasonable application — if the applicant chose to make it — could be unreasonably refused or the terms of any consent could be so onerous as to be unacceptable.

The judgment was made in favour of the applicant because, in the opinion of the judge, they had indicated a viable argument to the broad effect that in considering whether or not the new OZP had brought a *de facto* deprivation of property, the TPB has to look to the applicant's existing user rights in the land, not to any speculative means by which the applicant may be able to seek and through a method of private negotiation perhaps obtain a modification of such user rights so as to comply with the new OZP.

The decision of the TPB was accordingly quashed and the matter remitted for a new hearing at which the TPB, contrary to the court's decision, decided to retain the existing zoning!

On the basis of the decision in future the Planning Department will have to seriously take into account existing user and development requirements before proposing any major changes that would result in a *de facto* deprivation of property rights.

There have been two further High Court decisions where the question of the need to strike a fair balance between private property rights and public interest was considered. In *Capital Rich Development Ltd. & Anor v. Town Planning Board* [2007] 2 HKLRD 155 it was found that although the TPB had relied on both financial and planning considerations as the basis for its decision the evidence indicated that the financial consideration had a substantial or material influence on the decision to reject the Appellant's objection and that without the financial consideration the TPB would not have reached the same conclusion. Accordingly it was held that the decision of the TPB was *ultra vires* and had to be quashed. This was followed by *International Traders Limited v. Town Planning Appeal Board & Anor* [2009] 4 HKC 411 which was an application for judicial review where it was held that the TPB's discretion was constrained by the terms of the plan and by taking into account considerations which fell outside the parameters of the plan TPB had taken into account irrelevant considerations that rendered their decision *ultra vires* and was therefore to be quashed. The Court said: 'Just as the Town Planning Ordinance protects the Community, it protects property owners as well. An owner is just as entitled to rely on a DPA plan as the Government. That is the *raison d'etre* for the existence of the Board and the Appeal Board.'

Legitimate Expectation

The application of the doctrine of legitimate expectation in Hong Kong was initially considered by the Privy Council in *Attorney General of Hong Kong* v *Ng Yuen Shui* [1983] AC 629 when it was held that even where a person had no general right to a fair hearing, where a government department charged with the duty of making a decision, promised to follow certain procedures before reaching that decision, that procedure should be followed unless it conflicted with the department's statutory duty.[1]

This then raises the question of whether or not developers have a legitimate expectation for the Lands Department to approve the necessary lease modification once they have received planning consent. Legitimate expectation usually applies as a procedural remedy, it is therefore necessary to refer to the Lands Department's mission statements, performance pledge and practice circulars, which are published from time to time, to see if there is any clue as to how the department will respond in such instances. If the Lands Department were to deviate from what they had published and publicized as regular practice and as a consequence a developer or other applicant was adversely affected, the doctrine of legitimate expectation could, possibly, be invoked. However, as Mr Justice Keith in the Court of First Instance recorded in the case *The Hong Kong and China Gas Co. Ltd.* v *Director of Lands* [1997] HKLRD 1291, 'the doctrine of legitimate expectation is still in an embryonic stage of its development'.

This case arose because the Director of Lands declined to extend the applicant's special purpose lease on the grounds that the land was not being used for the purpose for which the lease was originally granted (see p. 30). The applicant argued that the government's 1987 policy statement on the renewal of such leases created a legitimate expectation that the lease would be extended. In upholding the Director of Land's decision, it was noted that a number of requirements, including the requirement for the statement giving rise to the expectation to be clear and unambiguous, must be established to justify the invocation of the doctrine of legitimate expectation. In the judge's view, the 1987 policy statement did not meet this requirement. However, it was noted that the policy statement clearly stated that the question of extending such lease would be considered on a case-by-case basis. Further, as there had been a significant change in the use of the land between the grant of the lease and the making of the policy statement, the applicant should have recognized the possibility that the lease might not have been extended for this reason.

The decision in the case of *Polorace Investments Ltd.* v *Director of Lands* [1997] 1 HKC 373, which related to an application for DD & H approval under lease, was however very clear and emphatic in stating:

In dealing with the appellant, the respondent acted as the Crown's land agent in its capacity of a private landlord. The public law concept of 'legitimate expectation' had no application to a private lease *Hang Wah Chong Investment Co. Ltd.* v *A-G* [1981] HKLR 336 followed.

The same point was made in the decision of *Ying Ho Co. Ltd. & Others* v *Secretary for Justice* [2005] HKLRD 135 as reported on pp. 68–69.

These two cases can be compared with the reference to legitimate expectation in the case of *Rita Enterprise Co. Ltd.* v *District Land Officer, Tai Po* [1996] 4 HKC 410, where the applicants argued that they had a legitimate expectation of the DLO issuing them an unconditional Certificate of Exemption, quoting 500 such previous applications. However, the judge noted that the 500 examples were all for houses to be built within 'Village' zones, whereas the subject application site was in a 'Green Belt' zone. The judge therefore concluded that the applicant did not have any legitimate expectation that the exemption certificate would be granted free of the requirement to seek planning permission prior to building. Accordingly he considered that the DLO had not departed from established practice.

Again, quoting from the *Rita* decision, 'Each case has to be 'examined individually in the light of whatever policy [the official] sees fit to adopt provided always that the adopted policy is a lawful exercise of discretion conferred upon him by statute. Any other view would entail the conclusions that the unfettered discretion conferred by the statute on [the official] can in some case be restricted so as to hamper, or prevent changes of policy' [per *Lord Scarman* – Re *Findlay* [1985] AC 318.

The decisions in these cases help clarify that the principle of legitimate expectation can only apply to broad public policy issues but cannot apply to the treatment or interpretation of individual leases which are considered to be in the private, not public, law domain.

Land Assembly for Redevelopment

The process of acquisition for redevelopment of land or properties in multiple ownership can be lengthy, frustrating and at times emotive. Recently, there has been more public discussion of the possibility of the government using its powers of resumption to assist private developers in site assembly for redevelopment in Comprehensive Development Areas (CDA) both in the urban areas as well as the NT. These powers exist under Section 4(2) of the Town Planning Ordinance (Cap. 131) whereby the Town Planning Board may recommend the resumption of any land that interferes with the layout of an area shown on a Master Layout Plan approved for a CDA. In practice even if the Board makes such a recommendation, the previous administration was reluctant to implement because of the sensitivities of being seen to openly assist developers. Even though such proposals are controversial, they could potentially bring substantial benefits to the community, in terms of both urban renewal and additional housing.

In order to facilitate the redevelopment of lots on which there are existing older buildings in multiple ownership, the government enacted the Land (Compulsory Sale for Redevelopment) Ordinance (Cap. 545) in 1999 with the objective of enabling the owners of not less than 90% of the undivided shares in a lot to make an application to the Lands Tribunal for an order to sell all the undivided shares in the lot for the purposes of the redevelopment of the lot. The Lands Tribunal is empowered to make such an order, having first heard any objection from the persons who own the other undivided shares and having been satisfied that all reasonable steps to acquire all the undivided shares have been taken in particular that the negotiations for the purchase of those shares have been on terms that are fair and reasonable.

The Lands Tribunal in its decision in *Intelligent House Ltd. v. Chan Tung Shing & Ors* [2008] 4 HKC 421 spelt out some useful guidelines and tests when assessing 'age' and 'state of repair' of older buildings and accepted the concept of buildings coming to the end of their economic lifespan. However a subsequent Court of Appeal decision in *Fineway Properties Limited and Sin Ho Yuen, the Administrator of the Estate of Sin Yat* [2010] 4 HKLRD 1 (CA) cautioned that until the economic theories and tests formulated in *Intelligent House* had the *imprimatur* of a higher court they should be approached with a degree of circumspection and should not be applied as if they were part of the Ordinance itself'.

Since enactment, up until the end of March 2010, only 27 compulsory sale orders had been granted, arising from 65 applications, mainly because the 90% threshold is unrealistically high. For example, a six-storey building (which is quite typical in the older urban areas) can be divided into six separate legal interests; having acquired five of the six legal interest represents only 83%, so the Ordinance could not be invoked to buy the remaining interest. Fortunately the Ordinance is written such that with the approval of the Chief Executive in Council, this threshold can be lowered to 80% and on 1 April 2010 the Land (Compulsory Sale for Redevelopment)(Specification of Lower Percentage) Notice 2010 came into effect officially lowering the threshold to 80% for the following classes of land lots:

> (a)　a lot with units that each accounts for more than 10% of the undivided shares in the lot;

(b)   a lot with all buildings ages 50 years or above; and

(c)   a lot that is not located within an industrial zone and with all the buildings on its premises being industrial buildings aged 30 years or above.

As expected this has resulted in a significant increase in the number of applications with 29 being received by the Lands Tribunal up until 15 March 2011.This in turn should translate into an increased number of compulsory sale orders in the coming years.

The Court of Final Appeal (CFA), at the end of its decision in the case *Capital Well Limited* v *Bond Star Development Limited* FACV 4/2005, made some interesting comments and recommendations on the question of how to handle applications where more than one lot is involved. The relevant paragraphs are as follows:

> The Lands Tribunal (LT) had, on the respondent's application, ordered the sale of the six lots intended for redevelopment in a single batch. However, the Court of Appeal held that on the true construction of the Ordinance this was impermissible. It varied the LT's order to confine it to an order solely for sale of the Lot. The order as varied is not under challenge and stands as between the parties.
>
> There is, however, a danger that if the power is so confined the policy objectives of the Ordinance may be undermined. As the Court of Appeal recognized, the minority owner, if sufficiently funded, might be able to bid up the single lot to a highly inflated price thereby exercising 'ransom power' through the medium of the public auction. And if the minority owner or a third party actually acquired the auctioned lot, the intended redevelopment might have to be abandoned or face lengthy delays subject to the uncertainties of negotiations with the new owner of the lot. Such consequences plainly run counter to the statutory objectives.
>
> If, on the other hand, it were open to the majority owner to combine sale of the Lot with sale of the other lots already owned, the entire developable site would be put up for sale. Such an auction could be expected to attract only bids from genuine developers. There would be no room for ransom-motivated bids. An appropriate reserve price would have to be fixed to ensure that the minority owner receives a proper share of the redevelopment value of the site. But whether the successful bidder should prove to be the majority owner or someone else, a redevelopment of the entire site would be able to proceed without impediment, in line with the objectives of the Ordinance.
>
> Plainly, the power coercively to order sale is confined to ordering the sale of a lot or lots in which a majority owner and a minority owner each hold a proprietary interest. However, in cases where a majority owner qualifies for the making of such a compulsory order and wishes to have that lot put up for auction together with adjacent redevelopment lots wholly owned by him, the question arises as to whether, on its true construction, the Ordinance precludes the LT from making an order for sale in respect of the composite site. That

matter was not in issue and was not argued before us. In the light of the policy concerns noted above, we wish expressly to leave that question open for possible future consideration.

Additionally, if a restrictive construction of the Ordinance is required, we wish expressly to leave it open for possible future consideration whether the LT has a discretion to give suitable directions (under s4(6) (a) of the Ordinance or otherwise) concerning conduct of the sale designed to secure that the sale of the single lot, the subject of its order, can take place together with the sale of the other redevelopment lots, similar to the directions given by the Court of Appeal in *Golden Bay Investment Ltd.* v *Chou Hung [1994]* 2 HKC 197 at 200-202, or along analogous lines.

These issues raise difficult questions and the best course may be for them to be addressed by the legislature with a view to ensuring that the objectives of the Ordinance are not frustrated.

The new administration in passing this law has demonstrated that it is prepared to tackle the sensitive question of assisting developers with site assembly, and perhaps now it will be more prepared to use its existing powers under Section 4 (2) of Cap. 131 with regard to CDA sites as discussed above. However, particularly in view of the CFA's comments quoted above, there appears to be a need for some formal supplementary legislation to be enacted to ensure, in the words of the CFA, 'that the objectives of the Ordinance are not frustrated'.

Calculation of Plot Ratio (PR) of Development on Sites Straddling Land Use Zones

Practitioners need to be aware that the Planning Department have now issued their Practice Note for Professional Persons No. 4/2006 advising that in these circumstances any building development should be regarded as one development on one site and the PR of the whole development should be calculated on the lower of the PRs stated on the relevant OZP. Minor relaxations to such PR's impositions may be submitted to TPB by way of S16 application and considered on their individual merit. The development industry is very unhappy with this Practice Note and is pressing for its removal.

Notes

1.   See Cruden 1999, p. 508 and p. 509.

LAND MANAGEMENT AND LEASE ENFORCEMENT

As the following Government Proclamation dated 21 October 1844 indicates, there has been a management problem for the authorities from the earliest days of Hong Kong's settlement.

> Whereas a great number of Chinese and others have, without permission, and in direct opposition to law and custom, settled themselves upon the Queen's Road and at divers places along the coast of this island, and have there erected mat-houses, and in some instances even wooden houses, wherein they live and carry on business without paying any rent to the Crown for the land so occupied:
>
> This is to give notice, that the Surveyor-General of this colony has received my commands to give the aforesaid persons notice to remove themselves and structures within a reasonable time and at his discretion, and, in default of their doing so, to eject them and remove their mat-sheds and other structures.
>
> This proclamation to be translated into Chinese and circulated throughout the island.
>
> (Quoted in Kyshe 1971, p. 70)

Today the Land (Miscellaneous Provisions) Ordinance (Cap. 28) provides the authorities with the necessary powers to control the unlawful occupation of unleased land, including the building of unauthorized structure together with control of excavations in unleased land. The authorities are also given the power to issue, at an appropriate fee prescribed in the subsidiary Government Land Regulations, licences for the occupation of unleased land, and the powers of control including the levying of summary fines and the issuing of demolition orders in the event of there being a breach of the Licence Conditions. The power to order the demolition of unlawful structure is , by virtue of Section 12 of Cap. 28, also extended to cover leased land in particular the structures built without consent on 'agricultural' land in the NT.

Where an owner of an 'Old Schedule' agricultural lot wishes to erect buildings, the permission of the Land Authority (DLO) is required. If the buildings are to be used for agricultural purposes, then a Letter of Approval may be issued by the DLO free of charge subject to three months' notice. The Letter of Approval is, in effect, the 'Licence' referred to in the First Covenant of the Block Government Lease.[1] Where the buildings or structures are for non-agricultural purposes if approval is obtained, then the DLO will issue a Short Term Waiver (STW) for a term of one year certain and thereafter quarterly subject to an appropriate waiver fee being charged. Waiver fees are based on standard rates that are reviewed every three years. There are a few Modification of Tenancy (MoT) permits still in existence; these documents were used prior to STWs and serve the same purpose. However, they are no longer issued and are slowly vanishing.

The use of licences has now largely been overtaken by the use of the Abbreviated Tender System whereby the parcels of government land that are not required immediately for development are made available on short-term tenancy (STT). These STTs are either for terms of one, two or three years certain and then monthly or quarterly thereafter. Typical permitted uses are open car parks; storage of equipment, plant nurseries and similar activities which do not require large structures and can be set up and closed down with the minimum of cost and fuss. Apart from earning income, a further benefit is that by letting out land on tenancy it avoids the expense that would otherwise be incurred in fencing and guarding vacant land.

Particularly in the NT, there are a large number of squatter structures which are predominately occupied for domestic use. The majority of these temporary structures were covered by the Housing Department's General Squatter Structure Survey carried out in 1976 which has been periodically updated and covers both government land and leased agricultural land. All structures have been given a survey number and in addition may have a licence, permit or approval from the Land Authority. Provided the structure continues to be used for the same purpose identified in the survey and, if its existence does not run contrary to any approval from the land authority, then it is entitled to remain and will not be required to be demolished under the Land (Miscellaneous Provisions) Ordinance. If these squatter structures are at any time cleared by the government for development, they will receive ex-gratia compensation and domestic occupiers are rehoused into public housing. Since April 2006 Lands Department have taken over responsibility for all squatter control and clearance functions from Housing Department.

In 1998 the Lands Department established a Slope Maintenance Section and has gradually taken over the responsibility for the maintenance and emergency repairs of the thousands of man-made slopes and retaining walls that exist on unallocated government land where there is no obvious owner or beneficiary.

Public buildings such as hospitals, town halls, government offices and museums are dealt with by a simple land allocation procedure with straightforward engineering conditions and a site plan. Similarly, all the sites for Hong Kong's public housing programme are held on land vested in the Housing Authority, this vesting being a more formal type of land allocation. In all these cases, the DLO prepares the conditions of allocation or vesting which are then formally passed directly to the government department concerned.

There are two other government agencies other than the Lands Department who have extensive management responsibilities. The first such agency is the Hong Kong Housing Authority (HKHA) which, together with the Hong Kong Housing Society, is responsible for a combined total of over one million rental or subsidized sale flats that provide secure subsidized housing accommodation for about half of Hong Kong's 7 million population. The HKHA is far and away the biggest builder and the largest estate management organization in town.

Less publicized is the role of the Country and Marine Parks Authority which was established following the enactment of the Country Parks Ordinance (Cap. 208) in 1976 and the Marine Parks Ordinance (Cap. 76) in 1995. Currently there are 24 Country Parks designated under the Ordinance which, together with Special Areas that fall outside Country Parks such as Tai Po Kau Foresty Reserve, have a combined area of around 400 sq.km, most of which is government land, representing some 40% of Hong Kong's total land area. These parks are now attracting over 12 million visitors a year, providing an essential green lung and recreational outlet for the urban population. It is the job of the Country and Marine Parks Authority, together with its executive arm the Director of Agriculture, Fisheries and Conservation, to properly manage the parks and most importantly, to ensure they are protected against encroachment for development. This subject is considered more fully in Chapter 20.

Lease Enforcement and Control

The Government Rights (Re-entry and Vesting Remedies) Ordinance (Cap. 126) provides that when a right of re-entry has accrued to the government under the terms of a particular lease, such right may be exercised by registering a Memorandum of Re-entry against the lot in the Land Registry, whereupon the lot re-vests in the government. Where the breach of the lease conditions relates to a flat or other parts of a building, as distinct from the lot itself, a Vesting Notice may be registered against the flat in the Land Registry, whereupon the flat and its undivided shares(s) are vested in the Financial Secretary Incorporated (FSI). The most common reasons for re-entry procedures to be invoked are as follows:

(a) Non-fulfillment of the BC condition which stipulates the time permitted, normally 48 months, in which the site must be developed: this is a deterrent against hoarding of land;

(b) Non-payment of instalments: this problem is diminishing as fewer and fewer sites are being sold by the government with an option to pay the premium by instalments;

(c) Non-payment of rent: this occurs for example if an owner dies intestate and there is no proper administration of the estate;

(d) Breach of lease conditions: usually a significant breach of the user condition will warrant re-entry action.

The legislation provides for the former owner to petition the Chief Executive or apply to the High Court in its jurisdiction in equity for relief against forfeiture. The majority of cases are dealt with by way of petition and there is an administrative arrangement for considering them. The re-entry/vesting may be cancelled on agreement of terms including payment of all outstanding arrears, interest thereon plus administrative charges. These powers have been delegated to the Director of Lands except in cases where it is recommended to reject the petition when it must be referred to the Chief Executive in Council. A memorandum of Re-entry or Vesting Notice is cancelled by registering a memorandum to that effect in the Land Registry.

It is not uncommon in certain parts of the urban area, usually the older parts for owners and occupiers of buildings to carry out illegal alterations and extensions to their premises. The major concern is to preserve both the safety of the buildings and the environment of those who live or work in or near them. If such works is in breach of the lease the DLO can take action, but if not, the Building Authority have a Control and Enforcement Division which can deal with these cases under the Buildings Ordinance (Cap. 123) if they are in breach of this ordinance.

There have been a few cases which help to give guidance on how the law should be applied. The following is a summary of the case *Li Sui-Yuet* v *Attorney General* [1970] HKLR 428:

> The plaintiff was the tenant under a Crown lease, one of the covenants of which prohibited her from constructing residential premises on the land leased. She had, however, constructed buildings on the land and converted them into residential dwellings. After warnings were sent to the plaintiff the Crown re-

entered upon the land and a memorial of re-entry was registered in the district office. The plaintiff subsequently largely rectified the position and she petitioned the Governor for relief against forfeiture of her lease under the *Crown Rights (Re-entry and Vesting Remedies) Ordinance* (Cap 126). The Governor granted relief upon conditions, but one of the conditions — that a kitchen be demolished with one month — was not complied with and no memorandum of cancellation was entered on the memorial of re-entry. The plaintiff sought a declaration that the order of forfeiture had been cancelled and contended that conditions could only be imposed which required the tenant to remedy the breaches which formed the subject matter of the re-entry; further if conditions were permitted to extend beyond such matters, the conditions must be reasonable.

The court held that the Ordinance gave an unfettered discretion to the Governor and there was no reason why the Crown should not impose conditions that were unconnected with the grounds upon which the lease had been forfeited. Further (obiter), there was no requirement that the conditions had to be reasonable.

This decision pre-dates the *Hang Wah Chong Investment Co. Ltd.* v *Attorney General* [1981] HKLR 336, but nevertheless it set the tone for what was to follow.

The decision in the case *Lok On Co. Ltd.* v *Attorney General* [1986] HKLR 857 (CA) was also concerned with the alleged unreasonableness of the premium charged for a BC extension and the Court of Appeal emphasized that it would be slow to interfere, on any equitable grounds, with the contractual rights of fully competent parties. In particular, it had no jurisdiction to review the reasonableness of a premium which was simply not a justiciable issue. It was legitimate for the government, when granting a concession from the full rigours of contractual terms, to impose such conditions whether reasonable or unreasonable, as it might think fit.

The Court of Appeal also observed that any statutory relief could only arise upon the government exercising its rights of re-entry. After re-entry, a government lessee had the statutory right under Section 8 of the Government Rights (Re-entry and Vesting Remedies) Ordinance (Cap. 126) to apply to the courts for relief. As to the terms on which relief might be granted, in circumstances where default is made under a BC, Huggins JA, in the same case stated :

> Had there been a re-entry it may be that the court would have adjudged that relief should be granted upon payment of compensation and have assessed that compensation at a figure below that which the Crown demanded as the price of the extensions but the two sums would have been for two entirely different although distantly related, benefits.

In practice, it is unlikely that any developer would risk or encourage re-entry in the hope of a court, as a condition of relief, assessing a lesser sum than the government itself might contractually impose as a condition for granting an extension of time.[2]

Re-entry or vesting is a very drastic action to take and is usually only taken as a last resort. All 12 DLOs throughout Hong Kong have lease enforcement teams who constantly patrol and inspect premises, respond to complaints and other departmental referrals if a breach of lease conditions is suspected. In the majority of cases, the breach will be remedied voluntarily once it has been discovered as most owners are fully aware of the consequences should they fail to comply. Upon discovery, owners are given a period of time to remedy the breach, normally three months. During this period, they pay a forbearance fee in acknowledgment that the government is withholding action while they are remedying a breach. If more time is required and can be justified, further periods may be granted in which the breach may be purged, again on payment of forbearance fees.

There are occasions when the occupiers, sometimes the tenants, are alleged to be in breach of the user conditions of the lease and when lease enforcement action is taken by the DLO, they challenge the action in the courts. The summary of the following two cases give some insight into how the industrial/godown user clause is interpreted:

Mexx Consolidated (Far East) Ltd v The Attorney General [1987] HKLR 1210 (HCt): In a lease there was a covenant that limited the use of the premises to industrial or godown purposes. In addition to the manufacturing of garments, the tenant used the premises for research, design and testing of samples and the making of patterns and the government contended that the premises were being used for commercial purposes in breach of the covenant.

The court held that the tenant was not in breach, since the nature of the user was primarily industrial.

Cavendish Property Development Ltd v Attorney General (1988) M.P. No. 762 of 1987: Six floors in the Cavendish Centre were let to the plaintiff/tenant — the Bank of America National Trust and Savings Association — by the defendant/government lessee for use as a data processing centre for banking. The government alleged that such user was in breach of special condition 9(a) of the Conditions of Sale which restricted the user to 'industrial or godown purposes or both'. The plaintiff sought a declaration that there had been no contravention of the Conditions of Sale.

The court held that the use of the building as a data processing centre constituted a breach of the Conditions of Sale.

The *Mexx* decision spawned a number of related changes as to how the government dealt with and defined industrial/godown lots and the buildings standing on them. Prior to *Mexx*, when it came to lease enforcement, the Lands Department tolerated up to 20% of each individual industrial operation being used for ancillary office purpose as described in the *Mexx* decision. Some industrial/godown leases already specified the percentage of ancillary office space allowed but others are silent but they were nevertheless treated the same. After the *Mexx* decision, the percentage of ancillary office space permitted in new industrial/godown auction sites, and tolerated in old sites, was raised to 30% and in September 1997 this was, to reflect Hong Kong's continuing changing needs, increased to 50% of their floor space, without the necessity of planning approval under S.16 of the Town Planning Ordinance (Cap. 131). If the percentage of approved ancillary office exceeds 50%, then a premium or waiver fee will probably be charged. There are standard rates for both annual waiver fees or lump sum fees payable upfront for waivers for the lifetime of the concerned premises. Lands Department Practice Note 2/2003 sets out the schedule of permitted users and No. 3/2007 sets out the current rates to be charged.

The current planning definitions of Industrial Use and Ancillary Office are as follows:

1. **Industrial Use**

   Any premises, structure, building or part of building or place (other than a mine or quarry), in which articles are manufactured, altered, cleansed, repaired, ornamented, finished, adapted for sale, broken up or demolished or in which materials are transformed, or where goods and cargo are stored, loaded, unloaded or handled, **or where the training, research and development, design work, quality control and packaging related to the above processes are carried out.** The words in emphasis have been added recently as a result of the *Mexx* decision and it is hoped that the Lands Department will be using the same definition when it comes to lease enforcement.

2. **Ancillary Office**

   An office is considered ancillary to industrial use if the activities of a firm located in the same premises or building or in the same general industrial area are mainly industrial in nature and the office only serves this firm and no other unassociated industrial or non-industrial operations.

The legal definition of industrial use — and what constitutes ancillary use thereto as related to the user clause commonly adopted in industrial leases in the 1960s and 1970s — was thoroughly examined in the Court of Final Appeal judgment [2003] 3 HKLRD300 in the case of *Raider Limited* v *The Secretary for Justice.* The case involved the use by a tenant of a floor within an industrial building erected on a lot with such a lease that was used both for the manufacturing of pagers and the operation of a paging service the customers of which were supplied with these same pagers. The owner claimed that this use contravened the permitted use. The judge in the Court of First Instance (1998, No. MP2523) found in favour of the tenant but on appeal the decision was reversed. The following extract from the Court of Appeal decision is considered the most relevant:

> The use of parts of the premises for the manufacturing of pagers and of the other parts of the premises for the purposes of the paging service operation, are discrete uses. Neither one is 'ancillary' to the other. And the use of part of the premises for the purpose of the paging service operation cannot, by any stretch of the imagination, be described as use as a 'factory' nor even as a use 'for industrial purposes'. Only a use for manufacturing purposes (and uses genuinely ancillary thereto) will qualify as a permitted use and the use of parts of the premises for the purposes of a paging service operation is not such a use.

As can be seen the matter ended up in the Court of Final Appeal which upheld the Appeal Courts decision with the following remarks:

> The primary user of the Premises must be for industrial purposes, before compliance with the user covenant could be achieved. All of the appellant's activities within the suit Premises must be considered as a whole. Where it was technically possible to break down those activities into separate elements, it was still their cumulative effect and not their individual characteristics, which was more important (*Mexx Consolidated (Far East) Ltd.* v *A-G & Another* [1987] HKLR 1210 considered). Whilst research, design and testing prior to the process by which articles were actually made and then inspected were properly to be regarded as ancillary to the industrial process, as were the packing and dispatch from the factory of articles after they had been made and inspected, the paging service did not pertain to any of that. It was an activity distinct from manufacture and was not ancillary thereto *(Mexx Consolidated (Far East) Ltd. v A-G & Another* [1987] HKLR 1210 applied).
>
> Further, the link between the paging service and the process by which the pagers were manufactured could not be considered so close as to render the paging service itself 'industrial' within the meaning of special condition 2(a), unless such service was the final stage of that manufacturing process or at least ancillary to it. This was not the case here.

On the planning side, the Town Planning Board introduced a new concept of I/O, that is, mixed Industrial/Office building to reflect the changing use and demand for this type of space. Sites have been sold by auction with a new user clause and quite a few existing industrial/godown lot owners have applied for and obtained planning permission to change the use and a percentage have gone further and applied for and obtained a lease modification so as to permit this new type of building to go ahead. Typically the new user clause for this purpose in government leases, as extracted from the special conditions for New Kowloon Inland Lot No. 5927, reads as follows:

> Subject to these conditions the lot or any part thereof or any building or part of any building erected or to be erected thereon shall not be used for any purpose other than the following:
>
> a) industrial or godown or both;
> b) offices ancillary and directly related to an industrial operation;
> c) any combination of sub-clauses (a) and (b) of this Special Conditions.
>
> excluding any trade that is now or may hereafter be declared to be an offensive trade under the Public Health and Municipal Services Ordinance, and any enactment amending the same or substituted therefor.

It is also important to read this clause together with the clause that controls the design of the building; it requires that each and every unit within the new building is suitable for industrial (or godown) and offices ancillary to such industrial (or godown) use. In effect, this means that the buildings have to comply with a dual standard with the more stringent, and therefore more expensive, standard prevailing. In practice this has meant that virtually all I/O buildings are designed and used 100% as offices which then presents potentially difficult lease enforcement problems for the Lands Department because they, in theory, have to check to make sure that each office unit has an associated or related industrial activity. This industrial activity does not have to be in the same building and may not be in the same industrial area. It may be that the owner of a factory in Shenzhen could occupy his ancillary office space in Hong Kong.

However, this relatively new I/O concept was, in 2001, superseded by the introduction of the OU(B), Other Use (Business) zone. As a result, over 250 hectares of redundant industrial land can potentially be converted to this broader use — commercial, retail, offices or hotels — subject to any necessary lease modification. There are examples of older industrial lots being modified in the 1990s to permit I/O use, only having to modify again 10 years later to OU(B) use in order to keep up with these rapid changes, with a premium charged on each occasion! Lands Department Practice Note 2/2001 refers.

Lands Department Practice Note 1/2010 introduces a Special Waiver for Concession of an Entire Existing Industrial Building which is discussed in more detail on p. 164.

Waiver/Acquiescence by the Government in Respect of Restrictive Covenants in Lease Conditions

In what was one of the last Hong Kong cases considered by the Privy Council in London, *Attorney General* v *Fairfax Ltd.* [1997] HKLRD 243, the decision of the Hong Kong Court of Appeal was upheld and the government's appeal dismissed. It was held that the government had abandoned a covenant restricting building on a Mid-Levels plot to villas. The lease also contained a rate and range clause. The full text of the Privy Council decision is included in Appendix IX. Reading this decision with those of the lower courts, it seems relevant to point out that in this case the land had been divided into 28 sub-lots, each with buildings of differing height ranging from terraced houses, several six-storey buildings to two high-rise blocks. All were erected without comment or demur from the landlord. Furthermore, these styles of building had existed for at least 40 years, well over the 20-year upwards requirement needed to establish other rights by limitation, or prescription and to prove abandonment of a legal easement. This can be compared with the judgement in the case *Citiword Ltd.* v *Tai Ping Wing* [1995] 2 HKC 181 when it was ruled that the government's lack of enforcement action for five years did not amount to estoppel, even though a block of flats had been constructed in breach of the restrictive covenant in the government lease to erect 'one detached or semi-detached private residence' and an occupation permit issued.

The question of estoppel was at the heart of another case *Peter and Angeli Wong Co. Ltd.* v *Silverera Ltd.* [1995] 3 HKC 411, which held that the government had made a representation and an estoppel had been created when the developer subsequently acted upon it. A summary of the case is as follows.

A restrictive covenant in a government lease relating to land in Dianthus Road, Kowloon, provided that only a detached or semi-detached private residence of European type could be erected on the plot. Before embarking upon redevelopment of the site by way of erecting a block of flats, the developer's architects wrote to the government to confirm that a low-rise block of flats could be erected on the site and received a reply from the DLO saying that 'under current Government policy flatted development with 2 main entrances is allowed in this locality notwithstanding the restriction of one residence in the lease conditions only, I also confirm that the flats can be sold separately.' Following this letter, the developer submitted his building plans for approval and the block of flats was constructed. There was a further letter from the Legal Advisory and Conveyancing Office confirming that it was government policy not to take enforcement action under the covenants in the particular lease. When one of the flats came to be sold, the purchaser raised a requisition based upon the effect of the restrictive covenant.

The learned judge held that the government had made a representation and an estoppel had been created when the developer subsequently acted upon the representation by constructing the block of flats and disposing of them to tenants in common. He concluded that it would be unjust and inequitable for the government, at a future date, to require the owners to demolish their flats which they had acquired on the basis of such a confirmation from the government. The vendor's title was, therefore, good.

In another late Privy Council decision in the case of *Real Honest Investment Ltd.* v *Attorney General* [1997] HKLRD 880, an earlier Court of Appeal decision was upheld ruling that a waiver on height control given by the Building Authority in 1948 which permitted a building of over 80 feet high did not constitute a permanent waiver and that on redevelopment the lessee had to revert to the original height restriction contained in the lease of 35 feet. The decision rested on the wording of the 1948 correspondence when the various restrictions in the Conditions of Sale were being considered to be waived. Their Lordships concluded that 'if it had been the intention to grant a waiver of the restriction on height for any future building at any time during the future currency of the lease and its renewal that could have been done but it would require clear language to express that intention.' They concluded that the 1948 correspondence did not express such an intention so the appeal was dismissed.

Similarly, the case of *Jumbo Gold Investment Ltd.* v *Yuen Cheong Leung & Another* [2000] 1 HKLRD 763 involved a long standing breach of a lease condition that restricted the building to a height of 35 feet, when in fact a five-storey building had been erected, with an OP issued in 1955, clearly in breach of this restriction. The Court of Final Appeal was asked to consider whether the breach constituted a defect in title in respect of the flats that had been sold in undivided shares because of the residual possibility of lease enforcement action being taken by the government.

In unanimously upholding the vendors appeal that his title was good it was held that:

(1) In a case such as this, where concrete proof of the Government's knowledge and attitude was difficult to find, the court must look at the larger picture. It was too narrow an approach to require the vendors to show proof of knowledge of the breach before the Government could be taken to have

waived the restriction. Instead, the broader question of whether there was a real risk of enforcement should be asked.

(2) The answer to that question here must be no. The only 'enforcement' action the Government could take was re-entry under the lease in respect of the entire piece of land upon which the block was built, pursuant to s.4 of the Government Rights (Re-entry and Vesting Remedies) Ordinance (Cap. 126) (the Ordinance), extinguishing the interest of every owner therein.

(3) If the Government as lessor were dealing simply with the developer as lessee, the equitable considerations arising on a question of relief against forfeiture under s.8(1)(b) of the Ordinance would be decided by examining the conduct of those two parties. But where third parties had acquired units on the basis that permission to occupy the building for domestic purposes had been granted, and Crown rent paid and accepted for many years, to forfeit their interest because of some 'fault' of the developer was a wholly different matter.

(4) It was well-known to both conveyancers and Government officials that many Crown Leases in the relevant area contained at 35 feet height restriction. The excess height of the block could not be concealed. The Government could not aver that it was only recently aware that the block, as originally constructed, contravened the restriction; nor could it explain to the owners that their property has, due to something that happened many years ago, become forfeited to the Government, without compensation.

The individual comments by Bokhary PJ are also worth noting, as follows:

In my view, the evidence in this case did not exclude a reasonable possibility of an unwaived breach of condition which gives the Government a right of re-entry. The question is therefore whether, assuming that the Government has that right, there is any real risk that it would actually take the drastic step of enforcing it to the detriment of innocent owners. I entirely agree with Mr. Justice Litton PJ that the correct answer is in the negative. It is simply not in the nature of good government to harm innocent people unnecessarily like that.

Accordingly it is safe to proceed on the basis that the Government would never do so.

The way in which this Court has decided the present case will, I trust, prevent cases of this type arising in future. I agree with Mr. Justice Litton PJ that this appeal should be allowed in the terms which he proposes.

It is hoped that the lease enforcement teams of the various DLOs will heed the unambiguous statements of the highest court in the territory!

Notes

1. See Chapter 3, p. 18.
2. See Cruden 1999, p. 510.

LAND ADMINISTRATION PROBLEMS AND PRACTICE ASSOCIATED WITH THE NEW TERRITORIES

In Chapter 3, reference has been made to some of the special characteristics of land administration in the NT. In this section, the following topics are examined in a little more detail:

Not all these problem areas are unique to the NT but it is evident from the quoted case law that the vast majority do occur there. It is therefore important to be aware of the pitfalls particularly if one is involved in the development, valuation or assembly of sites. Some of the topics have only been covered in outline merely to make the reader aware of the potential problems that may occur. It is very likely that once a particular problem has emerged a more detailed investigation and in-depth analysis of the specific legal issues will be required with appropriate legal advice.

13 LAND EXCHANGE ENTITLEMENTS (ALSO KNOWN AS LETTERS A/B)

What Are Letters A/B?

Letters A/B were issued by the Hong Kong government during the period starting from January 1960 until 9 March 1983 as an alternative to cash compensation when private land was to be resumed in the New Town Development Areas of the NT. The use of Letter B should be seen as an adjunct to the procedures of the Lands Resumption Ordinance (Cap. 124). It was a system devised to facilitate the speedy acquisition of private land for public projects which avoided payments of cash compensation and/or lengthy arguments over the level of compensation with the attendant time spent in Compensation Board (which preceded the establishment of the Lands Tribunal) or Lands Tribunal referrals. They were first used for the resumption of land to form part of Tsuen Wan New Town.

In simple terms a Letter B offered to a landowner already affected by a Gazette Notice of resumption under Cap. 124 a choice of either a cash payment at a stated rate or an entitlement to future grant of land in building status in any urban development area in the NT at some unspecified time in the future. In spite of this open-ended risk, in practice, nearly all landowners opted for Letter B rather than cash.

With the thrust of the New Town Development programme in the early and mid- 1970s, the outstanding commitment of Letters A/B awaiting an exchange had risen to about 36 million sq. ft. As a large percentage of the new land created for the New Towns was being taken up by public housing, infrastructure, town halls, swimming pools, and schools, there was disproportionally less new land available for private uses to offer back to owners of Letters A/B. Recognizing the huge problem that this ever increasing commitment would have on future land supply, the government scaled back the offer of Letters A/B to 50% of land taken in July 1978 after the Sir Y.K. Kan Committee Report and by March 1983 stopped issuing them altogether.

What about Letter A? These were issued by the government when private land was urgently required for a public project and the landowners were prepared to voluntarily surrender the land with vacant possession without going through the process of statutory resumption. Therefore, the issue of Letter A and B were more or less identical in terms of redemption.

Letters A/B are essentially a government promissory note in respect of a future grant of land. The terms of each Letter A/B document (which have varied from District to District and from year to year) confer upon the holder an entitlement at an unspecified future date, to a grant of building land **by exchange** at the ratio specified in the document. The majority of land resumed was in agricultural status and the exchange ratio was 2 sq. ft. of building land for every 5 sq. ft. of agricultural land. For building land the exchange ratio was one to one.

How Were They Redeemed?

One of the early products of discussions in the Sino-British Land Commission was an undertaking that all outstanding commitments for Letters A/B would be cleared by June 1997. Good progress was made, by 1989 the figure was down to 10 million sq. ft. and by 1995 there was less than 3 million sq. ft. to be redeemed. By then the vast majority of the outstanding Letters A/B were in the hands of four major development companies. The remainder were in the hands of smaller owners, perhaps even original owners who may have misplaced, lost or inadvertently destroyed them. In order to meet their deadline, the government negotiated directly with the big four holders and three land exchanges were executed in early 1997 which absorbed all their outstanding holdings amounted to about 1.5 million sq. ft. For the remainder, estimated to be less than half a million sq. ft., the government enacted the New Territories Land Exchange Entitlements (Redemption) Ordinance (Cap. 495) in December 1996 to provide for the payment of redemption money in respect of land exchange entitlements to the owners, and for the extinguishment of their rights against the government under such documents to a future land exchange. This ordinance was gazetted into operation on 27 June 1997 with a claims procedure set down and redemption money set aside to deal with claims as and when they arose.

Given the huge backlog of unredeemed Letters A/B and the collapse of the property market in the early 1980s, the government introduced an alternative method to attract Letter A/B holders to surrender their holdings and it was called the monetized scheme. On 24 February 1984, the Lands Department issued a Practice Note for authorized persons, chartered surveyors and solicitors and set out the new policy. Subsequently by GN 720 dated 9 March 1984, they publicly announced the new arrangements whereby a number of NT related land transactions such as the payment of modification premia, building covenant extensions and short-term-tenancy rents could be paid for by the surrender of Letters A/B in lieu of cash. In March and September of subsequent years, the government published its up-to-date assessment of currency values in the Government Gazette for this purpose, together with the current compensation values, it would pay by way of ex-gratia compensation for land resumption purposes in the NT. These compensation values have had a significant influence on valuing land in the NT.

For a few years a small number of Letters A/B were redeemed in this way but as the market value for Letters A/B started to exceed the government's own assessed currency values, this method ceased to be popular, and with the cessation of the Letter A/B land exchange system, this method of redemption also ceased.

Letter A/B Tenders

These tenders were assessed on a 'vintage' basis where basically the 'oldest is best' principle applied. The site area for the new land to be exchanged was known, say 8000 m^2 which equated to 86 112 sq. ft. of building land. Using the 2:5 ratio, this required 215 280 sq. ft. of Letter A/B , whether agricultural or building that had an aggregate surrender area of 215 280 sq. ft. The winner was the bidder that submitted, again in aggregate terms, the oldest Letter B calculated backwards from the date of closing the tender to the operative date of the Letter A/B surrendered, thus those with the highest aggregate days age won. A premium was chargeable in respect of Letter A/B exchanges and was calculated as being the difference between: (a) the value of the land being granted as at the date when the original land was surrendered or reverted and (b) the surrender value specified in the Letter A/B document which represents the value of the land itself on the day it was surrendered or reverted. In order to simplify the assessment of the value of the land granted at some historic date, that is, as long ago as January 1960, a table known as Chart W, W being the initial of the surname of the government valuer who devised the first table, was established to cover average values of formed and serviced land for various uses and densities for the different areas within the New Territories.

It is evident that because of the way tenders were assessed and awarded, and premiums calculated, that the older Letters B had the greatest value, so a very active market developed for these instruments. They were freely assignable, not subject to stamp duty and in times of rising land values were traded in a very speculative and sometimes volatile way. Indeed at one point advertisements for sale were even seen in the *Financial Times* in London! When the values of Letters A/B crashed, probably to a greater extent than general property values in 1982, it made the government's decision to scrap them significantly easier to make.

Originally Letters A/B were not intended to be assignable but when this became the practice, the government set up a register called the Commitment Transfer Register to record transactions in these documents. These registers were unofficial and had no status; each page was stamped with a notice that any person using it did so at his own risk! In addition, Letters A/B were capable of being mortgaged, and were mortgaged, to secure loans. The documentation used to assign and mortgage these documents was based on that used for land in the NT and commonly the statutory form of assignment of land under the New Territories Ordinance (Cap. 97) was used for such assignments.

Other terminology used when dealing with this topic were Operative Date and Modified Letter B. Although Letters A/B ceased to be issued as from 8 March 1983, there are some circumstances both before and after that date when former owners of land resumed have been issued with a Modified Letter B considerably later than the date of reversion which is usually the operative date, for example, successors to deceased owners where they were in the process of obtaining probate, absentee landlords, inability to clear existing mortgages or other encumbrances in time, and so on. Whenever there is a Letter B dated later than 8 March 1983, it is necessary to check carefully the operative date as to date of reversion and for premium calculation purposes, as indeed all Letters A/B need to be carefully checked to make sure of the correct operative date.

The case of *Ho Sum Keung* v *Director of Lands* [2005] HKCU 680 and [2006] HKCU 423 relates to a judicial review of the decision of the Director of Lands not to grant Modified Letters B to the administrator of the estate of Tsang Fuk Lin who had passed away in 1961 and whose lands had been resumed between 1975 and 1981. The case hinged on the Director's consideration of the case in accordance with the wholly unavoidable delay criterion set out in his internal land instruction and which had been implemented, unchallenged, throughout the years. In the first decision, the court granted relief to the applicant to satisfy the criterion. The second decision records that no new evidence was adduced or additional justifications put forward, so the application was dismissed.

These documents have evolved over time and they varied slightly from district to district and from year to year. In checking Letters A/B, nothing can be taken for granted and each document has to be checked separately. For instance, there are some Letters B issued in Yuen Long that only entitle the owner an exchange of agricultural land not building land!

A number of reasons can be adduced for the creation of the Letter A/B system, the best being that in the 1960–70s the government was not so well placed financially as it was in the mid-nineties, and given the large tracts of land that needed to be resumed, particularly for the New Town Development programmes, the use of Letters A/B avoided large outflows of cash and the delays in obtaining vacant possession that were part of the normal resumption method. Furthermore, the use of these land exchange entitlements recognized the fact that the vast majority of the land being taken was traditional ancestral land belonging to indigenous villagers who always preferred land to money, even if there was a delay in the provision of the replacement land. The Letter A/B system avoided the confrontation between the villagers and the government which had marred certain earlier resumption and clearances of villages in the NT. Finally, as Hong Kong operates a leasehold land system where the government is also the land authority, it was, in theory, in a position to control and regulate the flow of new land onto the market to redeem the commitment.

Quite by chance, given the local propensity for gambling and speculating, the government unwittingly created a perfect instrument for the NT landowners. There is an anecdote from Shatin that in the late 1970s when the speculative price for Letters B was at its height, property agents, having found out when Letters B were to be issued, would follow the postman delivering the letters on the next day so they could immediately knock on the door and offer to buy them! Only in the extreme depths of despair during the 1967 riots were Letter A/B owners known to have come forward and asked the government to take them back and give them cash at their face value.

So it was a win-win situation; the government got land without paying cash or interest and without damaging confrontations; the landowners were given a speculative future in land which they could trade; the architects of this particular scheme could not possibly have envisaged the full consequences of what they created!

In practice, the vast majority of Letters A/B were purchased in the latter years on behalf of four major property development companies. With the outstanding commitment having risen to some 36 million square feet, this dictated that the majority of the government's NT land sales up until 1997 were by way of Letter A/B tender with disproportionally less land being made available for sale by public auction. Without doubt, this gave the four companies a very definite advantage as these sales were, in effect, a restricted tender. One of the benefits of the closure of this method of land disposal was that much more land in the NT could be sold by auction than has been in the past, and thus opening up the market to all development companies.

Since 1 April 2003 the Lands Department have maintained the Commitment Transfer Registers of Letters A/B. Before that the Land Registry maintained them.

14 SMALL HOUSE POLICY（丁屋）AND THE 300-FOOT RULE

The Small House Policy (SHP), which has been operated administratively by the government since late 1972, was started at about the same time that the government was beginning to significantly influence affairs in the NT, particularly with the expansion of the public housing programme. It became one way of compensating the indigenous population by ensuring that their needs and traditions were respected and that they could also benefit from the major changes that were being forced upon them, particularly the development of the New Towns and their associated infrastructure. The principal features of the policy are outlined as follows (note that in the NT, despite the government's best effort, there is still a strong preference for using imperial measurements rather than metric):

1. Any male over the age of 18 who can trace his ancestry through the male line back to 1898 as being an indigenous villager of an established village[1] in the NT at the time are entitled to a once-in-a-lifetime grant of a house site for occupancy by himself and his family. Such grants are made at nominal premium subject to strict restrictions on alienation other than a building mortgage for purposes of constructing the house itself. Only if the grantee subsequently pays to the government the full assessed market value of the lot is he then entitled to sell the lot and house for profit. Currently the grant permits the grantee to erect a house not exceeding 700 square feet (65.03 square metres) in area and 27 feet (8.23 metres) and 3 storeys in height, which does not require the employment of an Authorized Person (AP) or approval of building plans under the Buildings Ordinance (Cap. 123) (BO). This exemption applies to all landowners in the NT and is not presently limited to indigenous villagers.

    Previously the height limit was 25 feet (7.62 metres) and over the years the storey restriction has gradually been increased from two, to two-and-a-half, to three stories. Some of the older grants and buildings will reflect these conditions.

These dimensions are important because the moment they are exceeded then the exemption from BO falls away. In the case of *Chong Ping*（莊秉）v *Hung Ling Yuen*（孔令源）(HCA6481/1998), the building in issue was 7.92 metres high, and the vendor had, on payment of a fine, received a letter from the District Lands Officer (DLO) tolerating the breach of height under the lease. The High Court ruled that this could not be extended to being tolerated under the BO as the latter was a separate entity and there was no way the DLO could usurp the authority of the Building Authority (BA). As a consequence and because it could not be demonstrated 'beyond reasonable doubt' that the purchaser would not be at risk of enforcement by the BA, the absence of an Occupation Permit (as required under the BO) meant that the vendor had failed to prove good title to the property. Somewhat fortuitously for this case, the height of an exempt building has since been raised to 8.23 metres; so presumably this particular problem will fall away.

2. If there is insufficient government land in a particular village for the DLO to execute a Private Treaty Grant (PTG), then an alternative is for an indigenous villager who owns agricultural land within the village environs to apply to the DLO for a Free Building Licence (FBL) or Land Exchange (LE) in order to build his house. The PTG, FBL and LE will all contain similar conditions as described in Paragraph 1 above. One important difference, however, is that for a PTG the restriction on assignment, which can only be applied for three years after completion, is perpetual whereas for LEs and FBLs it is only for five years, which is significant when it comes to assessing the premium for relaxing this restriction.

3. The Buildings Ordinance (Application to the New Territories) Ordinance (Cap. 121), enacted in 1987, codifies the present position and provides for Certificates of Exemption (C of E) from certain provisions of the BO for building works, site formation works and drainage works or certain buildings in the New Territories. These C of Es are issued by the DLO, but where the proposed buildings are to be built on sloping ground or are for more than a few houses, a C of E for the site formation and drainage may not be given and a formal engineering submission under the BO will be required. In these cases, the DLO will only issue a C of E for the houses themselves once the site formation and drainage plans have been approved. In effect, this means that these houses can be built without the need to employ AP and without the need to submit formal building plans for approval. This important privilege enables these houses to be built very quickly with a significant saving in professional fees. It also

explains the other name by which they are sometimes referred to, that is New Territories Exempted Houses or NTEHs. As mentioned earlier, this privilege applies not just to indigenous villagers. All 'Small Houses' are NTEHs but not all NTEHs are 'Small Houses', for example NTEHs can be built on lots held under GN364 condition referred to in Chapter 3.

4. Section 9 of Cap. 121 enables the DLO, when issuing a C of E, to impose conditions relating to safety and health or such other reasonable conditions as he may impose. In the case *Rita Enterprises Co. Ltd.* v *District Land Officer, Tai Po* reported at [1996] 4 HKC 410, the applicant who owned some land in a Green Belt zone had sought permission to rebuild some houses there. However, when the DLO granted the C of Es, he imposed a condition that 'no building work shall commence until Planning Permission for village type development has been obtained'. The applicant sought a Judicial Review claiming there was a legitimate expectation that the C of E would be granted unconditionally, arguing that this was usually the case. The application failed as the court held that particularly as the land in question was zoned Green Belt, the imposition of such a condition passed the 'reasonable' test required in Section 9.

    In the main body of this decision there is a useful reminder that Cap. 121 only exempts the applicant from certain sections of the BO, not all, and in particular not subsection 16(1) (d) which requires that building works should not contravene any approved or draft plans prepared under the Town Planning Ordinance (Cap. 131). This point was also referred to in the Lands Tribunal decision in *Discreet Limited and Secretary for Transport* (LDMR 14/2002) dated 25 July 2003, when it also stated that Cap. 121 did not exempt applicants from the Town Planning Ordinance.

5. The special privileges of the indigenous villagers were recognized and extended by virtue of paragraph 2 of Annex III to the Joint Declaration (see p. 28) and Article 122 of the Basic Law which allowed their leases that were to expire on 30 June 1997 to be extended until 30 June 2047 but without the need for them to pay the new annual rent applicable to other leaseholders.

Shortcomings of the policy

From time to time the Lands Administration Office publishes its 'performance pledges' indicating the standard of service the public can expect from the Lands Department. Included in the current list is a pledge to complete 1200 Small House cases each year. Obviously the government is still very committed to the SHP despite its many shortcomings, some of which are discussed below:

1. *The definition is wrong.* Is a 700 sq. ft. by 3-storey house, that is, 2100 sq. ft. a small house? When compared with the traditional 436 sq. ft. by 2-storey Old Schedule houses common in the NT in 1898, it certainly is not; and when compared with the size of public housing units available to the non-indigenous members of our community it definitely is not. Today it represents inequitable preferential treatment.

2. *The commitment is open-ended.* Every day another male indigenous villager reaches the age of 18 and is, in theory, entitled to a house site. Where is all the land going to come from? For those established villages in or adjacent to the New Towns, the granting of such land represents an inefficient use of a scarce resource. Today the villagers are, for the most part, no longer rural people and should be housed in more efficient medium or high-rise apartments. Any review of land use in areas zoned for village development on an OZP would have to take into account the decision in *Wah Yick Enterprises Co. Ltd.* v *Building Authority* [1997] HKLRD 1177 M.P. 1623, when the Court of First Instance concluded that 'in a Village Type Development Zone the use "House" properly construed does not include the 33 storey block of flats which the plaintiff proposes to build'.

3. *The policy is discriminatory.* 'Ding' rights, as they are commonly known, literally means male rights. In today's society of equality this is an obvious anachronism. However, if female indigenous villagers were equally eligible for a small house grant, the pressure on scarce land resources would be impossibly greater!

4. *The system has been abused.* Perhaps the principal reason for criticizing the SHP is the way that it is abused by the villagers themselves who, in increasing numbers, only use the preferential land grant as a way of making a quick profit. The Audit Commission's Report No. 39, issued on 15 October 2002,[2] found there were on average 533 cases a year of approved removal of the restriction on alienation during the previous five financial years, representing about 43% of the 1247 Certificates of Compliance issued on average during the same period. This makes a mockery of the original reason for granting the land which is to enable the villagers to provide homes for themselves within their own village. This high percentage of onward sales is an area of concern that needs to be addressed and will, hopefully, be considered in the government's ongoing review of the whole policy.

Another way the SHP can be abused is to make use of the name of an indigenous villager to apply for the necessary FBL to develop a piece of land beneficially owned by a developer, or any other non indigenous owner.

In order for the development scheme to be carried out it is necessary for the indigenous villager to make a false statutory declaration to the DLO that he is the legal and beneficial owner of the land in question and he has not entered into any private arrangement for his rights under the SHP to be sold to another developer or individual. A number of such arrangements have ended up in court and the cases of *Best Sheen Development* v *Official Receiver* [2001] 1 HKLRD 866 and *Chung Miu Teck* v *Hang Tak Buddhist Hall Association Ltd.* [2001] 2 HKLRD 471 (CA) (applied in, for example, *Cheung Chi Fai* v *Wan Hang Ping,* HC 193/2002) have confirmed that the court will not lend itself to the enforcement of such a contract for any party. This is because the making of the false declaration is illegal and involves the commission of the tort of misrepresentation, either of which renders the agreement unlawful and unenforceable under common law.

These cases serve as a warning as to the pitfalls of entering into such agreements.

The 300 foot rule

There is another administrative policy closely related to the SHP which also needs to be reviewed — the '300-foot rule'. It has been used by the various land authorities for many years to describe the environs or outer limits of the villages in the NT, usually measured as 300 feet from the edge of the last house built before December 1972. In the old days, before the advent of the New Towns in the 1970s, and more recently in the 1991 introduction of statutory planning to large areas of the New Territories, this '300-foot rule' was a useful administrative planning tool to control the spread of village development. However, in today's scenario of planned development, it should now be considered redundant.

There is now an increasingly worrying conflict emerging in the NT between the Lands Department's policies and the Planning Department's and Town Planning Board's land use zonings and approvals. If unresolved, the conflict has the potential to frustrate many important developments. Taking Sha Tin as an example, there exists many established villages within the New Town layout; their boundaries are prescribed by the Outline Zoning Plan (OZP) and there should be no question of the '300-foot rule' being applied to override the OZP. Now with the introduction of Development Permission Area (DPA) plans in the rest of the NT and their subsequent replacement by OZPs, more village zones are being clearly prescribed on statutory plans that are subject to gazetting, public display, and so on. Indeed, both representatives from interested parties, the villagers and the Lands Department will have had an equal opportunity to comment on or object to such plans including the notes attached thereto. Once a statutory plan is properly authorized and the boundaries of the village zones have been established, it is questionable that the Lands Department should subsequently seek to override such a plan by the administrative measure of the 300-foot rule.

There are examples where the Lands Department is still following the 300-foot rule irrespective of the planned zoning or the planning approval and, also significantly, irrespective of who owns the land. In one case the villagers sold their land to an outsider who then obtained the necessary planning consent, but the Lands Department frustrated implementation by refusing to process a land exchange. This attitude is inequitable because not only does it ignore proposals for which planning consent has been given, it is also ignoring the fundamental point of land ownership. It should be remembered that the Buildings Ordinance (Application to the NT) Ordinance (Cap. 121) applies equally to indigenous and non-indigenous villagers, so if the villagers have sold their land to outsiders and the new owner obtains the requisite planning consent, there is no logical reason for the Lands Department not to process the necessary land documentation.

The reasoning behind the Lands Department's attitude is undoubtedly 'political' and there is a reluctance to open this issue with the Heung Yee Kuk (HYK) which is the body, set up by statute, to act as the representative of the indigenous villagers to negotiate with the government on all aspects involving traditional village life, small houses, burials, and so on. The HYK, as evidenced by the drafting of paragraph 2 to Annex III of the Joint Declaration, is very influential and was, during the 1967 riots, credited with assisting the government in keeping the NT calm, but surely that historical debt has now been paid. Today there are more serious needs, such as the efficient and proper planned use of land and the abuse of the present inequitable system, that needs to be urgently addressed.

Privilege or right?

As the SHP has been in operation for over 30 years, the indigenous population has come to view this as an entitlement or right even though the policy is clearly an administrative one. In addition they can now refer to Article 40 of the Basic Law which states 'The lawful traditional rights and interests of the indigenous inhabitants of the "New Territories" shall be protected by the Hong Kong Special Administrative Region'.

A counter argument could be that these 'traditional rights and interests' should be those that existed in 1898 not those that have subsequently accrued.

There is clearly much room for discussion and argument. Following the Audit Commissions Report published in October 2002,[3] the Secretary for Housing, Planning and Lands promised to undertake a much needed comprehensive review of this complex subject within five years. This is clearly a delicate operation balancing the different interests and needs of the various stakeholders because at the time of going to press the review is still awaited![4]

Notes

1. Now defined in Part III of the New Territories Leases (Extension) Ordinance (Cap. 150)
2. At http://www.aud.gov.hk/eng/pubpr_arpt/rpt_39.htm
3. At http://www.aud.gov.hk/eng/pubpr_arpt/rpt_39.htm
4. In September 2003 Civic Exchange, a locally based independent think tank, published a report entitled 'Rethinking the Small House Policy' which gives an in-depth critique of this whole subject, how it started, evolved and where we are today. This report should greatly assist the Government in its own review of this subject. For further information visit their website at www.civic-exchange.org

15 LIMITATIONS ORDINANCE AND ADVERSE POSSESSION

By the very fact that the NT land administration system was designed to admit, as far as possible, customary Chinese law, the question of adverse possession, which can enable long-term occupiers of land to establish permanent rights, has inevitably arisen and practitioners need to be aware of the problems that may arise particularly if they are involved in site acquisitions of rural land. The doctrine of an adverse possession is founded on long established British law and precedents on which our legislation is based. The relevant law is Section 7 of the Limitations Ordinance (Cap. 347) which is set out below:

Limitation of actions to recover land

1) No action shall be brought by the Crown to recover any land after the expiration of 60 years from the date on which the right of action accrued to the Crown or, if it first accrued to some person through whom the Crown claims, to that person;

2) No action shall be brought by any other person to recover any land after the expiration of 12 years from the date on which the right of action accrued to him or, if it first accrued to some person through whom he claims, to that person:

Provided that, if the right of action first accrued to the Crown through whom the person bringing the action claims, the action may be brought at any time before the expiration of the period during which the action could have been brought by the Crown or 12 years from the date on which the right of action accrued to some person other than the Crown, whichever period first expires. (Amended 31 of 1991 s.5)

The period specified in Section 7(2) was previously 20 years but was reduced to 12 years in 1991. In the High Court judgment *Sung Mei Chi v Stone Target Ltd.* [1995] HKLY 777, it was clarified that the 12-year limitation period applies only to the commencement of adverse possession from 1 July 1991.

Another case that is significant in the context of adverse possession is that of *Chung Ping Kwan & Ors* v *Lam Island Development Co. Ltd.* [1996] 2 HKC 447 which ended up at the Privy Council. The lower courts had decided that because of the wording of the New Territories (Renewable Crown Leases) Ordinance (Cap. 152), all the 75-year leases that were extended by virtue of this legislation were, in 1973, granted a *new* lease rather than *renewals* or *extensions* of their expiring leases although this was contrary to the intention as stated in the 1969 Bill introducing the legislation. This meant that anyone claiming adverse possession could not carry over any accrued time prior to 1973 and they would have to start afresh from 1973 to accrue the required time to justify any claim. The Privy Council overruled the local courts; this was significant because it meant that any time accrued before 1973 can now be included in any claim for adverse possession and this could result in more successful claims than before.

Unsurprisingly the same issue has arisen as a result of the New Territories Leases (Extension) Ordinance (Cap. 150), raising the question of whether this Ordinance gives a lessee a new lease and source of title to evict a squatter, notwithstanding the fact that the squatter had accrued the statutory period of possession under the Limitation Ordinance (Cap. 347) over the property.

There was a rash of lower court decisions on this point, *Unijet Limited* v *Yiu Kwan Hoi*, unreported HCA 13637 of 1998, 21 June 2002 *(Unijet)*; *Mutual Luck Investment Limited* v *Yeung Chi Kuen & Others* (No. 2) 1 HKC90 *(Mutual Luck)* and *Chan Tin Shi* v *Li Tin Sung & Others* [2003] HKEC 54. In view of the decision in *Unijet* being in conflict with *Mutual Luck* and *Chan Tin Shi*, the latter case was granted leave to appeal to the Court of Final Appeal so the matter could be settled. From the court judgment [2006] HKLRD 185. The following extracts are considered the most relevant:

> Firstly referring to Cap. 150 'The language of s.6 is in my opinion clear. It says that the term of the existing leases is extended from the date on which they would otherwise have expired i.e. 27th June 1997 until 30th June 2047. Every existing lease, instead of being for a term expiring on 27th June 1997, is by force of statute to be for a term expiring 30th June 2047. But it continues to be the same lease. If it were a new lease whether from 28th April 1988 or from 28th June 1997, it could not be said that *its* term had been 'extended'.
>
> Such an interpretation would also be consistent with paragraph 2 of Annex III to the Joint Declaration where it is stated 'All leases of land granted by the British Hong Kong Government not containing a right of renewal that expire before 30th June 1997 Ö may be extended if the lessee so wishes for a period not later than 30th June 2047 without payment of an additional premium.'

The decision also compares Cap. 152, referred to earlier, with Cap. 150 and notes that in the former the language of deemed grant was used but in the latter the language of extension was used which strengthens the argument that no new lease had been granted under Cap. 150.

So there is now a consistent ruling in respect of both Ordinances which means that any time accrued before the passing of either law can now be included in any claim for adverse possession.

The operation of the limitation period does not give the adverse possessor title to the land. Instead, it merely bars the true owner from seeking recovery. In legal terms, to qualify as 'adverse possession', the adverse possessor must show that his occupation has been with *animus possidendi*. This requires him to show that he had continuous physical control inconsistent with the rights of the true owner and the use for which the true owner intends to put the land. There must also be factual evidence of this possession, presumably rate demands and payments for public utilities would be admissible.

The Court of Final Appeal's decision in the case of *Cheung Yat Fuk v Tang Tak Hong &Others* [2004] 7 HKCFAR 70, in dismissing the appeal, held that:

(1) The argument that a squatter could be in adverse possession of land through a licensee but not through a tenant was rejected;
(2) A squatter could be in adverse possession through a tenant by the receipt of rent, and
(3) When a squatter granted a tenancy and received rent, he was acting inconsistently with the title of the paper owner and that put the squatter in adverse possession of the land through his tenant. The squatter could in this way acquire possessory title to the land through his tenant's occupation of the land.

On the passing of the limitation period, the adverse possessor who then wishes to formalize his possessory title can either obtain a Court declaration order vesting the land in himself or can deal with the land as possessory owner. If the adverse possession is against the government, then presumably the adverse possessor would seek the grant of lease in order to regularize his occupation. A title obtained by adverse possession against the government can be resumed under the Land Acquisition (Possessory Title) Ordinance (Cap. 130).

A number of other cases involving the question of adverse possession have been decided as follows: *Chung Yeung Hung & Others v Law Man Nga & Another, Court of Appeal CA Nos. 29 to 32* [1997] HKLRD 1022 where it was established that the plaintiffs had established an arguable case for a prescriptive right to use an access road to their lot; *Sze To Chun Keung v Kung Kwok Wai David & Another, Privy Council Appeal No. 30* [1997] HKLRD 885 where it was held that the grant of a Crown Land Permit issued by the government in 1961 up until 1988 to the defendant did not interrupt the period of adverse possession. The grant of this permit may have transferred possession to the

Crown but it did not stop the running of the limitation period. Also in *Wong Tak Yue* v *Kung Kwok Wai & Another, Court of Final Appeal* [1998] 1 HKLRD 241, the occupier of the land, by declaring that at all times he was ready and willing to pay rent to the owners, had no intention of excluding the owners and thereby failed to show an arguable case on one of the essential ingredients for establishing adverse possession.

In the case of *Kan Kam Cho and Kan Chiu Nam* (2008) 11 HKCFAR 538 the Court of Final Appeal held that for the purpose of the law of adverse possession under the Limitations Ordinance, a letting to a tenant did not stop the running of the limitation period which had started running against the paper owner before the letting occurred. Contrast this with the situation where the adverse possession had commenced during the currency of the tenancy: in such a situation the tenant would be dispossessed not the landlord and this could only take place at the expiry of the tenancy.

In *Wong Lai Man v. Wong Tat Kwong & Anor* [2010] 3 HKC 328 there was a discrepancy between the boundary on the ground and the boundary shown on the plans within the Land Registry. The plaintiff's father found out that a portion of the subject land had a house built on it which the second defendant had occupied for about 50 years without interruption or interference from others. The plaintiff's sought possession of the subject land on the ground of common mistake and the second defendant counter-claimed on the basis that she had acquired the land by adverse possession on the ground of factual possession of the subject land for over 50 years.

The court found in favour of the second defendant on the basis of the 50 years of factual possession which met the criteria to demonstrate adverse possession noting that the mistake by the plaintiff of not knowing he owned the subject land had never been a ground to defeat a claim for adverse possession.

16 TSOS AND TONGS AND THEIR IMPACT ON LAND ASSEMBLY

A particular aspect unique to the NT which practitioners may well come across is when land is held by *Tsos* and *Tongs*. These are two very traditional Chinese institutions of landholding which come within the ambit of Section 13 of the New Territories Ordinance (Cap. 97) (NTO) that requires the administration 'to recognize and enforce any Chinese custom or customary right affecting land'.

The government recognizes nearly 4000 *Tsos* and over 2000 *Tongs* which collectively control some 6000 acres of land. Some of these institutions existed before the British took over administration of the NT in 1898. However, the government now discourages their formation.

Tsos received judicial recognition in the judgment of the case *Tang Kai-Chung v Tang Chik-Shang* [1970] HKLR 276 as follows: 'A Tso may be shortly described as an ancient Chinese institution of ancestral land-holding, whereby land derived from a common ancestor is enjoyed by his male descendants for the time being, living for their lifetimes and so from generation to generation indefinitely ... '

The decision in the case of *Leung Kuen Fai v Tang Kwong Yu (or U) Tong or Tang Kwong Yu Tso* [2002] 2 HKLRD 705 gives us some more contemporary clarification on the nature of *tsos* where it was held that the concept of trust was applicable to a *tso* with the managers as trustees and the members of the *tso* as beneficiaries. With regard to the application of Section 13 of Cap. 97, the ruling was that the court did not have to apply Chinese customary law, even for land in the NT. The case in question involved a claim for adverse possession and the court ruled that Section 13 should not be applied in a manner which allowed Chinese customary law to prevail over the relevant limitation statutes particularly as the decision on the trust argument had already placed the *tso* in a much better position than other owners of land in the NT.

Generally, the *Tso* is a customary land trust for the worship of a named ancestor and the unkeep of his grave. A *Tong* could have a similar purpose but would be more usually designed to provide funds for educational and welfare purposes of the 'beneficiaries'. It could also be extended to business ventures. A *Tong* may also build a hall to house ancestral tablets, whereas *Tsos* have no halls. *Tongs* may use a family's lucky name or other name but *Tsos* will always use the name of the common ancestor.

In land matters, *Tsos* and *Tongs* are the same in that it is the intention of the founders that the parcel or parcels of land or property must be perpetuated and not be disposed of. In *Tsos* and family *Tongs*, the interest of the member begins when he is born and ends when he dies. There are no problems of succession and no death duties are levied. Business or religious *Tongs* require the appointment of managers.

Tsos and *Tongs* are administered by managers and Section 15 of the NTO requires that these appointments be reported to, approved and recorded by the Secretary for Home Affairs (SHA). The same section confers on managers the power to dispose of or in any way deal with the said land as if he were the sole owner thereof, subject to the consent of the SHA. The SHA must also be satisfied that the sale is for a 'good purpose' (undefined!) and that all the members have signified their unanimous agreement to the transaction.

It is the latter requirement that makes the private purchase of *Tso* or *Tong* land virtually impossible because usually the consent of many people will be required but it only requires one member to object and the sale will be frustrated. Bearing in mind the original purpose of perpetual landownership within the *Tso* or *Tong*, the SHA may not be satisfied that a sale of land is for a 'good purpose', therefore this can also frustrate a sale. These factors can present insurmountable problems to developers who wish to try and assemble rural land for development and are well illustrated in the case *Tong Yau Yi Tong* v *Tang Mou Shou Tso* [1995] HKLY 788. Only the government can overcome these obstacles by the use of their statutory resumption powers. Indeed, in a government report issued in June 1994 on the question of land supply, one of the recommendations was that where a developer had succeeded in purchasing 85% of private interests, then subject to certain criteria, the government should be prepared to use its powers to assist in the complex task of completing site assembly.[1] This subject is covered in more detail in Chapter 11, pp. 94–96.

The decision in the case of *Brisilver Investment Ltd.* v *Wong Fat Tso & Another* [1999]3 HKC 567 gives some guidance where a parcel of *tso* land is co-owned by a person who is not a member of the *tso*. The circumstance in the case was that the owner of two-thirds of a property in the New Territories who was not a member of the *tso*, sought an order for its sale pursuant to the provisions of the Partition Ordinance (Cap. 352) (PO). The *tso*, which owned one-third of the property, argued that the Court did not have jurisdiction to make such an order because Chinese customary law prohibited the disposal of *tso* land by its members in the absence of the unanimous consent of those members; that this prohibition applied whether or not the application for sale was made by a *tso* member; and if there was a conflict between Chinese customary law and the PO, under Section 13 of the NTO, Chinese customary law overrode the PO. They also argued that under Section 15 of the NTO the consent of the registered manager of the *tso* and the SHA was required, and in order to protect *tso* members, the Court should not authorize a sale of land which dispensed with the Section 15 protection. The Court ruled that it had jurisdiction to order the sale, and held that:

(1) The question of Chinese law, custom, and customary rights was a matter of evidence.

(2) The evidence adduced in the cases cited by *tso* was only that Chinese law and custom prohibited a disposal of *tso* land by *tso* members. There was no evidence that this prohibition extended to outsiders unrelated to the *tso*, and in the absence of such evidence, the Court could not conclude that it did. As the other owner was not a *tso* member, the apparent conflict between their claim for a sale order and Chinese law and custom did not in fact exist.

(3) On the wording of s.15 of the NTO, the event that triggered its operation was a disposal by a *tso* manager, the provision had no application. It also followed that the Court could exercise its discretion (in appropriate circumstances) to order sale of *tso* land in these proceedings despite the lack of consent of the Secretary for Home Affairs.

Note

1. Task Force Report on Land Supply & Property Prices — June 1994 Planning, Environment & Lands Branch.

17 SUCCESSION

Until 1994, under S.17 of the New Territories Ordinance (Cap. 97), male heirs could succeed to land in the NT in accordance with customary Chinese law of the Qing Dynasty on approval by the SHA, without the necessity of obtaining Administration or Probate from the Supreme Court and without being subject to the provisions of the Intestates Estates Ordinance (Cap. 73) which provides a statutory right of succession on intestacy including widows and female heirs, nor to the requirements of the Probate and Administration Ordinance (Cap. 10). Under S.18 of Cap. 97, where land vests in a minor (for example, on succession) some fit person may be appointed by the SHA to be a trustee during the minority and the land cannot be disposed of by the trustee without the consent of the SHA. Under S.15 of Cap. 97, land held in the name of a clan family or Tong can be administered only by a manager(s) whose appointment has been approved by the SHA and such manager(s) may deal with the said land as if he were the sole owner thereof subject only to the consent of the SHA.

With the absence of Probate or Letters of Administration and where succession followed customary Chinese law, this could result in family disputes as to whom was considered to be the rightful heir and successor to a particular piece of property. The problem are well illustrated in the case *Wu Koon Tai and Anor.* v *Wu Yau Loi* [1996] 3 HKC 559 where an alleged owner of land tried to sell and another member of the family challenged his right to sell. The time taken to resolve such disputes could cause frustration and delay for any developer or purchaser wishing to buy, so again there is a need to be aware of the potential problems involved in such cases.

As from 24 June 1994, this system of NT succession was, in spite of the strong objections of the Heung Yee Kuk, abolished by the passing of the New Territories Land (Exemption) Ordinance (Cap. 452). The old procedure continues to apply in respect of persons who died before the date S.17 of Cap.

97 was repealed. Otherwise all succession in the NT is now subject to Intestates Estates Ordinance (Cap. 73) and the Probate and Administration Ordinances (Cap. 10). Under these ordinances females may apply for Administration or Probate and may now succeed on intestacy.

Two recent cases have thrown some more light on when Chinese customary law may, or may not, apply on succession. In *Leung Lai Fong and Ho Sin Ying* (2009) 12 HKCFAR 581 the Court of Final Appeal had to decide whether 'mother' in the context of the deceased, a childless widower who had died intestate, referred to the natural mother of an intestate or his 'legal mother' under Chinese customary law. It was held that the word 'mother' in S.4 (7) of Cap 73 meant the natural mother of the intestate and the natural mother only. It was explicitly stated that it was inappropriate to refer to any Chinese customary law status for which no express provision had been made.

The decision in *Lai Hay On and Commissioner for Rating and Valuation* [2010] 3 HKLRD 286 set out the principle that generally lawful succession could only take place by will or on intestacy by letters of administration and did not include an *inter vivos* gift or Chinese customary succession.

18 | FUNG SHUI（風水）AND GRAVES

Fung Shui, which literally means 'wind and water', is an ancient Chinese philosophy that seeks to guide people into achieving a harmonious balance with their surroundings. The belief is based on the solar calendar and mathematical systems and incorporates astronomy, geography, the environment, magnetic fields and physics.

Although *Fung Shui* goes back thousands of years it is still alive and well in today's technologically advanced and scientifically driven world, including the NT where it has always played a significant part in village affairs. Therefore anyone who has any dealings in the NT needs to be aware of its implications. The following paragraph was included in the Report on the New Territories 1899–1912 which was laid before the Legislative Council on 22 August 1912; the observations and comments made then are as relevant today as they were in 1912:

> The general religious beliefs as to the relations of the spirits with the land are embraced under the name 'fung shui', meaning 'wind and water' — the two great moving elements in nature. The whole earth, with all that grows out of it, is full of spirits good and bad, which have their own prejudices about the use and occupation of their haunts, and require proper attention from the human beings in their neighbourhood; so it clearly behooves anyone intending to build a house or a grave, a road or a railway, to ascertain on the best authority what site or direction he should choose. In its origins, fung shui can undoubtedly claim to be based on feelings and ideas natural to human nature, and there is much wisdom in it, which even our modern science cannot entirely ignore. Thus 'fung shui' forbids the overlooking of other houses or places, and the setting of one grave just above another: for such an action would show a spirit of arrogance and presumption. It sets great store by wild trees, which are for this reason carefully preserved and even worshipped near the villages, and certain large or ancient trees are objects of special veneration. When a site is duly chosen, and afterwards found to be un-healthy, it is discredited; and thus in time fung shui is modified or built up by a kind of case law; and in fact the popular opinion of 'good

fung shui' is very seldom mistaken. It is not surprising that in course of time the ideas of 'fung shui'; have been complicated and overlaid with numberless small observances and superstitions, employed by necromancers and geomancers and the whole host and fung shui professors in order to increase their own repute and mystify the people: but in its general principles it is a sane and simple idea, and is readily adapted by the common sense of its votaries, in accordance with the teaching of experience, and the needs of the time.

The very fact that *fung shui* is so hard to define and yet is still of such significance results in it being used as a bargaining chip in negotiations particularly when buying land from indigenous villagers. It is very hard to quantify and value *fung shui* as it remains a very subjective art and therefore it can be used to seemingly inflate values by an unreasonable degree.

The question of *fung shui* and its effect on statutory compensation was considered by the Lands Tribunal in the case of *Chow Chi Keung* v *China Light and Power Co. Ltd*. LTMR 1/82 when the Tribunal held, *inter alia,* 'If the need arose, there is no reason why the courts in Hong Kong, in appropriate compensation cases, might not recognize *fung shui*. However, in this case we do not need to consider *fung shui* as a separate head of compensation for if it is, as alleged, a factor in the price of land in the New Territories, it would be reflected

Graves may affect planning and development.

in the open market value. The only evidence on *fung shui* was from the applicant himself. He was a relatively young man, who did not claim any expertise in *fung shui*, but merely made the general assertion that *fung shui* is a dominant factor in land transactions among villagers in the villages in the New Territories and that the *fung shui* of his property had been adversely affected. On that evidence, alone, if it were necessary, we would be unable to find that the order has diminished the value of the property because of the alleged detrimental *fung shui* effect.[1]

The question of *fung shui* payments related to work on the express railway to Guangzhou caught the attention of both the media and the Legislative Council at the end of 2010 when investigations by the South China Morning Post[2] established that $72 million had been paid by Government to geomancers, *fung shui* practitioners, contractors and village chiefs over the past decade. Legislators were asking for, and were promised, great transparency and better monitoring of these claims to ensure they were properly assessed and justified before being paid.

The quality of *fung shui* in relation to the positioning of graves is highly sensitive particularly if the grave has to be removed or exhumed for new development. The level of compensation demanded in these circumstances can sometimes be exorbitant especially if it is an ancestral or clan grave of historical importance. In particular there will be very strong resistance to touching any grave that is less than seven years old. If it is possible, a new scheme should be designed to minimize the removal of such graves or better still to cater for their retention *in situ*. A good example of this is the alignment of the Tsin Long Highway (Route 3) which was adjusted in order that the traditional clan grave pictured was not over shadowed by the road structures and so could be retained *in situ*. It follows that a thorough inspection of any site is essential to see if there are any potential problems of this nature; and if there are, an accurate site survey should be obtained as soon as possible in order to locate the graves and to assist in future planning.

On the subject of graves and burials, it must be remembered that this is another area where the government, again recognizing traditional Chinese customs, has given privileges to the indigenous villagers by formally defining burial grounds and permitting traditional burials rather than encouraging cremation. The granting of these privileges has put the indigenous villagers in a strong negotiating position when it comes to the removal of any graves.

Note

1. See Cruden 1999, p. 193.
2. SCMP 3 and 16 December 2010.

BOUNDARY DISPUTES, MISSING LOTS, MISSING DOCUMENTS, AND SECONDARY EVIDENCE

Boundary Disputes

The Block Government leases are now over a century old and their deficiencies, particularly in relation to the accuracy of the plans attached to them, now come into sharper focus as more and more land has been converted from predominantly agricultural use to various forms of building use.

The original surveys were not done to today's high technical standards, in particular they lack co-ordinates. A sample survey was carried out by the Hong Kong Polytechnic University Research Project G-T574 in 2002 which covered 4 Demarcation Districts in the NT. Using the criterion that a difference in area within 0.005 of an acre was considered acceptable, it was found that the registered and physical areas of about 25% of the lots surveyed could not match each other.

These results led to pressure from some professional land surveyors for the Survey and Mapping Office of Lands Department to carry out a systematic survey of the whole of the NT. This would be a very costly and time consuming exercise which, although on the face of it may appear logical and sensible, may create as many problems as it may solve as there would be as many 'losers' as 'winners'!

There would certainly be a need for fresh legislation to implement any new plans which would need to properly reflect current land ownership rights and have adequate compensation arrangements for the 'losers'.

In the meantime owners of individual lots, and potential purchasers, can avail themselves of the services of an Authorized Land Surveyor (ALS), whose work is now governed by a Code of Conduct spelt out in the Land Survey Ordinance, Cap. 473 (LSO), in order to resolve or clarify any boundary disputes. As a last resort it may be necessary to go to the Courts for a final resolution, as in the case *Tam Mo Yin v Attorney General* [1996] HKC 379 which relates to a case where in fact the plan to which the grant related has been lost. The Court agreed that extrinsic evidence should be admitted to assist resolving the dispute. A summary of the case is given below because it provides positive guidance to practitioners having to resolve similar disputes.

In 1931, Lot 1510 in the New Territories had been sold by government auction by way of a New Grant and the area of the lot was stated to be 126 acres. Reference in the grant was made to a plan deposited in the District Office, but this plan was now lost. In 1950, the lot has been divided into two sections. Part of section A measuring 1,344,000 square feet (although it was not known how this measurement has been arrived at) was sold off and the plaintiffs eventually became owners of the remaining portion of section A. When they claimed possession of two fish ponds, the government contested this claim, arguing that the ponds lay outside the boundaries of the lot.

Yam J, relying upon expert evidence, concluded that the acreage stated in the auction particulars, and hence the acreage of the remaining portion of Section A, could not be relied upon for delineating the land boundaries, since it has probably been based upon an earlier DD Control Sheet on which the area had only been roughly calculated by a non-qualified person. Extrinsic evidence as to the extent of the lot should, therefore, be admitted. After admitting extrinsic evidence including the oral testimony of residents, aerial photographs and the location of a bund, Yam J concluded that the fish ponds did, in fact, lie within the boundaries of the land.

Reference can also be made to the case *Wong Lai Man v. Wong Tat Kwong & Anor* reported on page 138 where there was a discrepancy between the boundary on the ground and the boundary shown on the plans in the Land Registry and the question of adverse possession arose.

Missing Lots

A Missing Lot arises when a landowner who has a lot properly entered in the Schedule to the Block Government Lease but cannot trace the corresponding lot number on the plan requests the government to locate the boundaries of the lot. It is now defined in the LSO as follows: 'missing lot' arises when its landowner requests the government to locate the boundaries of a lot but a search of government records fails to establish their position. Where the government has accepted continual payment of the Ground Rent, it is considered that they have an obligation to locate the lot and there is an established procedure to handle such situations on application to the appropriate DLO.

There are also 'missing' house lots where many old schedule house lots were depicted collectively on the DD sheet in the form of hatched blocks and not recorded as individual house lots. This type of house lot may be re-established by means of the missing lot procedures.

Then there are numerous cases involving off site development or with overlapping lots where houses built in a row are in a misplaced position compared to their legal boundaries, or the same piece of land has been granted to different owners. These cases require a formal land exchange in order to rectify the boundaries and difficulties arise in both locating all the affected owners and then obtaining their unanimous consent. This could alternatively result in adverse possession claims and impede redevelopment.

Missing Documents

There are also cases in the NT, usually attributed to the Japanese occupation of Hong Kong during the Second World War, when many documents were destroyed and where the government cannot trace the original lease conditions. In such cases, it is not safe to assume that grants would have been made subject to the GNs current at the time of grant but secondary evidence such as a copy of the original GN advertising the sale of the land may be used to help establish the Conditions of the Grant.[1] In all cases where secondary evidence has to be relied upon, legal advice should be obtained before any action based upon their terms of the conditions is taken. In the absence of original or secondary evidence, the position on the ground and/or the action of the parties will need to be taken into account. For example, it should be established if there is a long history of the government and the lessee treating the land as being subject to certain conditions, plus any other extrinsic evidence as admitted in the case *Tam Mo Yin v Attorney General* quoted above.

In the cases of *Wu Wing Kuen* v *Leung Kwai Lin Cindy* and *Ip Foo Keung Michael & others* v *Chan Pak Kai* [1999] 3 HKLRD 738, the Court of Appeal has helpfully ruled on the status of secondary evidence where the original title deeds or certified copies are missing. In the first case, the respondent-vendor was unable to produce documents of title (i.e. the original of an agreement) for the grant of a government lease and therefore relied on the secondary evidence. It was held that Section 13 of the Conveyancing and Property Ordinance did not make any change in law as to the quality of the evidence which a purchaser of land was entitled to require from the vendor as proof of title to the land. Unless there was an express provision in the contract to the contrary, when primary evidence was not available, the purchaser must accept sufficient secondary evidence. The secondary evidence must provide clear and cogent proof of the contents of the missing document; its due execution; and the fact of its loss or destruction. Accordingly, the purchaser was bound to accept the secondary evidence offered as proof of the agreement.

In the second case, the respondent-vendor was unable to produce the original instrument conferring a power of attorney to act for a predecessor in title, upon a donee to assign the property and the secondary evidence produced by the vendor comprised two statutory declarations. It was held that for secondary evidence to be capable of proving the contents of a missing document, all that was required was clear and cogent proof of its contents; the best evidence rule no longer applied. Here the vendor's evidence did not prove the contents of the power of attorney, as *inter alia*, he had not stated that he had actually seen the power of attorney. It was also held that there was no evidence that the power of attorney had been duly executed. It was therefore *prima facie* the case that the secondary evidence was deficient since an essential element, namely proof of due execution, was lacking. Accordingly, the secondary evidence in relation to the missing power of attorney was deficient regarding proof of due execution.

Notes

1. See Chapter 3, p. 24, Fig. 3.2.

IV | FUTURE DEVELOPMENTS IN LAND ADMINISTRATION

The second edition of this book contains two new chapters, which reflect the latest development in land administration in Hong Kong.

Since the start of the new millennium, a number of topics have moved higher up the public agenda, in particular the preservation of our natural environment and the conservation of our built heritage. Because of Hong Kong's unique leasehold land system, the potential solutions to these problem areas lie in making revisions to the current land administration policies which are discussed in more detail in Chapter 20.

The passing of the Land Titles Ordinance in 2004 heralds a completely new system of guaranteed title to replace the current deed registration system for conveyancing. The implications of these changes, which will occur over the ensuing 12 years, are considered in Chapter 21.

HOW PLANNING AND LAND POLICY COULD BE USED TO ENHANCE CONSERVATION IN HONG KONG

An appropriate starting point is to understand Hong Kong's conservation obligations under international treaties which may be summarized as follows:

> In May 1984, the United Kingdom ratified the Convention for the Protection of the World Cultural and Natural Heritage 1972 ('the Convention') and extended it to Hong Kong. The PRC also ratified the Convention in December 1985. The Convention remains in force in relation to Hong Kong after 1997.
>
> Article 2 of the Convention defines 'natural heritage' to include, *inter alia*, 'natural sites of outstanding universal value from the point of view of science, conservation or natural beauty.' Article 4 of the Convention provides that each State Party undertakes the duty of ensuring, to the utmost of its own resources, the identification, protection, conservation, presentation and transmission to future generations of natural heritage. Article 5 requires the State Party to take appropriate legal, scientific, technical, administrative and financial measures necessary for the identification, protection, conservation, presentation and rehabilitation of natural heritage. Article 6 further requires the State Party not to take any deliberate measures which might damage directly or indirectly the natural heritage. Article 12 provides that the fact that a property belonging to natural heritage has not been included in the World Heritage List in Article 11 does not mean that it does not have an outstanding universal value that deserves to be protected, conserved and transmitted to future generations.
>
> In *Queensland* v *The Commonwealth* (1989) 167 CLR 232, the High Court of Australia held that the Convention imposed a legal duty to take measures for the protection, conservation, presentation and transmission to future generations of the cultural heritage and natural heritage. This obligation arises out of identification by the contracting state of its cultural or natural heritage, and does not depend on whether the site is listed on the World Heritage List. Under Article 4 of the Convention, a contracting state is under a duty to make identification of cultural or natural heritage.
>
> In October 1999, the UNESCO 12th General Assembly of State Parties to the Convention adopted a resolution that invites the contracting parties to give the highest priority to the adoption of a general policy which aims to give the cultural and natural heritage a function in the life of the community and to

integrate the protection of that heritage into comprehensive planning programme according to Article 5 of the Convention.[1]

Very recently, and most significantly, the Central People's Government on 9 May 2011 extended the decisions and Conferences of the Parties to the Convention of Biological Diversity (CBD), that was originally ratified in 1993, to Hong Kong which will demand a complete rethink of Government's policies particularly with regard to the criteria for designating Country Parks, the proposed measures for protecting Country Park enclaves and the treatment of privately held land associated with these activities.

In July 2003, the government published its review of Nature Conservation Policy in a document entitled 'Nature Outlook' which can be downloaded from the website of the Environment, Transport and Works Bureau.[2] The Review is presented as follows:

- Introduction — setting the scene
- Review of Existing Policy and Measures
- Improvement Proposals
- Public Support and Consultation
- The Annex sets out options considered impractical.

The situation today is probably not as bad as some environmentalists and green groups would have us believe, considering that since the enactment of the Country Parks Ordinance (Cap. 208) in 1976, We now have 24 Country Parks (CPs) plus 22 special areas for not use conservation which cover some 40% of the territory's total land mass. The Land Utilization map on the inside back cover also helps to clarify our understanding of the position.

Country Parks are designated for the purpose of nature conservation, countryside recreation and outdoor education. Special Areas are created mainly for the purpose of nature conservation. They now attract over 12 million visitors annually.

In 1995 the Marine Parks Ordinance (Cap. 76) was enacted which provides for the designation, control and management of Marine Parks and Marine Reserves. Currently there are four such parks and one reserve so designated.

Interestingly this 1995 legislation has provision for the government to resume private land for the purposes of marine parks or reserves and such resumptions are deemed to be for a 'public purpose'.

Surely the same logic and principles should now be applied to the Country Parks Ordinance particularly in the light of recent events described below.

Under the existing Environmental Impact Assessment (EIA) Ordinance (Cap. 499), designated project proponents are required to obtain environmental permits (EP) from the Director of Environmental Protection (DEP) before construction or operation of the project commences. In October and November 2000, the DEP rejected two applications for an EP. One application was for the proposed Lantau N-S link between Tai Ho Wan and Mui Wo cutting through the Lantau Country Park. The other, more famous case, was for the former Kowloon Canton Railway Corporation (KCRC) proposal to construct a spur line from Sheung Shui Station to the new border crossing at Lok Ma Chau which involved passing through Long Valley. The KCRC appealed against the DEP's decision and in September 2001 the Environmental Impact Assessment Appeal Board dismissed KCRC's appeal.

The Appeal Board's decision included the following relevant paragraphs:

1. During the public consultation period for the KCRC, EIA the DEP received 225 submissions from the public each of which opposed the project;
2. Under the paragraph entitled 'The Implementation of the EIA Process' the following words occur:

> There are two main matters of public interest involved. Both are important. The first is the public interest in the protection of the environment upon which the quality of life in Hong Kong will increasingly depend. The second is the public interest in ensuring that major designated projects are brought to fruition in a timely and efficient manner. ....'

In the light of all these events we can safely say that the protection of the environment, which must include conservation, is now a 'public purpose'. It would not have been possible to make this suggestion ten or even five years ago but today we can. This subtle shift from public interest to public purpose is most important because 'public purpose' is one of the criteria under the Land Resumptions Ordinance (Cap. 124) that can trigger a compulsory acquisition of private interests by the government, and in any new policy initiative the government must recognize and acknowledge it may need to use this tool to achieve effective conservation. It is regrettable that the government has failed to do so in this review.

The purpose of the EIA Ordinance is expressed in its title: to provide for assessing the impact on the environment of certain projects and proposals, for protecting the environment and for incidental matters. However, it does not cover conservation *per se* where no development is intended and it is this gap which needs to be addressed by any new policy.

The present conservation framework is well described by the Conservancy Association's August 2000 paper entitled 'Achieving Conservation – A Positive Conservation Policy for Hong Kong',[3] and is echoed in the government's consultation document, as follows:

The current legal framework for conservation is embodied primarily in the Country Parks Ordinance and the Town Planning Ordinance. In the case of country parks, conservation is the stated objective and this objective is by and large served by the Ordinance. For areas of conservation interest which fall outside Country Parks, the conservation intention is expressed through zoning the sites as Conservation Area (CA) under the Town Planning Ordinance. Both Country Parks and CA zones can cover large areas. Within these areas some specific sites may be designated Sites of Special Scientific Interests (SSSI), which provides more stringent control over land use, and hence greater protection of the sites from disturbance. The Agriculture, Fisheries and Conservation Department (AFCD) are the expert department within government for conservation, country park management and the designation of SSSI's. In fact these CA/SSSI zones now cover over 6600 hectares which is a further 5% of HK's land area so together with the Country Parks some 43% of our total land area is now protected.

Unfortunately this framework is too simplistic and ineffective because, first, it does not cover areas with high conservation value that fall under other zonings. A case in point are areas zoned Agriculture, which may consist of areas of high cultural or ecological value but which would not be protected because conservation is not the stated intention of the agriculture zone. Similarly, other zoning such as the Village zone and the Residential zones may contain buildings of high heritage or cultural value which may not be protected under their respective zonings.

Second, even for areas zoned CA or SSSI, the planning intention of conservation may not be realized if the conservation value is progressively diminished, either through willful destruction (e.g. war games) or as a result of natural degradation or by the misuse of pesticides. In other words, although conservation is the stated objective, such objective can be defeated either by lack of land management or by the inability of enforcement over destructive or inappropriate uses.

Third, even if the conservation objective is well served (naturally or through active management), the areas may still yield to development due to competing uses, such as improvement in transport or demand for housing (for example, to accommodate the rising demand for houses for indigenous villagers). There are strong advocates within the government for these competing objectives, all of which are backed by strong policy frameworks. By contrast, the present conservation framework is incomplete and does not provide a strong enough basis for the conservation department (AFCD) to be an effective advocate for the conservation objective commensurate with its value to society.

It is important to consider the land use zoning in the context of land ownership because in recent years there has been a subtle but significant shift in the way the Planning Department deals with new land use zoning. Consider that when the Country Parks were originally set up 30 years ago, they only ever covered government owned land. Private land, usually village land, was excluded. Today the position has changed; the Planning Department is prepared to rezone large areas of privately owned land, usually described for agricultural purposes on the Block Government Lease, usually to CA or conservation zoning. A lot of this land is lying fallow and unused and with the CA zoning that is how it will remain. Agricultural activities can often be incompatible with Conservation objectives and the ownership rights must be respected and treated fairly. Under this system they are not. At Wu Kau Tang in July 2000, 87 hectares out of a total area of 103 hectares had been zoned CA; similarly at Tai Long Wan in October 2001, 46.5 hectares out of 50.5 had also been zoned CA. In both cases large percentages are privately owned.

Let us also consider the new Outline Zoning Plan (OZP) that in February 2002 was approved for Sha Lo Tung,[4] which was designed to protect its important ecological (currently 68 species of dragon flies are recorded in the area) and cultural features. The 57 ha area designated in the OZP comprises about 22 ha as SSSI (covering the streams, a 30 m buffer on either side and freshwater marshes in the northeast of the site), about 12 ha of conservation area covering the freshwater marsh, fung shui woodland behind Cheung Uk and mature tree clusters behind Lei Uk and Lo Wai, about 22 ha of green belt covering foothills, lower hill slopes, spurs, isolated knolls, woodland or vegetated land, and about 2 ha of village type development. Provision of sewerage and emergency vehicle access may be necessary for the village development areas. To preserve the Hakka village houses any demolition, addition, alteration to the existing village houses require planning permission.

The fundamental weakness in the present framework can be summed up by saying that conservation by zoning alone is far too passive. Further, because these zonings now include large tracts of private land, for conservation to be done in a meaningful way it requires mechanisms for active management and/or a system for bringing private land into the scheme. This may, or may not, involve resumption but the private land owners should be assured of adequate compensation or encouraged to actively participate.

THE WAY FORWARD

As Civic Exchange concluded in their Nature Conservation – A New Policy Framework for Hong Kong, January 2011, 2010 will remembered as a landmark year for conservation in Hong Kong. Over 80,000 people joined a *Facebook* site to protest against a development of a private site in Tai Long Wan in Sai Kung, heralding a new level of public involvement in nature conservation that social media marketing has unlocked. In fact the owners had done nothing against the law but the existing passive approach, this site being outside the Country Park boundary with no land use zoning, to conservation is now clearly outdated and in the light of CBD needs to be radically rethought.

Following on from the Tai Long Wan case that first emerged in the summer of 2010 the Government was stung into action that resulted in May 2011 with the Country and Marine Parks Board receiving a Working Paper entitled Review of the Criteria for Designating Country Parks and Proposed Measures for Protecting Country Park Enclaves. The paper noted that there were 77 country park enclaves similar to Tai Long Wan with a total area of 2076 hectares. 23 of these sites were covered by OZP's and 54 were not however seven of these sites, including Tai Long Wan, have since August 2010 been covered by DPA plans gazetted under the TPO in order to protect the areas from incompatible development.

The updated criteria for designating country parks now states that conservation value, landscape and aesthetic value and recreation potential remain as the three main themes of intrinsic criteria in identifying suitable areas for country park designation. Other factors such as size, proximity to existing country parks, land status, and existing land use are relevant to demarcating boundaries but, importantly, the mere existence of private land will not be automatically taken as a determining factor for exclusion from the boundary of a country park.

All these new factors, including CBD, lead to the inevitable conclusion that the protection and expansion of the country parks should now rightly be considered as a 'public purpose' such that the Government could exercise statutory resumption powers over those parcels of private land that fall within the new criteria. Even though most of the private lands that will be so affected are restricted to agricultural use under the Block Government Leases such uses are, never the less, incompatible with the new conservation objectives so the owners need to be adequately compensated. Under the Basic Law there is a responsibility to protect the rights of private property owners and the government needs to respect this. It cannot expect to reach its new conservation objectives and standards free of charge and must now start to allocate substantial financial resources to meet the new challenges. Fortunately this is a wealthy Government that can well afford these costs which pale into insignificance when placed beside the expenditure for the new cruise terminal or the cost of the high-speed rail link to the mainland!

If public money is to be used to acquire such land then it is right and proper for the ongoing management of these lands to remain in the public domain. The

Department of Agriculture, Fisheries and Conservation already has the existing infrastructure in the shape of Country Park management centres scattered throughout the territory to play an expanded role in properly managing these expanded country parks. They also need to be given sufficient monies each year to ensure a high standard of management is achieved going forward.

With the new criteria now being put forward the idea of Public Private Partnerships (PPP) suggested in the 2003 Review are now seen to be contradictory and should no longer be pursued. The 2003 Review identified 12 priority sites but it is now revealed that seven of these are enclaves that should, more appropriately, be placed inside the adjoining country park and should not be subjected to any form of significant private development .Sha Lo Tung is the most egregious example of a proposed PPP that should simply not be allowed to proceed.

The expansion and protection of the Country Parks now being proposed would represent a magnificent legacy to future generations the cost of which would no doubt be enthusiastically supported by the community.

BUILT HERITAGE CONSERVATION

In the urban areas the main focus on heritage conservation has been on government-owned buildings which are looked after by the Antiquities and Monuments Office (AMO) of the Leisure and Cultural Services Department.[5] In the NT, there are a number of Chinese temples, usually sited on *tso* or *tong* land that have been repaired, upgraded and preserved. Recently the Ping Shan Tang Clan Gallery, housed in an AMO restored two storey building built by the British in 1899 as the first police station in the NT, was opened. The project represents a desire of some indigenous villagers to support heritage conservation. As one local leader said, "Conservation isn't just about preserving the past but also managing the pace of change. Too big a change can radically alter the character and appearance of the village, putting heritage ar risk."

Currently the government's thinking on nature conservation of privately owned land is more advanced than that on heritage conservation. Again there is an ongoing public debate initiated by the issuing of the government's consultation document published in early 2004 entitled 'Review of Built Heritage Conservation Policy'.[6]

There are regrettably very few concrete solutions put forward in this document to assist the debate but this is, to some extent, understandable because of the overriding need to respect the existing development rights of the present owners and the need therefore to adequately compensate them for any loss that may arise should their land be taken. Although it is clear that the government wishes to find solutions without incurring payments, there has been a relatively recent precedent when in 2004 it acquired a building in the Mid Levels known as Kam Tong Hall for $53m. This building was erected in 1914 and had been well maintained over the years with most of the original fittings surviving with minor alteration. In 1990 the Antiquities Advisory Board accorded a Grade II status to the building in recognition of its outstanding heritage value. The intention was to convert the building into a Dr. Sun Yat-san Museum, which was opened in January 2007. So a 'public purpose' must have been established to justify the acquisition?

An alterative to outright acquisition is the use of Transfer of Development Rights (TDR) as an incentive to preserve other historical buildings. John C Tsang, the then Secretary for Planning and Lands, addressed the Hong Kong Institute of Architects in December 2001 on this subject in the following clear and simple terms:

> The success of Hong Kong is couched in the operation of market forces. We cannot expect the developers to turn away from their objective to maximize profits and to volunteer to preserve historical buildings in the community without any return. They just don't behave like that. Nor can we expect Government to acquire all the historical buildings in the open market or to resume them under the Lands Resumption Ordinance. That is not the best use of public revenue and is, any way, just too expensive. It would be better if we can employ market forces to pay for the preservation of these historical buildings. Providing an incentive for property owners to encourage them to preserve these historical buildings is one way and TDR could be such an incentive.
>
> The purpose of a TDR scheme is to create a 'win-win' solution. With TDR, the owners of historical buildings of value will be able to keep their existing buildings, and use or sell the unused development rights as they see fit. The community would also benefit from the preservation of these buildings without having to buy or resume the properties.
>
> TDR is nothing new. Many overseas cities and communities, such as New York City and Vancouver, operate such schemes. The question is: can TDR work in Hong Kong?
>
> The existing framework of density control under the Buildings Ordinance and the statutory town plans does not allow any TDR to apply across sites that are not contiguous. At present, 'transfer' of development rights or permissible gross floor area (GFA) is only allowed between different parts of the same development site. This method should actually be more accurately referred to as clustering of GFA, rather than transfer of GFA.
>
> The idea of a TDR Scheme is to enable property owners to 'deed-restrict' their properties that are of historical value against future development, and to transfer the unused development rights to other sites of the same land use category in the same statutory town plan area, i.e. the area covered by an Outline Zoning Plan. In exceptional cases, the unused development rights could also be transferred to a contiguous Outline Zoning Plan.

The basic principle behind this idea is relatively simple. Under such a TDR scheme, historical buildings may be declared as monuments, and become eligible 'sending sites'. The owners of such properties could apply to modify their land leases against future redevelopment and obtain a right or entitlement to the unused development rights in exchange for the deed restriction or lease modification. The entitlement would be calculated by deducting the existing GFA of a historical building from the maximum GFA permitted under the land lease, the Outline Zoning Plan or the Buildings Ordinance, whichever is the least. The unused GFA permissible could then be transferred to other 'receiving sites'. A certificate of entitlement specifying the amount of transferable GFA, or GFA credits to be more precise, would be issued to the owner. These GFA credits could then be used in approved receiving sites or sold to other owners or developers.

By obtaining or buying such GFA credits, owners or developers could apply to a designated authority to use such rights to build at a higher density ratio, or plot ratio, than the development controls would normally permit for a building development on the receiving site.

The size of the building development should be commensurate with the size of the site in order to prevent excessive building bulk and should not overload infrastructure facilities. Under the proposed scheme, receiving sites would not be allowed to receive too much GFA credits. The total GFA of a building development on a receiving site should not exceed 20 per cent of the maximum GFA normally permitted.

This shows a very clear appreciation of the issues plus a very positive method of resolving the problem in a way that is cost neutral. It is worthy of serious consideration in the generation of solutions to this problem. If TDR cannot be made to work, for example if the owner of the subject property did not own any other suitable 'receiving' development sites, then a non-*in-situ* land exchange, as recently used in the case of King Yin Lei on Stubbs Road proved to be a suitable alternative mechanism. This is worth considering particularly if a high quality building has to be preserved and may well be used again, as in the latest case of Ho Tung Gardens on the Peak, where the government is reluctant to pay the estimated $3b needed to buy out the owner!

Conclusion

It is most unfortunate that even after the 1 July 2007 reorganization the conservation of the natural environment comes under the Environment Bureau whereas the conservation of Hong Kong's built heritage remains under the Home Affairs Bureau.

Interestingly the newly created Development Bureau is now taking a more proactive role in trying to strike the right balance between the delivery of major infrastructure projects against the interests of heritage conservation. In

November 2007 they launched a pilot scheme entitled 'Revitalizing Historic Buildings through Partnership Scheme', making available seven government-owned historic buildings for adaptive reuse, indicating a policy shift away from the Home Affairs Bureau.[7] Hopefully this new 'super' bureau will now take on the essential cross-sectorial policy coordination role with regard to all issues related to Hong Kong's natural and built heritage.

Another point in relation to sustainable development is that in the absence of other significant tax incentives that are available to the HKSARG to advance sustainable development, the one area they can administratively influence matters is through the level of land premium Lands Department charges for land use conversions. Lands Departments Practice Note No.1/2010 introduces a Special Waiver for Conversion of an Entire Existing Industrial Building and sets out the criteria whereby the owner of such buildings can apply for a special waiver at nil fee for the change of use, usually to permit non-industrial uses, for the lifetime of the existing building or until the expiration of the term of the current Government lease of the lot whichever is the earlier.

This new policy represents a radical change in Government thinking, being prepared to forego land premium in the interests of promoting and encouraging sustainable development, and must be seen as a very positive step. The Chief Executive in his 2011–12 Policy Address reported that as at the end of September 2011 Lands Department had approved 26 such cases with 23 in the pipeline; a very encouraging start.

A robust and effective conservation policy is an essential ingredient of Hong Kong's ambition to become 'Asia's World City' and the proposals being suggested are consistent with contemporary international thinking that market-based conservation may well be the best hope for reconciling future economic growth with the need to preserve both our natural and built heritage.

Notes

1. Paras 66 to 69 of the judgment in HCAL 19/2003 in the matter of the Town Planning Board and Society for the Protection of Harbour Ltd.
2. Nature Outlook – Consultation Document Review of Nature Conservation Policy — July 2003.
   Download from http://www.etwb.gov.hk.
3. The Conservancy Association Achieving Conservation — A positive conservation policy for Hong Kong — August 2000.
   Home page: http://www.conservancy.org.hk.
4. Civic Exchange — Conservation in Hong Kong — June 2002.
   Conservation of Sha Lo Tung — A way forward.
   Home Page: http://www.civic-exchange.org.
5. www.amo.gov.hk.
6. www.hab.gov.hk/en/pulications_and_press-releases/consultation.htm.
7. www.devb.gov.hk.

21 | THE LAND TITLES ORDINANCE 2004[1]

Introduction

On 7 July 2004, the Land Titles Ordinance (LTO) was enacted. The Ordinance (Cap. 585) will change the deeds system of conveyancing currently in force in Hong Kong to a system of registration of title. When fully implemented, the important consequence of this change will be that an executed assignment, which at present passes title to land, will have no effect in relation to the land, merely creating contractual rights. Instead, title to the land will require the registration of a statutory form of transfer in the Land Registry. Consequential amendments will result in a statutory form of instrument for all registrable dealings. This will have the effect that instead of having to search a chain of title deeds to establish title, only the register needs to be searched. Any state of title certificate issued by the Registry will reflect only the state of the title at the time of issue. The Register of title itself will be the authoritative statement of title, containing all current notifications and registrations.

What Type of System Is Being Introduced

The main features of the new system are:
a. a paramount register requiring registration of dealings in statutory form to effect title to or an interest in land;
b. an indefeasible title, subject to a proviso in the case of fraud by the registered owner, which is good from attack by all;
c. statutory protection by way of entry of a caveat for an unregistered dealing. As equitable interests are to be barred from the system, some device was needed to give protection to an interest prior to registration, and the caveat fulfilled this function;

d. the possibility of rectification of the register where necessary, either at the initiative of the registrar or under court order;
e. an assurance system providing compensation to a party suffering loss in certain cases; and
f. dealings with the land, such as mortgages and leases, requiring registration.

When will the Legislation take effect?

Enactment of the LTO in 2004 was made subject to condition that the government review a number of matters and report back to the Legislative Council before proposing a commencement date. In May 2007 the government reported to the Legislative Council that it has concluded from the review that amendments are needed before the LTO takes effect. The government is now preparing the amendment bill, which will cover both substantive changes and extensive redrafting and reorganization to make the legislation clearer and more user friendly for legal and other professionals as well as for the public. One major change indicated is that the limited provisions on updating of land boundary plans contained in section 94 of the LTO are likely to be removed and replaced with comprehensive new provisions in the Land Survey Ordinance that will apply to all land, irrespective of whether it has yet been brought under the LTO.

The government has indicated that it intends to introduce the amendment bill after the start of the next Legislative Council Term, which begins in September 2008. The bill will be accompanied by all draft regulations and forms needed for the operation of the system. Since the bill is likely to be subject to lengthy scrutiny in the Bills Committee, it is unlikely that the LTO will now come into force until after 2010 since time will have to be allowed for final practical preparations after enactment of the amendment bill. Even when the LTO does commence, for an initial period of 12 years it will apply only to what is termed 'new land', which is newly granted land or land regranted after surrender. The Land Registration Ordinance (Cap. 128) (LRO) will continue to apply to all existing land during this period, which may be seen as an 'incubation period' since amendments have been made to the LRO to allow certain protective action to be taken by claimants to interests that have not yet been registered under that Ordinance. These include provisions for a caveat and a caution against conversion of land to the new system. It is possible that the length of the incubation period may be varied after initial experience with the title register and the complete change-over to title registration may take place more quickly than expected.

The Incubation Period

During the incubation period, the LTO will apply to new grants land to dealings in any properties built on land granted after the commencement date. The amended LRO will apply to dealings in all previously registered land and property.

There will be one major change in respect of certain transactions which are not protected at present under the LRO but by reference to common law principles. This relates to the manner in which unwritten equities are to be dealt with.

Unwritten Equities

At present, a person claiming an interest in land under a transaction which has not been reduced to writing cannot register the claim in the Lands Registry because only written claims to land may be registered. Once the LTO operates to affect LRO land, the claim behind the unwritten equity will be lost if previously it had not been registered under the LRO. To enable this, the LRO has been amended by the LTO to introduce a caveat procedure which on registration gives notice of the claim. During the incubation period a claimant under an unwritten equity may register a caveat but this is not essential to retaining a claim during that period.

One example of an unwritten equity is that referred to as 'the bus driver's interest' which was considered in *Wong Chim-ying* v *Cheng Kam-win* [1991] 2 HKLR 253. That interest was said to be a beneficial interest under a resulting trust. As only interests which were registered under the LRO were recognized in a contest with a bona fide purchaser of the subject land, the unwritten equity was able to be ignored by such a purchaser, even one who took with notice of it, that is, who knows the existence of the equity. However, in a radical decision, the Court of Appeal held that the claim to the interest was to be protected under non-statutory notice provisions, largely perhaps because it was said that the purchaser in that case had had notice of the possibility of a claim. Despite the failure to register the interest, it was binding on the purchaser because common law principles would bind the purchaser in equity.

Once the incubation period ends and the LTO binds LRO land, an unwritten equity will not be permitted to affect land unless it had been 'caveated' during the incubation period. On conversion to the LTO, the caveat will become a 'non-consent caution'. Without registration, the claim will be lost as proprietary interest in the land, and the position will be the same as that prevailed prior to 1991; at most the interest will be contractual.

Anyone holding such a claim, whether a current interest or one created prior to the end of the incubation period, should register a 'caveat' against the land even if it is not clear that the interest does affect the title to the land or an interest therein. There is a wide variety of circumstances which can give rise to such equities and if the interest is thought to be proprietary, then the holder should caveat. This is so even though the owner of the land or interest can take action to have the caveat removed. Further, if the caveat was wrongfully registered, the owner can seek damages against the caveator for loss suffered by its registration.

Caution against Conversion

During the incubation period, anyone who has not been registered as owner under the LRO but who claims title to the land, or a beneficial interest in it, will need to register a 'Caution against Conversion', thereby putting the owner on notice of an attack on the owner's title or on the interest. The cautioner will need to take timely court action to advance his or her claim. So if it has not been removed earlier, this caution lasts for one year, although it can be extended for another year by the court. Where action to support the claim has been undertaken during the currency of the caution, and a *lis pendens* has been registered, the life of the claim will be thereby extended. The owner of the land can take action to have the caution removed, and if it has been wrongfully registered the owner can seek damages against the cautioner for loss suffered.

The caution does have a short life so as to cause claimants to take timely action to pursue their claims.

The Full Conversion

Once the incubation period has passed, then subject to certain exceptions all LRO land will be converted into LTO land. The main exception applies to land which is subject to a valid 'Caution against Conversion' which had been registered when the land was still LRO land.

The second exception is that if registration under the LRO of a dealing is in progress, there will be no conversion until the completion of that transaction.

From the full conversion date all dealings with the land must comply with the terms of the LTO and title will be indefeasible within the terms of section 25.

Indefeasibility of LTO Land

The feature which distinguished a registration of title system from all others is that under that system, title to the land or to an interest in the land comes from registration of an instrument in statutory form in the land registry: section 25. Without registration the interest can be the subject of a caution — either consent or non-consent — but no title passes to the claimant and the claimant's rights are compensable in contract only.

Once a person is registered as owner of the land, or of an interest in the land, that title is indefeasible. This means that it is good against attack from 'the whole world' (meaning from any other party) unless the owner had obtained registration through fraud (the owner's fraud or the fraud of another to which the owner was a party or by which the owner was bound), or where a mistake or omission had been made, or where the registered instrument was void or voidable: sections 25 and 82. In any of these cases, the registered title is liable to be set aside when action is taken against the owner and the register is ordered by the court to be rectified under section 82.

The indefeasible title is subject to certain interests even if they have not been created by the owner. These include:

a. covenants, exceptions, reservations etc in the government lease: section 25 (2) (b);
b. any registered matter affecting the land: section 25 (2) (b);
c. any overriding interest affecting the land as provided for in section 28: section 25(2) (c).

There is a large list of these overriding interests including:

a. Chinese custom or customary rights in the NT;
b. any public rights;
c. easements registered under the LRO, rights of way and rights of water;
d. easements of necessity;
e. a wide variety of statutory rights including those for resumption, demolition, or redevelopment;
f. a first charge under the Stamp Duty Ordinance;
g. leases for terms not exceeding three years; and
h. rights acquired by adverse possession.

The title is subject also to any dealing entered into by the owner where the other party has registered a 'consent caution'. It is also subject to the claim to an interest in a 'non-consent caution'.

There is no indefeasibility for land boundaries: sections 18 and 94.

Section 53 provides for the registration of a Deed of Mutual Covenant as an encumbrance against title. This will act as a further exception to the indefeasible title.

New Grants will become indefeasible, subject to the exceptions mentioned, on registration during the incubation period; LRO land will become indefeasible on the conversion when the incubation period ceases and the LTO comes into full force.

Long Leases

The LTO seeks to distinguish 'Long Leases', that is those for a term of not less than 21 years remaining at the time of registration, granted at rack rent and for which a premium has been paid, granted by the owner of the land. In substance a 'Long Lease' is a sub-lease by the government lessee and does not confer any greater rights than usual for a sub-lessee. However, the reason why the 'Long Lease' is distinguished under the terms of the LTO is that it is often treated more as giving rights of 'ownership' than those of a sub-lessee; the payment of the premium encourages this view. Dependent on its terms, the lease can be sold, mortgaged or the subject of the sub-sub-lease and it has a marketable value.

The reference to the 'Long Lease' means that in effect there will be three types of leases capable of affecting land. These are the 'Long Lease' (which must be registered: sections 26 and 49), the lease for a period of more than three years (which also must be registered: section 48), and the lease for a period not exceeding three years at market rent without payment of a premium where the lease takes effect in possession (which cannot be registered but which acts as an overriding interest under section 24). The current rule that an option in an unregistrable lease must be protected by registration will continue to operate.

Preparing for the Change-over

It is not too early to start thinking about how the LTO will affect land dealings once the incubation period commences.

The party creating an unwritten interest which may affect land will need to be aware that that interest will be capable of protection under the LRO. At the same time, the recipient of that interest will need to be careful to caveat and then to be prepared to justify the caveat, as representing the recipient's claim to a proprietary interest in the land, in court. This could result in expensive litigation. Landowners should then be careful in their dealings with their land and their interest therein. The *Wong* v *Cheng* situation showed that the court will apply equitable principles to indicate that the party paying for the land, but who failed to protect his or her interests, may well end up as owner of that land. It thus behooves owners, and persons dealing with landowners, to be more precise in their transactions, and to reduce the transaction to writing.

Any person claiming title to land or an interest in land (created under a written instrument) will want to consider registration of a 'Caution against Conversion.' Cautioners will want to make sure they are correct in their assessment of the situation because the registered owners do have the right to damages for loss caused by that caution.

The new landowner who takes under a New Grant, will be operating under the LTO for all transactions with the land. The new landowner must be aware of all overriding interests affecting the title because it may be within his or her power to reduce this liability. Contractual principles will continue to operate in the same way as at present so that any unsupportable warranties in the Sale and Purchase Agreement as to the state of the title may result in the owner being liable for damages to a purchaser due to failure to monitor title.

In the run up to the enactment of this new Ordinance it was recognized that there would need to be additional legislation in order to fine tune and clarify certain aspects of the new law. However substantial revisions are now to be made to the Ordinance and it is not known when the amending legislation will be submitted to the Legislative Council.

Note

1. The author is grateful to Messrs. *Simmons & Simmons for their agreement to substantially incorporate their August 2004 article into this chapter and also to the former Land Registrar, Mr Kim Salkeld, for his* contribution.

APPENDICES

APPENDIX I

Public Notice and Declaration of 1 May 1841

"The following Notice is published for general information. But the necessary particulars not having yet been obtained regarding the portions of land already surveyed, the blanks relating to number and extent of allotments and period of sale, cannot yet be filled up.

"Arrangements having been made for the permanent occupation of the Island of Hong kong it has become necessary to declare the principles and conditions upon which allotments of land will be made, pending Her Majesty's further pleasure.

"With a view to the reservation to the Crown of as extensive a control over the lands as may be compatible with the immediate progress of the establishment, it is now declared that the number of allotments to be disposed of from time to time will be regulated with due regard to the actual public wants.

"It will be a condition of each title that a building of a certain value, hereafter to be fixed, must be erected within a reasonable period of time on the allotments; and there will be a general reservation of all Her Majesty's rights. Pending Her Majesty's further pleasure the lands will be allotted according to the principles and practice of British laws upon the tenure of quit rent to the Crown.

"Each allotment to be put up at public auction at a certain upset rate of quit rent and to be disposed of to the highest bidder: but it is engaged upon the part of Her Majesty's Government, that persons taking land upon these terms shall have the privilege of purchasing in freehold (if that tenure shall hereafter be offered by Her Majesty's Government), or of continuing to hold upon the original quit rent, if that condition be better liked.

"All arrangements with natives for the cession of lands, in cultivation, or substantially built upon, to be made only through an officer deputed by the Government of the Island; and no title will be valid, and no occupancy respected, unless the person claiming shall hold under an instrument granted by the Government of the Island, of which due registry must be made in the Government Office.

"It is distinctly to be understood, that all natives, in the actual occupancy of lands, in cultivation, or substantially built upon, will be constrained to establish their rights, to the satisfaction of the land officer, and to take out titles, and have the same duly registered.

"In order to accelerate the establishment, notice is hereby given, that a sale of town allotments, having a water frontage of yards, and running back yards, will take place at Macao on the instant, by which time, it is hoped, plans, exhibiting the water front of the town, will be prepared.

"Persons purchasing town lots will be entitled to purchase suburban or country lots of square acres each, and will be permitted, for the present, to choose their own sites, subject to the approval of the Government of the Island.

"No run of water to be diverted from its course without permission of the Government.

(Signed).   "CHARLES ELLIOT."

"Macao, 1st May, 1841."

[Hongkong Gazette, 1st and 15th May, 1841.]

APPENDIX II

Public Notice of 7 June 1841 and Terms of Sale on 14 June 1841

On the 7th June, 1841, a Notice under the hand of Sir CHARLES ELLIOT was advertised of the proposed sale of the annual quit rents of 100 lots of land with water frontage and of 100 town or suburban lots, as follows:-

PUBLIC NOTICE OF 7TH JUNE, 1841.

"Notice is hereby given, that a sale of the annual quit rent of 100 lots of land having water frontage will take place at Hongkong, on Saturday, the 12th instant, as also of 100 town or suburban lots. The dimensions of the respective lots will be specified and defined on the spot by the Commanding Officer of Engineers, to whom parties are referred for further particulars.

"The titles will be delivered on payment of the rent, and the minimum value of the buildings to be erected on the lots, and the period allowed for erection, will also be then declared.

(Signed),   CHARLES ELLIOT,
Chief Superintendent,

charged with the Government of Hongkong.

"Macao, 7th June, 1841."

The sale advertised for the 12th was postponed to the 14th June, 1841, when it had been found impossible to put up the number of lots (200) as advertised in the Government Advertisement of the 7th of that month, and only 50 lots having a sea frontage of 100 feet each, or nearly so, were offered for sale, and it will be observed, from the following copy of the terms of that sale, that not only was the frontage not defined, but the depth from the sea to the road (the present Queen's Road), was stated to necessarily vary considerably, and that the parties, (intending purchasers), would have the opportunity of observing the extent for themselves.

TERMS OF SALE ON 14TH JUNE, 1841

"1. Upon a careful examination of the ground, it has been found impossible to put up the number of lots named in the Government Advertisement of the 7th instant, and only 50 lots, having a sea frontage of 100 feet each, can at present be offered for sale. These lots will all be on the seaward side of the road. Lots on the land side of it, and hill and suburban lots in general, it will yet require some time to mark out.

"2. Each lot will have a sea frontage of 100 feet, nearly. The depth from the sea to the road will necessarily vary considerably. The actual extent of each lot as nearly as it has been possible to ascertain it will be declared on the ground. And parties will also have the opportunity of observing the extent for themselves.

"3. The biddings are to be for annual rate of quit rent, and shall be made in pounds sterling, the dollar in all payments to be computed at the rate of 4s. 4d. The upset price will be £10 for each lot, the biddings to advance by 10s.

"4. Each lot having been knocked down to the highest bidder, he will receive an acknowledgment that he is the purchaser of the lot; and this acknowledgment will be exchanged for a more formal title, as soon as the precise measurement and registration of the lots shall be completed.

"5. Upon delivery of the titles, the purchasers will be called on to pay the rent for the first year reckoning from the date of sale.

"6. They will also be required to erect upon each lot a building of the appraised value of $1,000 or to incur upon the land an outlay to that amount, within a period of six months from the date of sale. As security for the performance of this engagement a deposit of $500 shall be paid into the hands of the Treasurer to the Superintendents within one week from the day of sale, the deposit repayable as soon as an equal amount shall have been expended. Non-compliance with these terms will incur forfeiture of the deposit and allotment.

(Signed), J ROBERT MORRISON,
*"Acting Secretary and Treasurer to the
Superintendents of Trade."*

APPENDIX III

Extract from Land Commission Report 1886–87

The sales of Crown Land which have taken place since the year 1869, have been at a fixed annual rent with an upset price, the highest bidder above the upset price being declared the purchaser at the fixed annual rent.

ACREAGE OF HONGKONG.

The acreage of Hongkong has been estimated to be as follows:—

	Acres cultivated.	Acres uncultivated.	Total.
Hong Kong (exclusive of Victoria,)	406	16,796	17,202
Victoria	—	—	900
Kowloon	412	1,309	1,721
Stonecutters's Island	—	192	192
Totals	818	18,297	20,015

These figures, however, are only estimated in so far as they relate to the cultivated area, and the inquiries of the Commissioners would lead them to believe that the lands actually in possession of villages, squatters, and trespassers, &c. greatly exceed the estimate.

NUMBERS AND RENTALS OF LEASED LOTS AND THE HOUSES STANDING UPON THEM.

The following shows the number and description of leased lots with their rental as existing on the 25th December, 1886:—

					No.	Annual Rental.
Marine Lots,	(for	999	years	),	276	$62,143.69
Inland Lots,	("	999	"	),	947	71,019.63
Quarry Bay, Marine,	(for	999	years	),	1	2,534.44
Victoria Farm,	("	75	"	),	42	1,067.88
Rural Building,	("	75	"	),	43	3,013.01
Aberdeen, Marine,	("	999	"	),	5	579.16
Aberdeen Inland,	("	999	"	),	56	329.36
Apleehow, Marine,	("	999	"	),	19	142.26
Apleehow Inland,	("	999	"	),	19	186.84
Sowkewan Lots,	("	999	"	),	91	1,087.50
Stanley, Inland,	("	75	"	),	1	1.00
Kowloon, Marine,	("	999	"	),	15	10,748.85
Kowloon, Inland,	("	75	"	),	113	3,270.35
Kowloon, Farm,	("	999	"	),	9	240.37
Kowloon, Garden,	("	14	"	),	68	2,017.32
Hunghom, Inland,	("	75	"	),	143	1,139.00
Total					1,847	$159,520.66

The Commissioners are of opinion that it is desirable in the interests of the Colony that all the land granted upon lease (except for agricultural or pastoral purposes, or for garden lots), should be granted upon the same tenure. Before very long it will be necessary that something should be done in reference to the Leases for 75 years. The same difficulties will soon arise in dealing with there as arose with the 75 years Leases granted in the early days of the Colony, when the lot holders looked forward to the fact that the termination of their Leases was within a measurable distance; to remedy which the term was extended for a further period of 924 years. The lots become unmarketable, tenants will do nothing towards repairs, or in the improvements or sustenance of their dwellings; if they were habitable towards the expiration of the term that is as much as they would be. No one has bought land on a 75 years Lease only, with the idea that the Crown would enforce its right of re-entry at the end of 75 years and turn them out. Nor does it appear why there should be any distinction on one side of the harbour to the other: or on lands in the town or in the country. It may be urged that parties should be kept to the strict performance of their engagements with the Crown, and that where land has risen in value the landlord should be entitled to the unearned increment, at least proportionably with the tenant.

In modern days it has been strenuously urged that the landlord, even if a private individual, has no right to this unearned increment. In case the Crown insists upon its rights, however, the Crown will, at the expiration of 75 years, take not only the unearned increment, but the whole value of the improvements effected by the tenants.

The Crown in dealing with Crown Lands is not like some private persons selfishly seeking to drive a hard bargain at the expense of an individual, but to dispose of its lands in the best interests of the whole community.

The Crown, as the Commissioners have endeavoured to point out in another part of this Report, has the entire monopoly of all ungranted land, and in the ease of the settlers at Kowloon, and on the Hills, purchasers were and are, compelled either to accept the terms that are offered by the Crown, or to go without the land.

The Commissioners feel sure that the same reasons which decided Earl GREY to sanction the extension of the Town Lots from 75 to 999 years would apply equally to the extension of the Leases of all other lots from 75 to 999 years.

APPENDIX IV

Attorney General v Melhado Investment Ltd. [1983] HKLR 327

Attorney General	Appellant

AND

Melhado Investment Ltd.	Respondent

(Court of Appeal)
(Civil Appeal No. 79 of 1982)

Huggins, V.-P., Leonard, V.-P. & Fuad, J.A.

8th–9th, 13th March 1983.

Property law — New Territories land — Block Crown lease with schedule attached describing use of the land as it was at time lease granted-schedule descriptive only and not limiting as to the use which may be made of the land.

A New Territories landholder sublet its land to be used for the storage of steel girders. The Crown objected that such use was contrary to the terms of the Crown lease of which the landholder was the assignee. The landholder disagreed and commenced these proceedings seeking a declaration to the effect that the storage of the girders would not constitute a breach of the terms of the lease. The landholder succeeded at first instance and the Attorney General appealed on behalf of the Crown.

The land had been included in a Block Crown lease granted in 1905. In a schedule to the lease the use of each lot was described as it then was. There were descriptions such as "Padi", "Waste", "Grave", "Dry Cultivation" and "Broken Latrine".

It was argued on behalf of the Crown that the descriptions of use in the schedule to the Crown lease were more than merely descriptive. It was said that they limited the use which could lawfully be made of the land. It was also argued that there was an implied covenant in the lease against use of the land for any purpose other than that for which it was used at the time the Crown lease was granted. And it was argued that in any event there was a custom that there should be no change of use of land in the New Territories without the consent of the landlord. These restrictions, it was said, were additional to the express provision in the lease requiring a licence to build on the land.

Held:
1. The use of the land as listed in the schedule to the Crown lease was descriptive only. The purpose of the schedule was to identify the lands to which the lease related. If the schedule had been intended to be other than descriptive it would not have been necessary to include in the body of the lease restrictions on building without a licence. It would be absurd to construe the lease so as to compel a lessee to maintain a lot as a broken latrine for 75 years.
2. There was no implied covenant of the type contended for. Again, if such a term had been intended to be implied, it was unnecessary to express the general restriction on building. In any event the conditions necessary to be fulfilled before a covenant will be implied had not been met in this case.

3. There was no evidence to support a finding of a custom of the type contended for.

Appeal dismissed.

B. G. J. Barlow, Assistant Principal Crown Counsel & N. L. Strawbridge, Senior Crown Counsel for the Crown.
H. Litton, Q.C. & W. Poon instructed by Ho & Wong for the respondent.

The judgment of the Court of Appeal was delivered by Sir Alan Huggins, V.-P.

Cases cited in the judgment:-
1. Watford Construction Co. v. Secretary for the New Territories [1978] HKLR 410
2. B.P. Refinery (Westernport) Pty. v. President, Councillors and Ratepayers of the Shire of Hastings [1978] 52 ALJR 20
3. Directors etc. of the London and South Western Railway Co. v. Blackmore [1870] 4 HL 610

Sir Alan Huggins, V.-P.:-

The respondent took out an originating summons for the construction of a Block Crown lease relating to land in the New Territories. The issue concerned the use to which the lease permitted the land to be put.

All the lots listed in the originating summons are now held by the plaintiff respondent for the remainder of a term of 24 years less 3 days from 1st July 1973 pursuant to a Block Crown lease dated 24th January 1905. It is common ground that the lease has to be construed in the light of the circumstances existing at the time of its execution. In 1898 the Crown had concluded the Convention of Peking, under which the area which was to be known as the New Territories was leased to the Crown. It was agreed, inter alia, that the existing inhabitants of the New Territories would not be disappropriated, but their rights had to be fitted into the framework of the British legal system and this was to be done by the grant of Crown leases to those who were able to establish their claims to the satisfaction of a Land Tribunal. To this end a survey was carried out of the entire area and, to avoid the necessity for separate leases to each individual, the device was adopted of the Block Crown lease, which set out in a schedule the name of each "owner" in a particular district, details of his holding and the initial rent which he was required to pay. The lease contained a provision for review of the rent after ten years and also provided —

> "that in the event of any building being erected on any premises expressed to be demised as agricultural or garden ground the rent payable in respect of such premises shall be such sum as shall be specified in the licence for the erection of such building to be granted in manner hereinafter appearing;"

The need for a licence arose from a term that the lessees would not

> "convert any ground hereby expressed to be demised as agricultural or garden ground into use for building purposes other than for the proper occupation of the same ground as agricultural or garden ground without the previous Licence of His said Majesty, His Heirs, Successors or Assigns, signified in writing by the Governor of the said Colony of Hongkong, or other person duly authorized in that behalf".

The schedule contained a column for indicating "Description of Lot" and in this column were inserted descriptions such as "Padi", "Waste", "Grave" and "Dry cultivation". Another similar, Block Crown lease was before the judge, without objection, in which one lot was described as "Broken latrine".

The plaintiff, as the successor in title of one of the original grantees, entered into a sub-lease which purported to allow the sub-lessee to use the land "for storage of steel only" and the evidence showed that a large quantity of steel girders had been stacked upon the land. It was not in dispute that these were intended for construction purposes. The Crown objected and these proceedings resulted.

Mr. Justice Jackson-Lipkin granted the declarations sought, to the effect that the storage of these girders would not constitute a breach of the terms of the Block Crown lease, and the Attorney General appealed to this court. The judge appears to have thought that his decision was, to his regret, hampered in some way by the decision of this court in **Watford Construction Company v. Secretary for the New Territories** [1978] HKLR 410, although he observed that it would be improper of him to dissent from that decision. He did not indicate how he would have differed and we are unable to see how he was in any way hampered by that decision when it is properly understood. The case arose out of a claim for compensation following a resumption of land. The land was described in the schedule to the relevant (but similar) Block Crown lease in a manner which was accepted to be "agricultural". No licence to build had been given. The owner sought compensation on the basis that it had the right to build otherwise than for the proper occupation of the same ground as agricultural or garden ground, whilst the Crown contended that the assessment should be made on the basis that no buildings could lawfully be erected without a licence — for which an enormous premium would be charged. No other possible use of the land was in contemplation. The only conclusion reached which is germane to the present case was that the description of the land in the schedule was what it purported to be — merely a description — and was not to be construed as, of itself, limiting the use which could lawfully be made of the land: the limitation on use was imposed by the covenant against building without a licence. We see no reason to doubt the correctness of that decision and none has been suggested to us.

What may have caused difficulty is the ambiguity of the phrase "demised as agricultural or garden ground". As is apparent from **Watford Construction Company v. Secretary for the New Territories** [1978] HKLR 410 that could mean, on the one hand, that the land was demised on terms which prohibited its use for anything but agriculture or gardening, or, on the other, that it was land which was described as agricultural or garden ground.

In our view the contention on behalf of the Attorney General that the words in the schedule are something more than descriptive is completely untenable, even if we were not bound to follow the earlier decision on the point. The lease itself contains the words "that piece or parcel of ground ... set out and described in the schedule". The whole purpose of the schedule was to identify the lands and the parties to which the lease related, and then to particularize the terms and the rents which had been reserved by the body of the lease. If anything more were required to show conclusively that the descriptions in the schedule were not intended to constitute a limitation on the use of the lands during the terms, it is to be found in the fact that the body of the lease does contain a restriction on building without a licence: if the lessee of every plot expressed to be demised as "padi" was obliged by the schedule to maintain it as padi, the restriction on building would be unnecessary. The ultimate absurdity of the suggestion can be seen when one sees the contemporaneous and identical Block Crown lease, the schedule to which describes one lot as "Broken latrine". We decline to adopt a construction which would compel the lessee to maintain that lot not merely as a latrine but as a broken latrine for 75 years.

The second argument advanced on behalf of the Attorney General was that there was an implied covenant against use for any purpose other than that which apparently existed at the time of the letting, at least without the previous licence of the Crown. Again, if such a term is to be implied, it was unnecessary to express the general restriction on building. The conditions which have to be fulfilled before a covenant will be implied are succinctly stated in **B.P. Refinery (Westernport) Pty. Ltd. v. President, Councillors and Ratepayers of the Shire of Hastings** [1978] 52 ALJR 20, 26D:

> "... for a term to be implied, the following conditions (which may overlap) must be satisfied: (1) it must be reasonable and equitable; (2) it must be necessary to give business efficacy to the contract, so that no term will be implied if the contract is effective without it; (3) it must be so obvious that 'it goes without saying'; (4) it must be capable of clear expression; (5) it must not contradict any express term of the contract."

The suggested covenant certainly does not fulfil conditions (2) and (3).

The final submission for the appellant was that there was a custom that there should be no change of use of demised land in the New Territories without the consent of the landlord. It was argued that such a custom did exist under the Common Law in England in relation to agricultural land. If there was such a custom, it required (as do all customs) to be proved by evidence. We can find no jot or little of evidence to support a finding of such a custom here, nor was it ever suggested before Mr. Justice Jackson-Lipkin that there was such a custom. Indeed, the only evidence upon which reliance is now placed is the existence of the schedule itself. The most that could possibly be inferred from that is that the use of the land was as described in the schedule both at the date of the survey and at the date of the lease. That does not begin to establish a custom of the kind contended for. Yet again, if there was such a custom, was it necessary expressly to restrict building on the land?

The reality of the matter is that in 1905 no one ever imagined that land in the New Territories might be wanted otherwise than for cultivation or building; therefore the Crown did not think it necessary to cover such a possibility by express provision in the lease. The law is clear and was stated by the late Mr. Justice Pickering in **Watford Construction Company v. Secretary for the New Territories** [1978] HKLR at p.413 thus:

> "No doubt a demise simpliciter of land which happened at the time of the demise to be agricultural land would leave the lessee free to change the user and character of the land ... "

It will have been observed that we have throughout assumed that, where the restrictive covenant in the Block Crown lease refers to ground "hereby expressed to be demised as agricultural or garden ground" those words are appropriate to include ground demised as "padi" and "dry cultivation". The term "padi" is commonly used to describe not only the crop grown in a padi field but also the field itself. "Dry cultivation", it is true, is not strictly descriptive of land but of a use to which land may be put, but we think it would be unjustifiable to construe those words in the present context otherwise than as intended to describe the land by reference to its existing use.

We must further make it clear that no issue was raised before us whether the storage of the steel might be "use for building purposes" on the basis suggested in **Directors etc. of the London and South Western Railway Company v. Blackmore** [1870] 4 HL 610, 616/7 and that for that reason there was a breach of the restrictive covenant. We can readily conceive of circumstances in which storage of building materials would be so closely associated with the work of construction as to constitute a building purpose. This aspect of the matter was not canvassed in the affidavits.

Appeal dismissed.

W.S.C.

APPENDIX V

Winfat Enterprises (H.K.) Co. Ltd. v Attorney General [1984] HKLR 211

Winfat Enterprises (H.K.) Co. Ltd.	Appellant (Plaintiff)

AND

Attorney General	Respondent (Defendant)

(Court of Appeal)
(Civil Appeal No. 76 of 1983)

Roberts, C.J., Cons & Fuad, JJ.A.

10th–11th, 14th–17th November; 14th December 1983.

Administrative and constitutional law — colonial Governor — proclamations made by the Governor in 1899 with respect to property rights in the New Territories — do not have the force of law.

Administrative and constitutional law — colonial legislature — powers — the power of the Hong Kong legislature to make laws for the "peace, order, and good government" of the New Territories is not ambiguous or uncertain in extent — the words confer the widest law — making powers on the legislature — it is not permissible to look to the Convention of Peking, 1898 (L.H.K. App. IV, I1) to define the ambit of the power — New Territories Order-in-Council, 1898 (L.H.K. App. IV, J1).

Administrative and constitutional law — colonial legislature — powers — the statutory provisions governing land tenure and resumption in the New Territories are intra vires the Hong Kong legislature — Crown Lands Resumption Ordinance, Cap. 124; New Territories Ordinance, Cap. 97.

Administrative and constitutional law — colonial legislature — Royal Instructions — requirement that the Governor not assent to certain types of bills — non-compliance — legislation valid notwithstanding failure to comply — Hong Kong Royal Instructions, 1888, art. XXII(7) (now Hong Kong Royal Instructions, 1917, L.H.K. App. I, D1, art, XXVI(6); Colonial Laws Validity Act, 1865, c. 63, s. 4.

Administrative and constitutional law — treaties — breach of a treaty obligation of the Crown is not capable of redress at the instance of a subject in the domestic courts of Hong Kong.

Property law — Crown lands — New Territories — proclamations made by the Governor in 1899 with respect to property rights — do not have the force of law.

Property law — Crown lands — New Territories — all land in the New Territories having been vested in the Crown by statute, the Crown has the right to deal with such land as it sees fit, and accordingly may impose any condition in a Crown lease.

Property law — Crown lands — New Territories — the statutory provisions governing land tenure and resumption in the New Territories are intra vires the Hong Kong legislature — Crown Lands Resumption Ordinance, *Cap.* 124; New Territories Ordinance, *Cap.* 97.

Property law — Crown lands — recovery of possession — New Territories — the power of the Governor to order the resumption of New Territories land is not fettered by the provisions of the Convention of Peking, 1898 (L.H.K. App. IV, I1) — Crown Lands Resumption Ordinance, *Cap.* 124.

The plaintiff had purchased the residue of a Crown lease in the New Territories. The lease included a prohibition against building on the land without permission. The plaintiff sought but was denied permission to develop the land as high class housing. The plaintiff then sublet part of the land, with the permission of the District Officer, to be used for the parking of vehicles.

In 1981 the Governor ordered the resumption of part of the land pursuant to the Crown Lands Resumption Ordinance, *Cap.* 124. The land was required for a public purpose, temporary housing. Cash compensation in excess of $15 million was offered to the plaintiff on condition that the land be surrendered free of encumbrances. The plaintiff was unable to meet this condition because of the sublease it had granted. Therefore its only claim to compensation was under the Crown Lands Resumption Ordinance, by which the potential development value of the land was required to be discounted, such that the amount of compensation was likely to be significantly less than the value of the land on the open market.

The plaintiff commenced action seeking a series of declarations to enable it to escape the terms of the ordinance and related legislation. The plaintiff's action was dismissed at first instance (see [1983] HKLR 211) and this appeal was brought.

The plaintiff's argument was based on the "no-expropriation" clause of the Convention of Peking, 1898 (L.H.K. App. IV, I1) by which the New Territories were leased from China. It is there provided that if New Territories land is required for public purposes it shall be bought at a fair price. The plaintiff conceded that the terms of the convention are not in themselves enforceable as part of the domestic law of Hong Kong, but argued that the no-expropriation clause had been imported into the constitutional law of Hong Kong so as to take precedence over any ordinance inconsistent with its terms.

The plaintiff sought to establish the following propositions —

(1) that the no-expropriation clause of the Convention of Peking had been embodied in the law of Hong Kong by virtue of two proclamations made by the Governor at the time the New Territories were incorporated into Hong Kong. These proclamations contained assurances that the property rights of the inhabitants of the New Territories would be respected. It was argued by the plaintiff that these proclamations had the force of law as having been made in exercise of a residuary prerogative power of the Sovereign "sole", that is the Sovereign acting outside her Privy Council. The plaintiff contended that this power had been exercised by the Governor on the direction of the Queen;

(2) that the system of land tenure imposed on the New Territories as part of Hong Kong was in breach of the Convention of Peking, 1898. In particular some of the terms imposed in Crown leases infringed the convention, and so did those provisions of the Crown Lands Resumption Ordinance which provide for compensation at less than the full market value of land compulsorily acquired;

(3) that the power of the Governor to make laws for the "peace, order, and good government" of the New Territories as part of the Colony (New Territories Order-in-Council, L.H.K. vol. 24, App. IV, p.J1) did not authorise legislation in breach of the Convention of Peking, 1898. This submission was put upon two grounds:

(a) first, on a reading of the Order-in-Council as a whole, in particular the preamble, it could be seen that the purpose was to implement the convention. Therefore, argued the plaintiff, the Governor's power to make laws must necessarily be restricted to laws which do not offend against the convention;

(b) secondly, the plaintiff contended that the phrase "peace, order, and good government" is ambiguous, uncertain or unclear, and that therefore the court should construe it in accordance with the terms of the convention;

(4) that the legislation was ultra vires for failure to comply with the Royal Instructions to the Governor of Hong Kong. Article XXII(7) of the Royal Instructions, 1888, which was in force at the relevant time (now Royal Instructions, 1917, L.H.K. App. I, D1, art. XXVI(6)) provided that the Governor should not assent to any ordinance inconsistent with a treaty obligation of the Crown, but should reserve such ordinance pending signification of the Royal pleasure. This had not been done in the case of the legislation concerned here, and therefore, argued the plaintiff, the legislation was ultra vires insofar as it was in breach of the Convention of Peking;

(5) that even if the legislation concerned were valid, it had not authorised the Governor of the day to impose restrictions as to the use of New Territories land. This being so, the plaintiff was entitled to develop the land as it pleased, without seeking a modification of the lease, and on resumption of the land it was consequently entitled to full market value compensation under the Crown Lands Resumption Ordinance.

All of the above points were disputed by the defendant. It was submitted that even if the legislation were defective by reason of the Governor having given his assent when he should have reserved for the Royal pleasure, such defect would in any event have been cured by the exercise of the Crown's power of non-disallowance. The trial judge had accepted this argument and found that the ordinances complained of were ratified by non-disallowance amounting in law to express authorisation. The defendant argued that for this and other reasons the legislation was valid and further that it empowered the government to act as it had done in this case.

Held:

1. The Governor's proclamations promising that the property rights of the inhabitants of the New Territories would be respected do not have the force of law —

   (a) the wording of the proclamations is inappropriate to a legislative instrument. It is clear that they were meant only to give the inhabitants of the New Territories due warning of the government's intentions;

   (b) in any event, assuming that the Queen retains a prerogative power to legislate by herself, outside her Privy Council, as contended by the plaintiff, she did not purport to exercise such a power in the case of these proclamations. And assuming that it would be open to the Queen to authorise the Governor to exercise such a residuary prerogative power on her behalf, no such authorisation had in fact been made.

2. It was not necessary for the court to decide whether the Convention of Peking had been breached in the manner contended by the plaintiff, because even if it had, such breaches would not be capable of redress at the instance of a subject in the domestic courts of Hong Kong. The right to enforce a treaty is only with the high contracting parties.

3. The power to make laws for the "peace, order, and good government" of the New Territories is wide enough to support the legislation complained of in this case —

(a) the power is not restricted by the reference to the Convention of Peking in the preamble to the Order-in-Council. The preamble does no more than recite, by reference to the convention, the source of jurisdiction;

(b) there is abundant authority that the words "peace, order, and good government" confer the widest law-making powers. The words are not ambiguous or uncertain in extent and therefore it is not permissible to look to the Convention of Peking to define their ambit.

4. Even if the Governor breached the Royal Instructions in assenting to the ordinances concerned, the legislation is nevertheless valid. Section 4 of the Colonial Laws Validity Act, 1865 provides that no colonial law shall be void or inoperative by reason only of the failure of a Governor to comply with instructions. The plaintiff's argument that s. 4 applies only to specific instructions and not the general directions contained in the Royal Instructions, was not correct. The section clearly applies to both.

5. The restrictions imposed in the Crown lease were valid. All land in the New Territories had been vested in the Crown by statute. This had the effect of conferring on the Governor power to deal as he thought fit with New Territories land. Clear words would be necessary to take away this unrestricted power, and such words could not be found. Therefore the Governor has authority to insert in a grant of Crown land any term which he thinks appropriate to the case.

Obiter dictum:

The trial judge, commenting on the Privy Council's decision in *Attorney General v. Ng Yuen-shiu* [1983] 2 WLR 735, and considering the proclamations made by the Governor at the time the New Territories were incorporated into Hong Kong, had suggested that at the time occupiers of land in the New Territories might have been entitled to call upon the government to redeem the promises embodied in the proclamations. In *Ng's* case it was held that a public promise as to the manner in which a discretionary power would be exercised was binding on the government even in the absence of a legal duty to act as promised. The trial judge had not, however, suggested that it was open to the plaintiff to rely on that decision now, and in any event their Lordships could not see how the plaintiff could do so. The legislation considered by the Privy Council was neutral as to how the discretion should be exercised but here the action complained of was specifically authorised by statute. If there was a promise here it could hardly be enforced in the face of specific legislation to the contrary.

Dubitante:

It was not necessary for the court here to pronounce a view on the defendant's argument that the ordinances complained of had in any event been ratified by non-disallowance. However, their Lordships would not like it to be thought that they agreed with this argument since there must be grave objections in principle to attributing to the Crown, in its prerogative guise, power to give force to an otherwise invalid law, by the mere act of deciding not to disallow it.

Appeal dismissed.

D. G. Widdicombe, Q.C. & A. Neoh instructed by Raymond Tang & Co. for the appellant/plaintiff.

J. C. Griffiths, Q.C. & R. A. Oshorne, Senior Crown Counsel for the Crown.

The judgment of the Court of Appeal was delivered by Roberts, C.J.

Cases cited in the judgment: —
1. Campbell v. Hall (1774) 98 ER 1045
2. Vajesingji Joravarsingji & ors. v. Secretary of State of India [1924] LR 51 IA 357
3. Chau Kwai-chiu & anor. v. Wong Shin (The Shell case) 9 CILC 298 (30 June 1900)
4. Secretary of State in the Council of India v. Kamachee Boye Sahaba (1859) 7 Moo Ind App 476
5. Attorney General v. Ng Yuen-shiu [1983] 2 WLR 735
6. Ibralebbe v. R. [1964] AC 900
7. Riel v. R. [1885] AC 675
8. Chenard & Co. v. Joachim Arissol [1949] AC 127
9. Saloman v. The Commissioners of Customs and Excise [1966] 3 All ER 871
10. Rediffusion Hong Kong Ltd. v. A.G. and anor. [1970] HKLR 231
11. Poon Wai-ting v. A.G. [1925] HKLR 22
12. Watford Construction Co. v. Secretary for the New Territories [1978] HKLR 410

APPENDIX VI

Hang Wah Chong Investment Co. Ltd. v Attorney General [1981] HKLR 336

Hang Wah Chong Investment Co. Ltd.	Appellants

AND

Attorney General	Respondent

———

(Privy Council)
(Privy Council Appeal No. 16 of 1980)

———

Lord Wilberforce, Lord Edmund-Davies, Lord Keith of Kinkel, Lord Scarman & Sir John Megaw

23rd March 1981.

Administrative law — limitation on building height and type — whether Director of Public Works empowered to demand premium to amend those limitations.

Local Government — limitations on height and type of building permitted — Director of Public Works entitled to demand a premium as a condition of granting a development concession.

Contracts — Conditions of Sale — Crown Land — meaning of conditions.

In 1931, a parcel of land was sold by the Crown at auction. Among the Conditions of Sale were limitations on buildings to be erected on the land. A further condition provided for the grant of a Crown lease but none was in fact ever executed. In 1953, the appellants' predecessors in title wished to purchase the land from the purchaser. They wanted to erect "Apartment Buildings" of a height no greater than that of an adjacent set of apartments. Permission was sought from the Director of Public Works, who agreed. The land was purchased and the apartment building erected. The building was called Grand Court.

In 1973, the appellants acquired the site and wished to demolish Grand Court and redevelop the site. The Director of Public Works advised that he was only prepared to grant permission to redevelop the site on the payment of a premium. The appellants applied to the High Court seeking a declaration that no consent was needed from the Director of Public Works and hence no premium was due. Yang, J. dismissed the application and this was confirmed by the Court of Appeal. The appellants appealed to the Privy Council.

For the appellants, a number of alternative submissions were made. First, it was argued that under the terms of the Conditions of Sale, no permission was necessary to erect Grand Court.

Secondly, they argued that permission was never in fact sought or granted. Hence, the appellant submitted, the building was erected and occupied for 20 years without protest from the responsible authorities and therefore with their implied acquiescence, and that in consequence they could not now object to the redevelopment of the land.

The appellants' third argument was that the permission given in 1953 should be regarded as consenting to the erection of flats as a class of unlimited height.

Next, they argued that in offering to grant approval for the redevelopment upon payment of a premium, the Director of Public Works was raising revenue rather than relating his approval to matters relevant to the contract and particularly to his control of the type of buildings to be erected. His discretion under the terms of the Conditions of Sale was limited to these latter matters only.

Finally, they argued that in demanding a premium, the Director of Public Works, who was also the Building Authority and hence acting in the public domain, was imposing an unsupportable condition on his compliance with the appellants' request amounting to an abuse of power.

Held:
The appeal would be dismissed for the following reasons: —
1. Under the terms of the Conditions of Sale, permission was needed to erect Grand Court and this permission was sought and given.
2. The permission granted in 1953 included a restriction on height.
3. (Applying *Viscount Tredegar v. Harwood* [1929] A.C. 72) The appellants' submission that any discretion as to the granting of approval must be limited to matters relevant to the contract and particularly to the Directors' control over the type of buildings was "piling implication upon implication" which was not "a legitimate mode of onstruing a very simple and plain condition".
4. The Director of Public Works plays many roles acting not only as the Building Authority but also as Government Land Agent. He was entitled to act and was acting in this latter role when offering to grant approval subject to a premium. There is no difference in this connection between a lease granted by a public body and a private lease.

Appeal dismissed.

M. Littman, Q.C., M. Miller, Q.C., I. Jakes & P. Fung instructed by Linklakers & Paine for the appellants.
G. Godfrey, Q.C. & B. Barlow, Senior Crown Counsel instructed by McFarlanes for the respondent.

The judgment of the Privy Council was delivered by Lord Edmund-Davies.

Case cited in the judgment: —
1. Viscount Tredegar v. Harwood. [1928] Ch. 59; [1929] A.C. 72.

Lord Edmund-Davies: —

This appeal is from an order of the Court of Appeal of Hong Kong dismissing the appeal of Hang Wah Chong Investment Company Limited ("the appellants") from a decision of Yang, J. in the High Court of the Supreme Court whereby he dismissed the appellants' originating summons seeking declarations concerning their proposed development of a piece of land off Kadoorie Avenue, Kowloon. This was part of a lot sold by the Crown at an auction in 1931 to the Hong Kong Engineering and Construction Company Limited ("Hong Kong Engineering"), and the Conditions of Sale provided for the grant of a Crown lease but none was in fact ever executed.

The following Special Conditions of Sale are of great importance and must be quoted in full:

"6. Save as provided herein the Purchaser shall not erect on the Lot any buildings other than detached or semi-detached residential premises of European type or such other buildings of European type as the Director of Public Works may approve of with garages and all proper outbuildings thereto. Provided that, subject to the provisions of Special Conditions 7 and 8, the Purchaser shall be at liberty to erect flats, with or without shops or self-contained garages on the ground floor, fronting to Argyle Street and Waterloo Road on that part of the Lot hatched red on the sale plan and having a frontage of approximately 350 feet to Argyle Street and approximately 125 feet to Waterloo Road.

Save as herein provided no buildings erected on the Lot shall be used otherwise than as a private dwelling-house without the written consent of the Governor.

7. The design of the exterior elevations plans height and disposition of any buildings to be erected on the Lot shall be subject to the special approval of the Director of Public Works and no building shall be erected on the Lot save in accordance with such approval.

. . .

21. Where under these conditions the consent or approval of the Governor or of the Director of Public Works is required the grant or with-holding of such consent shall be in the absolute discretion of the person named."

In 1953, the appellants' predecessors in title were minded to purchase from Hong Kong Engineering a vacant portion of the lot they had acquired in 1931 for the purpose of erecting a block of flats, and on December 9, 1953, their solicitor sent a letter in the following terms to the Director of Public Works:

". . . My client desires to purchase these Lots for the purpose of erecting Apartment Buildings of a height levelling to the roof of the Hillview Apartments....

"The said Lots are on the same level as the said Hillview Apartments but there is a clause in the Conditions of Sale ... which says [The wording of Special Condition 7 was then quoted in full].

"Before my client purchases the said Lots he desires to know whether your Department have any objection to the proposed height of the buildings to be erected on the said Lots . . . ."

The Director of Public Works is by definition also the Building Authority, and on December 31 a member of his staff replied:

". . . I am instructed to inform you that the Director of Public Works is prepared to approve the erection of buildings on the sites . . . at a level not higher than the roof level of Hillview Apartments."

It should be pointed out that the proposed block of flats would not be, in the words of Special Condition 6, "fronting to Argyle Street and Waterloo Road".

On May 26, 1954, the Building Authority sent to the appellants' predecessors in title a formal notice,

"To permit the buildings to be erected to the height shown on the submitted plans."

Thereafter the land was purchased, there was a further approval of plans as required by section 128 of the Buildings Ordinance, a 7-storey block of flats ('Grand Court') was built, and on September 23, 1955, the Building Authority issued a permit "to occupy and use for domestic purposes" the completed building, and Grand Court has been used as an apartment block ever since.

In March 1973 the site was assigned to the appellants, who were minded to demolish Grand Court and replace it by four new blocks of flats, three of them being 17 storeys high and the fourth 14 storeys. As in 1972 the Registrar General had circulated "To All Solicitors" a memorandum reminding them that a premium was exacted by the Government "for a modification of a Crown lease", the appellants' real estate representative wrote to the Crown Land and Survey Office on June 20, 1973, indicating the nature of the appellants' project and adding:

> "From the Conditions of Sale . . . it would appear that no modification premium will be payable in the event of redevelopment of the above lot. However, for the avoidance of doubt . . . we . . . request you to confirm if our understanding is correct. If, on the other hand, you are of the view that modification of the Conditions of Sale is required, please treat this letter and the enclosed plan as an application of our clients for the purpose of the said circular memorandum."

The material parts of the reply sent on August 23, 1973, by the Director of Lands and Survey was in the following terms:

> ". . . I am prepared to recommend a modification...of the Conditions of Sale...subject to the acceptance of the following provisional basic term:-
>
> (i)   Private residential use only.
>   . . .
> (iii)   No part of any building to exceed 170' Colony Principal Datum.
>   . . .
> (viii)   Payment of a premium."

A protracted correspondence then ensued, the appellants' representative contending on October 30, 1973, that no modification was called for and that accordingly no premium was exigible, the Chief Estate Surveyor indicating on October 28, 1974, that a reduced premium of $3,077,000.00 was chargeable, conditional upon the appellants' acceptance within one month. Timeous acceptance not being forthcoming, the premium thereafter reverted to $3,216,000.00.

In this state of affairs, on August 25, 1976, the appellants submitted to the Building Authority plans of the proposed redevelopment, and on October 26 a formal notice of approval was issued, but "subject to Section 14(2) of Buildings Ordinance", which provides that:

> "Neither the approval of any plans nor the consent to the commencement of any building works or street works shall be deemed . . . to act as a waiver of any term in any lease or licence."

The Building Authority also pointed out that:

> "A modification of the lease Conditions is required in order to permit the development you propose and you should therefore advise your client to apply for such a modification before proceeding further."

On the foregoing facts the primary issue relates to what happened in 1953, and turns on the construction of the Special Conditions of Sale already cited in this judgment. On the threshold is the question whether the appellants' predecessor in title had needed approval to erect the 7-storey Grand Court. For the appellant the contention is that the building came within the words "detached or semi-detached residential premises of European type" in Special Condition 6, and that the approval of the Director of Public Works under that Condition was, therefore, not necessary and was in fact never sought or granted. For the respondent, on the other hand, it is contended that a block of flats is not "a detached or semi-detached" dwelling, but that it comes within the following words, " . . . such other buildings of European type as the Director of Public Works may approve of with garages and all proper outbuildings thereto", and that this view is supported by the presence of the immediately succeeding provision in Special Condition 6 that "the Purchaser shall be at liberty to erect flats" on a site *other than* what for brevity may be called the Grand Court site.

These conflicting views have now been presented at length before three courts and were carefully and expansively considered by the Court of Appeal. No useful purpose would be served by traversing yet again what has become familiar ground, and it should suffice to say that in the unanimous opinion of their Lordships the submission of the respondent is clearly correct. In the result, they hold that in 1953 the approval of the Director of Works was required under Special Condition 6, just as his special approval was required in relation to the matters specified in Special Condition 7.

The Director's approval thus being required, was it ever granted? For the appellant it is submitted that it was never even sought, that Grand Court was nevertheless erected and occupied for over 20 years without protest from the responsible authorities and therefore with their implied acquiescence, and that in consequence they cannot now object to the proposed extensive redevelopment of the Grant Court site. It is common ground that the special approval required under Special Condition 7 was both sought and granted, but it is objected that the 1953–55 correspondence makes no express mention of Special Condition 6. That is true, but it in no way concludes the matter. For as the Director's approval was required, even without invoking any presumption of regularity it requires only slight evidence to lead to the conclusion that, the development having in fact taken place, the necessary approval had in fact been obtained. In this context, it is noteworthy that by their letter of December 9, 1953, the appellants had informed the Director not simply of the height of the proposed building but also that it was an "Apartment Building", a term which it is unchallenged clearly meant a block of flats. The Building Authority approval signified on December 31 therefore related not only to a building "with roofs at a level not higher than the roof level of Hillview Apartments" but to an "Apartment Building". Their Lordships are thus led to the conclusion that the Director's approval was obtained both under Special Condition 6 and under Special Condition 7.

But was such approval given in relation to the erection of an apartment building unrestricted as to height, or one not exceeding 7 storeys in height, or (as the appellants contend) has the Director's approval given in December 1953 to be regarded as consenting to the construction on the Grand Court site of flats *as a class* and of unlimited height? If the last of these is the right view to adopt, it follows that, provided only that plans are submitted and special approval obtained under Special Condition 7, the appellants are free to proceed with their extensive redevelopment and there can be no question of any premium being exigible. But in their Lordships' opinion it is a mistake to sever Special Conditions 6 and 7, just as it is a mistake to regard Condition 7 as relating solely to height. And their Lordships respectfully adopt the observations of Huggins, J.A., who said in the Court of Appeal:

> "I do not think it follows from the fact that Special Condition 7 refers expressly to the height of buildings for which special approval is required that a consent under Special Condition 6 may not also include a limitation as to height".

It accordingly appears that the proper construction of the appellants' solicitors' letter of December 9, 1953, is that they were there at least impliedly seeking the Director's approval under both Special Conditions and that the approval granted on December 31 was in truth restricted to the erection on the site of a block of flats not exceeding 7 storeys in height.

It follows from the foregoing that the extensive redevelopment now contemplated by the appellants cannot proceed without the consent of the Director of Public Works, and that, by virtue of Special Condition 21, the grant or withholding of that consent is in his absolute discretion. Even so, as he indicated on October 26, 1976, approval of the building plans (albeit "subject to Section 14(2) of Buildings Ordinance"), can payment of a premium of *any* amount be exacted as the condition of granting final permission to proceed? As the hearing of the appeal progressed, this proved the most troublesome of all the points raised. The appellants submitted that, were some modification of the terms of a lease involved, a landlord could legitimately extort a premium. But no lease was ever granted and, the appeal turning on the contract of sale and the necessity of obtaining thereunder merely the Director's *approval* and no modification of a lease, it was submitted that no premiums may be demanded. In their Lordships' opinion, however, this question cannot so simply be answered. It is necessary to consider carefully the terms of the contract of sale.

The appellants' next submission was that any discretion as to the granting of approval under Special Condition 6 possessed by the Director must relate to matters relevant to the contract and particularly to his control over the *type* of buildings, whereas in the present case the demand for a premium is wholly unconnected with any such consideration. The argument presented in the appellants' printed Case was that, ". . . the Director is not entitled to take into account matters which are wholly extraneous to the purpose of Conditions 6 and 7, such as the raising of revenue (any more than he could do so in the exercise of any of his other functions under the Conditions) and that if he does so and such a matter is the sole reason for the withholding of approval, the Appellants are entitled to act as if his approval had been granted". This submission is in substance similar to that upheld by the Court of Appeal in **Viscount Tredegar v. Harwood**[1] [1928] Ch. 59, but rejected by the House of Lords [1929] A.C. 72. There Lord Shaw of Dunfermline rejected the Court of Appeal's implication of a new clause in a lease to the effect that the lessor's consent to insurance of the leased property with any responsible insurance company was not to be withheld unreasonably, and added (at page 80):

> "The Court [of Appeal] then proceeds to attach to these terms and to this contract . . . that the lessor must furnish a justification for his refusal, and further that such a justification must be something incidental to the individual contract itself and also to the financial standing or responsibility of the alternative insurance company. I am humbly of opinion that this process of piling implication upon implication is not a legitimate mode of construing a very simple and plain condition. It is clogged neither by the one implication nor the other."

In the same way and for a like reason, their Lordships reject the objection taken in the present appeal that a premium is not exigible because it is "wholly extraneous to the purpose of Conditions 6 and 7".

Somewhat more formidable than the foregoing is the point (scarcely hinted at in the appellants' printed Case, but nevertheless spaciously developed by their learned counsel) relating to the role assigned to the Director of Public Works under the contract and particularly in relation to Special Conditions 6 and 7. It has already been observed that he is by definition also the Building Authority, and he is charged with many duties falling within the public domain, in relation to which it might well amount to an abuse of power were he to demand a premium as a condition precedent to acceding to a suppliant's request. Was the Director, ask the appellants, not operating in the public domain when saddling his approval of the appellants' building plans in 1976 with a demand for an extremely high premium which bore no apparent relation to the terms of the appellants' application? And, in consequence, was he not therefore imposing an insupportable condition on his compliance amounting to an abuse of power?

It has to be observed in the first place that it is common ground that the Conditions of Sale operate in lieu of the terms of the contemplated Crown lease which was never granted. Secondly, no difference relevant to the present appeal can be drawn between a lease granted by a public body, or indeed the Crown, and a private lease (*Wade*, 'Administrative Law,' 4th Edn. p.644). Thirdly, the view expressed by Huggins, J.A. in the Supreme Court that "The Director of Public Works has many responsibilities besides those imposed by the Buildings Ordinance" appears well established, one of those responsibilities being that of acting as the Crown's land agent. And appellants' counsel did not challenge the conclusion of Huggins, J.A. that " . . . the Director of Public Works can bind himself in his capacity as the Building Authority without binding himself in his capacity as land agent and vice versa".

The various Conditions of Sale well illustrate the wide range of roles played by the Director in exercising his discretion. As regards some of the Conditions, the Director's role may, almost certainly, be that of protector of the public interest. The vital question is whether for the purposes of Special Conditions 6 and 7 he can properly be regarded as being entitled to act in his capacity of land agent for the Crown. It is not open to serious doubt that those Conditions relate directly to the landlord's interests, economic and otherwise, and their Lordships conclude that the Director was entitled to act, and did act, in that role when granting his qualified approval to the appellants' plans in 1976.

On that view, can it properly be said that it is for the respondent to establish the reasonableness of the demand for a premium? In the light of **Viscount Tredegar v. Harwood**[1] [1928] Ch. 59 (ante), their Lordships are of the opinion that the question requires a negative answer. But they must not thereby be taken as holding that the requirement was capriciously advanced (and, indeed, appellants' counsel expressly disclaimed any such suggestion) or that, were it incumbent upon the respondent to justify the requirement, he would be unable to adduce good reasons for demanding a premium. It is sufficient, for present purposes, simply to say that, the appellants seeking a concession from their landlords in relation to the development of land leased, the landlords were entitled to make the granting of that concession conditional upon the payment of a premium.

It follows that in their Lordships' opinion the unanimous decision of the Court of Appeal to uphold Yang, J's dismissal of the appellants' originating summons should in its turn be upheld. They will therefore humbly advise Her Majesty The Queen that the appeal should be dismissed. The appellants must pay the respondent's costs of the appeal.

Appeal dismissed.

APPENDIX VII

Secan Ltd. v Attorney General [1995] 2 HKLR 523

Secan Limited	Plaintiff (Respondent)
AND	
Attorney General of Hong Kong	Defendant (Appellant)

(Court of Appeal)
(Civil Appeal No. 120 of 1995)

———

Litton, V–P., Bokhary and Liu, JJ.A.

13th–15th June 1995.

Administrative law—environment—noise—agreement made between the Developer and Crown agents to implement "such ameliorative measures as deemed necessary by the Director of Environmental Protection"—whether the Director of Environmental Protection could insist on developer to build a noise barrier—approach in construing Special Condition in the agreement—whether the Director's powers to require taking of ameliorative measures were "spent".

In 1988, the plaintiff, a developer, entered into an agreement with Government to carry out substantial redevelopment at Ap Lei Chau which included a residential areas called "South Horizons". The parties agreed certain Special Conditions including Clause 12(a) which provided that the developer *"...shall implement such ameliorative measures as deemed necessary by the Director of Environmental Protection"*. The development was shown as having residential blocks alongside a road leading towards proposed industrial areas.

In March 1988, the plaintiff was informed by the Environmental Protection Department about the environmental problems affecting the site. In July 1988, the plaintiff submitted an "environmental issues report" with certain proposals to deal with the problem but the proposal including weather-stripping the windows and double-glazing were not acceptable to Environmental Protection Department. In March 1989, the plaintiff was told to build a louvre tunnel to shield four residential blocks from the traffic noise. After meetings between various Government Departments and plaintiff, the proposal to build a louvre tunnel was abandoned but in November 1992, the plaintiff was required to build a large noise barrier. The blocks of flats were constructed and eventually, the plaintiff decided to insulate these flats instead of building louvre tunnel or noise barrier. The Government insisted the plaintiff build a noise barrier and said that otherwise permission to assign the flats would be refused. The plaintiff sought a declaration that it was not bound to construct the barrier. On 20th March 1995, Sears, J. granted a declaration saying that it was not bound to construct the barrier to the plaintiff.

The defendant appealed.

Held:

1. (per Litton, V.-P.) The agreement was a commercial agreement which intended to give the Government a very large measure of control over the development proposal. In construing the agreement, a court should not be too astute or subtle in finding defects and must give effect to what the parties by their agreement have clearly intended. In the present case, since the proposal submitted by the respondent was not accepted by the Director of Buildings and Lands, the respondent was bound to implement such ameliorative measures as were deemed necessary by the Director of Environmental Protection.

2. In construing Clause 12(a), it was not legitimate to "pile implication upon implication", (*Hang Wah Cheong Investment Co. Ltd. v. Attorney General of Hong Kong* [1981] 1 WLR 1141 applied).

3. Clause 12(a) empowered the Director of Environmental Protection to require ameliorative measures to be implemented but he was bound to act in good faith, exercise judgment and not act capriciously.

4. The power of Director was not "spent" at the time he required the noise barrier in about November 1992 since, when the proposal was eventually rejected, it was up to the respondent to come up with another proposal acceptable to the Director.

5. (per Liu, J.A.) There was no ambiguity in Clause 12(a). Accordingly, in construing Clause 12(a), it was not open to the parties to invite the judge to put himself in thought in the same factual matrix as that in which the parties found themselves at the time of the grant (*Reardon Smith Line v. Hansen-Tangen* [1976] 1 WLR 989 applied).

Appeal allowed.

P. Graham, instructed by Crown Solicitor, for the appellant.
N. Kat, instructed by Baker & Mckenzie, for the respondent.

Cases cited in the judgment:

Fawcett Properties Ltd. v. Buckingham County Council [1961] AC 636
Hall & Co. Ltd. v. Shoreham-by-Sea Urban District Council [1964] 1 WLR 240, [1964] 1 All ER 1, 62 LGR 206
Hang Wah Cheong Investment Co. Ltd. v. Attorney General of Hong Kong [1981] 1 WLR 1141
Pyx Granite Co. Ltd. v. Ministry of Housing and Local Government [1958] 1 QB 544, [1958] 2 WLR 371, [1958] 1 All ER 625, [1960] AC 260, [1959] 3 WLR 346, [1959] 3 All ER 1
Reardon Smith Line Ltd. v. Hansen-Tangen (t/a H.E. Hansen-Tangen) [1976] 1 WLR 989, [1976] 3 All ER 570, [1976] 2 Lloyd's Rep 621
Viscount Tredegar v. Harwood [1929] AC 72, [1928] Ch 59

APPENDIX VIII

Humphrey's Estate (Queens Gardens) Ltd. v Attorney General and Another [1986] HKLR 669

Humphrey's Estate (Queen's Gradens) Ltd.   Plaintiff
(Respondent)

AND

Attorney General and Another   Defendants
(Appellants)

———

(Court of Appeal)
(Civil Appeal No. 92 of 1985)

———

Li, V.-P., Yang and Fuad, JJ.A.

7th–10th, 13th–15th and 31st January 1986.

Contract — negotiations for grant of lease "subject to contract" and with no intention to create legal relations — equity to preclude a party from relying on such protective terms.

Land law — licence to occupy premises — whether party estopped from giving notice of termination.

The dispute out of which this appeal arose concerned certain Conditions for Exchange, negotiated over a long period of time but never formally executed, regarding the redevelopment of a site at Queen's Gardens (Q.G.). The parties to the negotiations, which commenced in 1979, were the parent company of the plaintiff (H.K.L.) and the Crown (H.K.G.). In April 1980 the Principal Government Land Agent wrote to H.K.L. outlining provisional basic terms for an agreement, stressing that at that stage there was no intention to create any legal obligation. In January 1981 by a letter headed "without prejudice" H.K.G. wrote to H.K.L. stating that "subject to contract" H.K.G. agreed in principle to grant the Q.G. site on specified terms and conditions. H.K.L. replied immediately, also "without prejudice", confirming that the basic terms were acceptable subject to the resolution of certain matters. On 1st June 1981 H.K.G. sent H.K.L. a copy of the draft Conditions of Exchange in respect of the transaction, again on the basis that there was no intention to create any legal obligation on the part of H.K.G. Essentially, it was agreed that the Q.G. site would be permitted to be redeveloped, together with any adjoining private land in H.K.L.'s ownership, on payment of a premium by H.K.L. This was to be satisfied partly in cash and partly by the assignment to H.K.G. of a number of flats in another of H.K.L.'s developments (Tregunter). On 29th June 1981 the first Tregunter flat was handed over to H.K.G. and the other flats were assigned between that date and 11th August 1981.

H.K.G.'s occupation of the Tregunter flats was on the terms of a draft licence which entitled H.K.L. to terminate the licence and resume possession should the proposed grant of a lease of Q.G. not be made. In November 1981 H.K.L. made the first payment on account of the premium for Q.G. and H.K.G. issued a licence for H.K.L. to enter the site and demolish the existing buildings. The licence expressly stated that it was not to be construed as having committed H.K.G. to the permanent grant of the licensed area.

In February 1982 H.K.G. sent H.K.L. a draft of the proposed Conditions of Exchange but no consensus was reached and correspondence and discussions continued. In August 1982 the final payment of the premium was made. By early 1983 H.K.L. was in serious financial difficulties but continued to seek agreement with H.K.G. over the Conditions of Exchange. In 1984, however, H.K.L. decided not to proceed with the acquisition of Q.G. on the basis that there was no legally binding contract between the parties. H.K.L. requested repayment of all sums paid on account of the premium and gave notice to terminate H.K.G.'s licence to occupy the Tregunter flats within 28 days.

In an action by H.K.L. to recover the sum of the premium together with possession of the Tregunter flats H.K.G. argued that an equity had arisen out of the words and conduct of H.K.L. in such a way that the "subject to contract" formula and the disavowal of an intention to enter into legal relationships became irrelevant. H.K.G. relied in particular on the handing over of the flats in Tregunter as an indication that thereafter neither party could withdraw. It was further argued that H.K.L. was estopped from determining the licence in respect of Tregunter because, by its conduct in not demanding possession of the Tregunter flats until 1984, H.K.L. had encouraged H.K.G. to act to its detriment with an expectation that H.K.L. would carry out its part of the bargain.

At first instance the judge held for the plaintiff, directing H.K.G. to repay the premium to H.K.L. and granting H.K.L. declarations that H.K.G.'s occupation of the Tregunter flats was as licensee only, that the licence had been determined and H.K.L. was entitled to possession of the flats. H.K.G. appealed.

Held:
1. The equity relied upon for the main part of H.K.G.'s case and promissory estoppel have their differences. The distinction to be addressed is not so much any difference there might be between the two doctrines but rather the nature of the "representation" relied upon. Where a representation is made by words (which may or may not be contained in a letter or other document) the principal issue before the court will be the true construction of the representation in the light of the surrounding circumstances, which is strictly a matter of law. But where words, conduct (and acquiescence) are in issue it is doubtful if the same degree of unambiguity can be insisted upon and it will be a question of mixed law and fact.

2. Great importance must be attached to the "subject to contract" principle. By the use of this reservation the parties have expressly stipulated that the execution of a further contract is a condition of the bargain they have reached, and there will be no enforceable contract while that condition remains unfulfilled. The court will not recognise a contract to make a contract. (Per Fuad, J.A.) Provided parties to an agreement in principle are aware of the significance of the "subject to contract" doctrine in property deals each must realise that either party might withdraw, even without good cause, and certainly if the "buyer" gets into financial difficulties before the transaction can be finalised. To "expect" otherwise will, normally, be fanciful. (Per Li, V.-P.) When the formula "subject to contract" is employed by the parties, such formula must be expunged clearly and unambiguously by the words or conduct of the same parties before equitable relief can be claimed. Where only one party seeks to expunge it, such expunction must be known to, and acquiesced in by, the other party so as to make it unconscionable for the other party to insist on its strict legal right.

3. The court is only entitled in the exercise of its equitable jurisdiction to disregard the clear understanding between the parties that neither shall be bound until the condition they have stipulated has been fulfilled, in very unusual circumstances (*Salvation Army Trustee Co. Ltd. v. West Yorkshire Metropolitan County Council* (1981) 41 P & CR 179 considered).

4. On the facts the "subject to contract" reservation was not a mere incantation in the documents and in the letters exchanged, as is often the case. It could not possibly be contended that H.K.G. did not understand or mean what was being said. If H.K.G. entertained the expectation or held the belief that by taking possession of the Q.G. site or the handing over of the Tregunter flats or both, H.K.L. would in no circumstances insist upon their legal right to withdraw from the transaction before formal completion, that expectation was unreasonable and unjustified.

5. When possession or occupation of property is a fact in issue in this kind of case, if any conditions or limitations are placed upon that possession or occupation, then unless something happens afterwards to indicate that the conditions have been waived or removed, or that the owner's words or conduct have led the occupant reasonably to believe so, they must prevail.

6. (Per Fuad, J.A. *obiter*). If H.K.L. had accepted the Q.G. site without restrictions, or handed over the Tregunter flats without conditions, the facts might have entitled the court to enforce the equity in relation to the entire transaction.

7. With regard to the licence to occupy the Tregunter flats, for an argument based on promissory estoppel to succeed, the conduct, promise or encouragement (indicating that the licence could not be revoked) must be clear and unambiguous. (*Woodhouse Ltd. v. Nigeria Produce Ltd.* [1972] AC 742; *E. & L. Berg Homes* v. *Grey* (1979) 253 EG 473 and *Spence* v. *Shell* (1980) 256 EG 55 applied.) Silence or inaction cannot be regarded as a "representation" unless a legal duty (a moral duty is not sufficient) was owed by the representor to the representee to take the steps, the failure to take which is relied upon as the creation of the estoppel. The court in examining the conduct relied upon as creating the estoppel has to bear in mind the practicalities of the situation. At the material time H.K.L. was seeking to re-negotiate the terms of the Conditions of Exchange and it could not be held against the plaintiff that H.K.L. did not demand possession of the Tregunter flats (and in this way assert legal rights) until it became plain that H.K.L. had to take the Conditions of Exchange as they stood or not at all. (*Shaw* v. *Appelegate* [1977] 1 WLR 970; and *E. & L. Berg Homes* v. *Grey* (supra) considered.)

Appeal dismissed.

G. Godfrey, Q.C. & D. Fleming, instructed by the Crown Solicitor, for the Crown.
R. Alexander, Q.C. & R. Ribeiro, instructed by Deacons, for the respondent.
Separate judgments were delivered by members of the Court of Appeal

Cases cited in the judgments:

1. Ramsden v. Dyson (1866) LR 1 HL 129
2. Taylors Fashions Ltd. v. Liverpool Trustees Co. [1982] 1 QB 133
3. Greasley & Others v. Cooke [1980] 1 WLR 1306
4. Gregory v. Mighell (1811) 18 Ves Jun 328
5. Plimmer v. Wellington Corporation (1884) LR 1 HL 129

APPENDIX IX

Attorney General v Fairfax Ltd. [1997] HKLRD 243

Attorney General of Hong Kong   Apellant

and

Fairfax Ltd   Respondents

———

(Privy Council)
(Privy Council Appeal No. 5 of 1996)

———

Lord Browne-Wilkinson. Lord Jauncey of Tullichettle, Lord Lloyd of Berwick, Lord Nicholls of Birkenhead and Lord Cooke of Thorndon
17 December 1996

Land law and conveyancing — Crown lease — building covenant restricting development to erection of villa residences only — whether abandonment of covenant by Crown by acquiescence

P was the owner of the leasehold interest in part of the land governed by a Crown lease, which restricted the development of the land to the erection of one or more villa residences only. The land comprised in the lease is now known as Nos 1–27 Hing Hon Road and 65 Bonham Road. Over the course of the years since 1957, there had been erected on the land a whole host of multi-storey residential buildings ranging from three storeys to 26 storeys in height. P intended to redevelop the site and erect a high-rise residential building. The Crown asserted that the proposed development would constitute a breach of the covenant and demanded a premium as consideration for the waiver by the Crown of its rights under the covenant. P contended, first, that the covenant in the lease did not, on its true construction, prohibit the erection of the multi-storey building and secondly that in any event the Crown, as landlord, had abandoned the covenant by acquiescing over many years in the development of the whole lot in a manner inconsistent with the covenant. P sought declaration that the Crown could not enforce the covenant. The trial judge declined to make the declarations sought. The Court of Appeal held that the covenant necessarily prohibited the erection on the land of anything other than villas but that the Crown had abandoned the covenant by acquiescence. It granted P a declaration that it was entitled to erect a multi-storey building on its site (see [1995] HKLY 769). The Crown appealed contending that P had to prove that the Crown had knowledge of the developments in breach of covenant before any question of abandonment by the Crown could be presumed.

    Held, dismissing the appeal, that:
    (1) The Court of Appeal was right in holding that this was the clearest possible case of abandonment. Whilst proof of knowledge was essential, there was here overwhelming proof. This case was not concerned simply with what was going on on P's site. The Crown was relying on a single covenant, which applied to the whole lot. Therefore conduct by the Crown inconsistent with its continuing reliance upon the covenant in relation to all parts of the lot was relevant to the

question whether the Crown had abandoned the covenant. Accordingly, the question was whether the Crown was aware of the wholesale development of the whole of the lot that had taken place over the years. (See pp.245J, 246A–246D.)

(2) In the absence of any explanation the only possible inference from the fact that over a period of forty years multi-storey blocks had been built over virtually the whole of the lot was that everyone, including the Crown, must have been aware of those facts. An area of 2 1/2 acres had been transformed into an area of high-density high-rise buildings. It would take compelling evidence, which was lacking, to rebut the inference that everyone concerned with that land was well aware that it was not being used for villas. The suggestion that the Crown as landlord did not know of the development was unrealistic. (See p.246C.)

Mr Michael Barns, QC and Mr Robert Andrews, instructed by Macfarlanes, for the appellant.

Mr Edward Nugee, QC, Mr Gabriel Fadipe and Ms Jennifer Tsui (of the Hong Kong Bar), instructed by L. Watmore & Co, for the respondents.

Cases cited in the judgment:
Gibson v Doeg (1857) 2 H & N 615
Hepworth v Pickles [1900] 1 Ch 108
In re Summerson (Note) [1900] 1 Ch 112

Cases cited in argument:
Banning v Wright [1972] 1 WLR 972; [1972] 2 All ER 987
Cheng (T.S.) & Sons Ltd v A-G [1986] HKC 607

Lord Browne-Wilkinson:
By a lease dated 16 June 1862, the Crown demised to the lessee approximately 2 1/2 acres of land in Hong Kong described as Inland Lot 757 for a term of 999 years. The lease contained the following covenant:

> That he [the lessee] shall and will, before the expiration of the first year of the term hereby granted, at his and their own proper costs and charges, in a good, substantial and workmanlike manner erect, build and completely finish fit for use, one or more good, substantial and safe brick or stone messuage or tenement, messuages or tenements, upon some part of the ground hereby demised, with proper fences, walls, sewers, drains and all other usual or necessary appurtenances, and shall and will lay out and expend thereon the sum of three thousand two hundred and thirty dollars, and upwards in the erection of one or more villa residences only, in accordance with the terms of sale which said messuage or tenement, messuages or tenements, shall be of the same rate of building, elevation, character and description, and shall front and range in an uniform manner with the messuages or tenements in the same street, and the whole to be done to the satisfaction of the surveyor of Her said Majesty, Her Heirs, Successors or Assigns.

Over the years, the land comprised in the lease has been subdivided into 28 sub-plots, now known as Nos 1-27 Hing Hon Road and 65 Bonham Road. The respondents, Fairfax Limited, are currently the owners of the leasehold interest in Nos 9 and 10 on which they propose to erect a high-rise residential building. Fairfax contend, first, that the covenant in the lease does not, on its true construction, prohibit the erection of the multi-storey building, and, secondly that in any event the Crown as landlord has abandoned the covenant by acquiescing over very many years in the development of the whole of Inland Lot 757 in a manner inconsistent with the covenant. On the other side, the Crown assert that the proposed development would constitute a breach of that covenant and has demanded a premium as consideration for the waiver by the Crown of its right under the covenant. It was in those circumstances that Fairfax started these proceedings against the Attorney General asking for declarations that the Crown could not enforce the covenant.

The trial judge, Mayo J, did not decide the question of construction. The Court of Appeal held that, despite the fact that the covenant was framed in positive terms [ie, the covenant to erect one or more villa residences only] it necessarily prohibited the erection on the land of anything other than villas. There is no appeal to their Lordships against that decision of the Court of Appeal on the construction of the covenant.

On the issue of abandonment, the Court of Appeal (reversing the decision of the trial judge) held that the Crown had abandoned the covenant and made a declaration that Fairfax is entitled "to erect a multi-storey residential building on the site of 9 and 10 Hing Hon Road". The Crown appeals to their Lordships against that decision.

The whole case turns on the developments which, over the years, have taken place on Inland Lot No 757. At the date of the lease, the southside of the lot fronted onto Bonham Road. At some date long ago, a road, Hing Hon Road was constructed so as to divide the land from east to west. It is not proved that "villas" were ever erected on the land. However it does appear that, at some stage, there were semi-detached houses on some of the plots, which houses were set right back from Hing Hon Road and stood in their own gardens. It may well have been that these houses constituted "villas". Before 1945 there were constructed on Nos 2, 19 and 20 three-storey attached terraces houses the front doors of which opened directly onto Hing Hon Road. Those houses are still there today. But they cannot, by any stretch of imagination, be described as villas.

The main developments took place after 1945. Between 1957 and 1959, six-storey apartments (containing 12 flats) were erected on Nos 5, 6 and 9–12. During the 1960s, similar buildings were erected on Nos 21–24 and Nos 26 and 27. In 1966, a 9-storey apartment building was erected on No 1. Since then developments have been even more striking: on Nos 3–4 a 14-storey apartment building (1975); on Nos 7–8 a 21-storey apartment building (1984); on Nos 13–17 a 26-storey apartment building (1973); on No 25 a 6-storey apartment building (1990); and on No 65 Bonham Road a 25-storey apartment building (1992). In consequence, the whole area of Inland Lot 757 bears no resemblance to what the original lease must have contemplated — a low density area of villa houses presumably each in single occupation — but is a high density, high-rise area of apartment blocks in multiple occupation.

The Court of Appeal held that, in these circumstances, the Crown must be presumed to have released or abandoned the covenant. They relied, in their Lordships' view correctly, on the principles established in *Gibson v Doeg* (1857) 2 H & N 615, *In re Summerson* (Note) [1900] 1 Ch 112 and *Hepworth v Pickles* [1900] 1 Ch 108. In the last of those cases Farwell J at page 110 stated the applicable principles as follows:

> . . . if you find a long course of usage, such as in the present case for twenty-four years, which is wholly inconsistent with the continuance of the covenant relied upon, the court infers some legal proceeding which has put an end to that covenant, in order to shew that the usage has been and is now lawful, and not wrongful.

The Court of Appeal held that this was the clearest possible case of a course of conduct wholly inconsistent with the continuance of the covenant contained in the lease of 1862.

Before their Lordships, the Crown contended that Fairfax had to prove that the Crown had knowledge of the developments in breach of covenant before any question of abandonment by the Crown can be presumed. A man cannot acquiesce in conduct of which he is ignorant. Whilst their Lordships accept that proof of such knowledge is essential, there is here overwhelming proof. It is true that Fairfax was unable to lead evidence showing specifically that any relevant servant or department of the Crown was aware of what was going on. But it must be borne in mind that this case is not concerned simply with what has been going on on the property belonging to Fairfax, Nos 9 and 10 Hing Hon Road. The Crown is relying on a single covenant which applies to the whole of Inland Lot 757. Therefore conduct by the Crown inconsistent with the continuing reliance upon the covenant by the Crown in relation to all parts of Inland Lot 757 is relevant to the question whether the Crown has abandoned the covenant. Accordingly the question is whether the Crown was aware of the wholesale development of the whole of Lot 757 which has taken place over the years.

In the absence of any explanation the only possible inference from the fact that over a period of forty years multi-storey blocks have been built over virtually the whole of Lot 757 is that everyone, including the Crown, must have been aware of those facts. An area of 2 1/2 acres has been transformed into an area of high-density high-rise buildings. It would take compelling evidence, which is lacking, to rebut the inference that everyone concerned with that land was well aware that it was not being used for villas. As Leonard J said in the Court of Appeal: "The suggestion that the Crown as landlord did not know of the development is unrealistic".

Their Lordships concur with the Court of Appeal in holding that this is the clearest possible case of abandonment and will humbly advise Her Majesty that the appeal should be dismissed. The appellant must pay the respondents' costs before their Lordships' Board.

GLOSSARY

It is a feature of Hong Kong business both inside and outside of the government to use initials as a form of abbreviation. Land administration is no exception and some of those more frequently used are listed below:

AP	Authorized Person, usually an architect but can also be an engineer or surveyor
ALS	Authorized Land Surveyor
BA/BOO	Building Authority, sometimes referred to as Buildings Ordinance Office
BC	Building Covenant, requirement under lease conditions
BCL/BGL	Block Crown Lease, now Block Government Lease (BGL), the first title documents used in the New Territories
BC3	Building Conference 3, the Lands Department's forum for considering plans under DDH or MLP conditions
CA	Conservation Area
CBD	Convention of Biological Diversity
CC	Certificate of Compliance, requirement under lease condition
CDA	Comprehensive Development Areas, a planning land use zoning
C of E	Certificate of Exemption, applies to small houses in the New Territories
CPD	Colony Principal Datum, benchmark for measuring height, see also HKPD
DLC	District Land Conference, the Lands Department's principal decision making forum
DB	District Boards, local advisory bodies
DD	Demarcation District, refer to the New Territories land registration
DDH	Design, disposition and height clause in lease conditions
DLO	District Lands Officer, the government's land administrators at district level

DO	District Officer, the government's district administrator of Home Affairs Department
D of L	Director of Lands, head of the Lands Department which includes LAO, LACO and SMO
DPA	Development Permission Areas, planning in the New Territories
EIA	Environmental Impact Assessment
ExCo	Chief Executive in Council, highest decision-making body in the government
FBL	Free Building Licence, part of Small House Policy
FSI	Financial Secretary Incorporated, used in cases of re-entry
GFA (gfa)	Gross floor area, development potential of a lot as may be specified in lease conditions
GIC	Government, Institute and Community uses, a planning use zoning
GN	Government/Gazette Notification, formal government announcements published in the weekly *Gazette*, usually on Fridays
HKPD	Hong Kong Principal Datum, benchmark for measuring height, also see CPD
HKSAR	Hong Kong Special Administration Region
HKSARG	Hong Kong Special Administration Region Government, since 1 July 1997
HYK	Heung Yee Kuk, a New Territories organization representing the indigenous villagers
JPN	Joint Practice Note
LACO	Legal Advisory and Conveyancing Office, the Lands Department's in-house solicitors
LAO	Land Administration Office of the Lands Department
LEE	Land Exchange Entitlement also known as Letter A/B
MLP	Master Layout Plan requirements either under lease conditions or planning permission
MoT	Modification of Tenancy, pre-dates STWs
NT	The New Territories
NTEH	New Territories Exempt House, exempt from the Building Ordinance
NWNT	Northwestern New Territories
OP	Occupation Permit issued under the Buildings Ordinance
OZP	Outline Zoning Plans as published by the Town Planning Board and approved by ExCo
PR (pr)	Plot ratio, the multiplier applied to the site area of a lot to arrive at the permitted

PTG	Private Treaty Grant
RC	Rural Committees representing villages in the New Territories
REDA	Real Estate Developers Association
R of W	Rights of Way usually forming part of the lease conditions
SC's	Special Conditions
SDU	Sustainable Development Unit
SHA	Secretary for Home Affairs, the government's policy bureau for DO's
SHP	Small House Policy applying only in the New Territories
SMO	Survey and Mapping Office of the Lands Department
SSSI	Sites of Special Scientific Interest
STT	Short-term tenancy as granted by DLOs
STW	Short-term waiver as granted by DLOs
TIA	Traffic Impact Assessment
TDR	Transfer of Development Rights
TDS	Territorial Development Strategy, the government planning studies
TPB	Town Planning Board, considers and approves OZP, rezoning and planning applications
URA	Urban Renewal Authority formerly Land Development Corporation LDC
VC	Valuation Committee/Conference, the Lands Department's forum for premium assessments
VR	Village Representative who serves on the RC

BIBLIOGRAPHY

Books

Cameron, Nigel. 1979. *The Hong Kong Land Company Co. Ltd.— A brief history.* Hong Kong.

Cruden, Gordon N. 1999. *Land Compensation and Valuation law in Hong Kong.* Singapore: Butterworths.

Endacott, G.B. 1958. *A history of Hong Kong.* London: Oxford University Press.

Nield, Sarah. 1988. *The Hong Kong Conveyancing and Property Ordinance.* Singapore: Butterworths.

Norton Kyshe, J.W. 1971. *The History of the Laws and Courts in Hong Kong from the Earliest Period to 1898.* With a new foreword by Sir Ivo Rigvy. Hong Kong: Vetch and Lee.

Roberts, P.J. 1975. *Valuation of Development Land in Hong Kong.* Hong Kong: Hong Kong University Press.

Sayer, G.R. [1937] 1980. *Hong Kong 1841–1862: Birth, adolescence, and coming of age.* Reprint, with new introduction and additional notes by D.M. Emrys Evans, Hong Kong: Hong Kong University Press.

Wesley-Smith, Peter. 1998. *Unequal Treaty 1898–1997: China, Great Britain and Hong Kong's New Territories.* Revised Edition. Hong Kong: Oxford University Press.

Government Reports and Publications

British Parliamentary Papers on China, with correspondence, dispatches, reports and other papers related to Hong Kong. 1971. Vol. 24, 1846–60; Vol. 25, 1862–81; Vol. 26, 1882–99. Irish University Press.

Notes for the Use in the District Land Offices, New Territories. 1908.

Report from the Hong Kong Land Commission of 1886–87 on the History of the Sale and Tenure and Occupation of Crown Lands of the Colony. 1887.

Report on the New Territories, 1898–1912 laid before the Legislative Council. 22 August 1912.

Special Committee on Compensation and Betterment. A Report. March 1992.

The White Paper: A Draft Agreement between the Government of the United Kingdom of Great Britain and Northern Ireland and the Government of the People's Republic of China on the Future of Hong Kong. 26 September 1984. London: Her Majesty's Government.

Sources Used for Court Cases

Reported Judgements

HKC	Hong Kong Cases
HKCFAR	Hong Kong Court of Final Appeal Report
HKCU	Hong Kong Cases Unreported
HKLJ	Hong Kong Law Journal
HKLR	Hong Kong Law Reports
HKLRD	Hong Kong Law Reports and Digest
HKLY	Hong Kong Law Year Book

Unreported Judgements

Where unreported judgements are mentioned in the chapters, the appropriate court file reference is given. Copies can normally be obtained from the High Court Library. The following abbreviations are used:

Privy Council (replaced by the Court of Final Appeal since 1 July 1997)

PCA   Privy Council Appeal

Court of Appeal

CA   Civil Appeal

High Court (replaced by the Court of First Instance[1] since 1 July 1997)

HCA   Civil Action

MP   Miscellaneous Proceedings

AL   Administrative List

---

1. Hong Kong Reunification Ordinance No. 110 of 1997

Hong Kong Conveyancing

Sihombing, Judith and Michael Wilkinson. 1993. *Hong Kong Conveyancing: Law and Practice Vol. 1, Cases and Material Vol. 2, 2(A)*. Singapore: Butterworths.

INDEX

CASES

TERMS

香港土地用途
LAND UTILIZATION
IN HONG KONG

本地圖是根據規劃署 2006 年的土地用途數據和其他有關資料，並使用衛星遙感及
地理信息系統技術編製而成。當中包括從 SPOT ⊛ 衛星圖像（版權持有者：CNES；
發行者：Spot Image）中取得的資料。本地圖旨在顯示香港的概括土地用途模式。

This map is compiled from the 2006 land use data of the Planning Department and
other relevant information, including data derived from SPOT ⊛ satellite images
(⊛ Copyright CNES; distributed by Spot Image), using remote sensing and
geographic information system technologies. This map is intended to show
the broad land use pattern of Hong Kong.

深圳市　SHENZHEN SHI

蛇口
SHEKOU

后海灣
（深圳灣）
DEEP BAY
(Shenzhen Wan)

羅湖
Lo Wu

落馬洲
Lok Ma
Chau

上水
Sheung
Shui

天水圍
Tin
Shui
Wai

新田
San Tin

石崗
Shek Kong

元朗
Yuen Long

屯門
Tuen Mun

龍鼓水道
URMSTON ROAD

深井
Sham
Tseng

荃灣
Tsuen Wan

青衣
Tsing Yi

欣澳
Sunny Bay

馬灣
Ma Wan

九龍
Kowloon

赤鱲角
Chek Lap Kok

竹篙灣
Penny's Bay

愉景灣
Discovery
Bay

東涌
Tung Chung

坪洲
Peng Chau

梅窩
Mui Wo

大　嶼　山
Lantau Island

大澳
Tai O

長沙
Cheung Sha

石壁
Shek Pik

長洲
Cheung Chau

西博寮海峽
WEST LAMMA CHANNEL

南丫島
Lamma
Island

大嶼海峽
LANTAU CHANNEL

索罟群島
Soko Islands

Edition 2007 版
Series LUM/HK/A3 組別

香港特別行政區政府規劃署編製及出版
© 2007 版權所有　未經許可　不得複製　政府物流服務署印
Prepared and published by Planning Department, the Government of the Hong Kong Special Administrative Region
© 2007 Copyright reserved - reproduction by permission only　　Printed by Government Logistics Department

Scale 1 : 170 000　比例尺

km 1 　　0　　　　　　2　　　　　　4